THE FOREST AND THE TREES

THE FOREST AND THE TREES

A Memoir of a Man, a Family, and a Company

The McGowins of Chapman, Alabama, and the Logging and Lumbering Business

BY FLOYD MCGOWIN

NEWSOUTH BOOKS
Montgomery

NewSouth Books
105 S. Court Street
Montgomery, AL 36104

Hank Williams's "The Log Train" is used by permission of Sony/ATV Music
Publishing. All photographs were provided by the author's family members, who
express their appreciation to J. MacDonald Russell Jr. for the scanning of the images.

Publisher's Cataloging-in-Publication data

McGowin, Floyd, 1931–2010.
The forest and the trees : a memoir of a man, a family, and a company /
Floyd McGowin.
p. cm.
Includes index.

ISBN 978-1-60306-374-6 (paperback)
ISBN 978-1-60306-375-3 (ebook)

1. Alabama—History. 2. Autobiography—Memoirs. I. Title.

2015937242

Printed in the United States of America
by Ebsco Media

Contents

Aerial view of Chapman, Alabama.

Preface

My grandfather, James Greeley McGowin, had a reputation for being both an astute businessman and a fair and ethical person in his dealings with people, regardless of the circumstances. Never small-minded or mean, though occasionally tough, he was well regarded and liked, if not loved, by just about everyone. Usually referred to as Mr. Greeley, he had a larger-than-life reputation in Butler County and south Alabama; in the little sawmill town of Chapman, where I have lived and worked most of my life, he had the status of patron saint and cult figure. He was president of the W. T. Smith Lumber Company, referred to as "The Company" by locals, which was the county's largest industry and landowner. After he and his older brothers and some relatives bought the company in 1905, my grandfather moved up from Mobile to Chapman to run it. The company, originally established in 1884 as the Rocky Creek Lumber Company by a man named Chapman, was bought by W. T. Smith from Birmingham who changed the name in 1891. The McGowins kept his name on the company since it was well regarded in the trade. They probably lacked confidence that the business would have much of a future, as sustained-yield forestry practices were unknown in this cut-out-and-get-out era common to the large lumber operations in the Lake States and the South.

When I was two and a half years old, my grandfather died prematurely on January 1, 1934, of pneumonia and complications from a ruptured appendix. I have a strong mental image of him holding me on his lap while he sat in a white rocking chair on the front porch of his faux-colonial mansion, Edgefield, which he built in 1927 on his farm two miles northeast of Chapman. Peter McGowin Moore, my youngest grandson, is now about the age I was in my recollection of my grandfather. He bears the name of Mr. Greeley's uncle, who died in 1863 near Mobile while serving in the

Confederate Army. Peter McGowin was one of five brothers who lost their lives fighting for the South in the War of Secession. Peter's brother Alex, my great-grandfather, married Peter's widow, Nancy Floyd, for whom I am named, when he came back from the war. Another brother, James, also survived and was taken for a ghost by one of the freed slaves when he showed up at the family plantation east of Brewton six months after the war's end. Another brother, Thomas, was too young to go to war. Young Peter bears a strong resemblance to his Confederate ancestors, not surprising since most of the men in our line bear the family mark in their facial characteristics.

I held Peter on my lap while I sat in my chair in the living room of my home one night not long ago. My place is called Eastwood for my mother's family name and is just down the hill from Edgefield in a stand of ancient pine trees overlooking the lake Mr. Greeley built in 1919. Peter can't talk yet, but I think he understands me. I wondered aloud about acting as a go-between, bridging the time from the death of Mr. Greeley to the present day, now that he is about to begin his own appreciation of people, places, and events. He is a handsome boy with personal dignity, and he looked me directly in the face and seemed to want me to do so.

I decided to take on this assignment by describing defining events in my life as I saw them, during periods of our region's and country's history that have encompassed momentous social, political, economic, and technological change. More took place in the last two-thirds of the twentieth century along these lines than probably during any comparable period. My life has been full and interesting, and I have been privileged to know a lot of people and be involved in situations that illustrate change in both the physical aspects of life as well as the values that affect it. Using my experiences, I have recorded some of these things so that Peter and other young people might better understand what is different and what is the same with regard to the past. Older readers are welcome to put their own interpretations on the things I describe, and many may take issue with my conclusions. For my part, I am in that era of my life between active employment and impotent geezerhood, where I see things with more clarity and truth than previously, and I hope that what follows will be of interest to more than a few people. All the stories are told as honestly and accurately as possible, but what I have written is not history in an academic sense.

I relate my story in three parts. The first, "Chapman Town," deals with my family, early education, and surroundings. Parts of it may be painful to various members of my family and offensive to some corporate types. "Wild Fire" covers my time at Yale University and in the Marine Corps. This period occupied only about 10 percent of my life to date, but the few years I spent growing up as a part of these great institutions marked me as much or more than anything else and pointed me in the right direction in life. "The Company," the third and final part, concerns my formative years in business where I learned the trade, soldiered in one of the most violent strikes in U.S. history, and became a professional pilot.

Each of us develops his or her own character born of inherited genes, the influence of others, and personal life experience. It is my hope that this book will pay adequate tribute to those people and times that have formed mine.

I STARTED THIS BOOK in 1998 when I realized I had probably been down enough roads less traveled to constitute an interesting story. That said, I needed to put it together while the memories were still vivid and the time available. I am old-fashioned in ways and values, so I used my idol Hemingway's technique of spending several mornings a week with a pen and legal pad. Temple Alexander, an attractive and talented housewife and mother of four, was helping me then as an administrative assistant and transcribed most of the original writing.

My friends Bobbie Gamble and Joan McCullough Scott read the manuscript as it progressed and tendered helpful criticism. My lawyer Elisha Poole and longtime U.S. Marines squadron mates and friends Dick Clough and Don Kelly gave encouragement that I was doing something worthwhile, as did my wife, Rosa.

The original manuscript grew impossibly long and detailed, and after some of my original optimism receded, I put it on the shelf. An independent bookseller in Birmingham glibly told me that my chances of getting it commercially published were about the same as getting struck by lightning, probably a reasonably correct assessment of such matters (plus, he didn't know me).

Fate works in strange ways, and I have always believed things happen for a reason. After a few more years had passed, the noted attorney/author Dan Meador came back home to Greenville to do a book signing of his latest novel, an event attended by my cousin Eleanor Adams. Dan told her he had heard about my manuscript and wanted to see it, probably because of its local flavor. He read it and wrote me a long, detailed critique and gave me a few encouraging phone calls. He also shared the manuscript with Jennifer Kelland, who had been an editor for several book publishers. Dan got us together by phone, and Jen and I struck a tentative deal for editing my manuscript.

About this time, I ran into an old friend, Lesa King. She had worked at my business, Rocky Creek Logging Company (as did her father), during its best days in the 1980s and had recently taken early retirement after twenty-five years as a computer troubleshooter for several large companies. Lesa joined the project, a valuable asset, as Jen does her thing from the Greek Isles. These two used Internet technology to make the editing give-and-take run smoothly. Jen deftly removed a third of the original without diminishing the core message or changing my style or choice of words and has always been positive to work with.

If all these stars had not lined up, you would not be reading this.

Part I

Chapman Town

The Log Train

If you will listen a song I will sing
About my daddy who ran a log train
Way down in the Southland in ole Alabam'
We lived in a place that they called Chapman Town.
And late in the evening when the sun was low
Way off in the distance, you could hear the train blow
The folks would come running and Mamma would sing
Get the supper on the table, here comes the log train.
Every morning at the break of day
He'd grab his lunch bucket and be on his way
Winter or summer, sunshine or rain
Every morning he'd run that ole log train
A sweating and swearing all day long
Shoutin' get up there oxens, keep movin' along
Load 'er up boys cause it looks like rain
I've got to get rollin' this ole log train
This story happened a long time ago
The log train is silent, God called Dad to go
But when I get to heaven to always remain
I'll listen for the whistle on the ole log train.

— HANK WILLIAMS (1924–1953)

1

Chapman Town and the McGowins

The Chapman Town in Hank Williams's last song was home base for the log train that his daddy, Lon, drove for the W. T. Smith Lumber Company, Butler County's largest industry and landowner, which locals referred to as "The Company." Hank recorded that song, "The Log Train," in Nashville in 1952 as a demo, probably his last. His cousin Taft Skipper, while logging for W. T. Smith in 1958, told me about the song being played at his house near Chapman. It took me almost twenty years to find it, even after talking to Hank Jr. (who had never heard of it). I had given up when Chubby Manning brought it to me. Bob Pinson of the Country Music Foundation confirms that Hank performed the song "for some family members in Alabama over the Christmas holidays that year and probably intended to perform it for his father when he went to visit him on Christmas Day. Unfortunately, Lon was not at home and was never privileged to hear the song." The Williamses lived in Chapman for several years in the twenties, when it was a thriving industrial community of nearly two thousand people, an incorporated "company town" with three sawmills (two cutting pine and one hardwood), as well as mills making heading and staves for the barrel trade—a big business in those days—and veneer used in shipping containers for apples, oranges, bananas, and various vegetables.

My grandfather, James Greeley McGowin, usually called "Mr. Greeley," ran the company as general manager from the time the McGowins bought it in 1905. His father, Alex, had operated a sawmill in Escambia County, so Mr. Greeley was no stranger to the business. At Mr. Greeley's death, my father, Floyd, took over, and he guided W. T. Smith successfully through the difficulties of the Depression, World War II, and postwar labor and family problems. He and his brothers Earl and Julian were lumber business pioneers in the phase that succeeded the cut-out-and-get-out period. Their most important legacy was establishing a sustained-yield forestry program. Each year they grew substantially more timber than they cut, and they accumulated an additional 80,000 acres for a total holding of 221,000 acres when the company was sold in 1966. The McGowins ran what amounted to a feudal empire, and my grandfather, followed by my father—both men of principle who followed the rule of law even at times when they didn't agree with it—were the benevolent manor lords. Company towns had a bad reputation, but Chapman was a happy place, given the conditions much of society in our part of the world lived in at that time.

I came along in the middle of all this and have lived my entire life in Chapman, except for a dozen years away at school and in the Marine Corps. My plan to be a military and airline pilot didn't work out, so I joined the lumber business as a fourth-generation player and spent more than thirty-six years in it: eleven in the family company, eleven as CEO of one I started, and fourteen running that business for the Fortune 500 company that bought it. Like my people before me, I was a boss for almost all of this time with responsibility for a substantial number of people and events, and this is my story.

A psychologist once said that one's character and personality is essentially formed by age five. I believe genetics and family environment contribute roughly equal shares to this development, and I'll tell you what I remember about my early days.

CHAPMAN WAS TWELVE MILES south of Greenville, the county seat of Butler County, on the main line of the Louisville & Nashville (L&N) railroad that ran from Chicago to New Orleans, and adjacent to U.S. Highway 31 that ran from the Canadian border in Michigan to the Gulf of Mexico. The railroad, built in the 1830s, and the highway, built in 1928, linked the town to Montgomery and Mobile and, by extension, to places like New York, Washington, Atlanta, Birmingham, and New Orleans. While deep in the rural piney woods, Chapman really wasn't isolated. The roads weren't much—Highway 31 and Alabama 10 (which ran east-west through

Chapman Mill in the early days.

Greenville) were the only paved ones—but the railroad made up for it. Few people outside the rich or middle class had cars, but several local trains in each direction stopped at Chapman every day, and travelers could board express trains to the major cities at Greenville or Georgiana, four miles south. Trains brought mail four or more times a day, so my father always had his *New York Times* the day after publication. Air travel was in its infancy, but the airmail route operated by Eastern Airlines, which linked Mobile and Montgomery, passed right by Chapman.

The town, which surrounded the mill site, was a self-contained community located close enough to the workplace so that most could walk to their jobs in a matter of ten or fifteen minutes; nobody lived more than half an hour away by foot. A company store in a large one-story building on the east side of the railroad tracks carried a complete line of fresh meats, fruits and vegetables, hardware and farm tools, dry goods, and school supplies, as well as a full line of clothing for men, women, and children. A small drugstore section also sold Southern Dairy ice cream and "Cow Chows" (chocolate-covered ice cream on a stick) much favored by us kids. The frequent train service from Mobile and Pensacola allowed fresh seafood several times a week. The store operated a delivery service using a mule-drawn dray, dropping off orders at customers' homes each day. In those days, the post office was located at the north end of the store building, and the filling station and grease rack were adjacent. Company stores, like company towns, are now history, and they mostly got bad press from labor leaders, liberal writers, and country music lyricists. As far as I could tell, the Chapman Mercantile Company, as ours was called, was much appreciated by most of its customers: black, white, rich, and poor. When I was thirteen, I had my first summer job working in the grocery department, and I remember it as a happy place and something of a social hub, particularly for the women of the community. Segregation was the law and custom at the time, but the store functioned as a sort of neutral zone where conversation and good cheer cut across racial and economic lines.

Besides the store, the company provided other basic services. The doctor's office was in the middle of town, as were the hotel, barber shop, and dry cleaners. Across the railroad from the store stood a park for white people with tennis courts, a picnic area under big, old shade trees, and a large swimming pool fed by a very cold artesian well. Both races had their own schools, churches, lodge halls, and ball fields, which the company built and maintained. The company also operated a large icehouse and later a Grade A dairy with a herd of fine Jersey cows, a project of my father's.

Neighborhoods were broken down along racial and class lines. The leading citizens of both races had better and larger houses located closer to the center of town, providing more convenient access to work, school, services, and shopping. Butler County was, and still is, about 43 percent black, and W. T. Smith's workforce was almost exactly 50-50. This may have been the norm in the lumber business, but it was *not* for most of the larger employers, like the cotton mills, utility companies, railroads, and transportation businesses, which employed relatively few blacks.

In Chapman the races lived and worked side by side in legally separate but harmonious constituencies. The jobs were typically assigned along racial lines, eliminating much cause for friction from people of different color competing for the same slot. Blacks indeed made up the majority of the common labor, but many also held semiskilled and skilled jobs, which they performed at high levels of proficiency and reliability. More than a few white Southerners, usually rednecks but also some educated and professional people, considered blacks a sort of subhuman species characterized by dull mentality and shiftless nature, lacking in morality and work ethic. Although I was aware that some felt this way, I saw little evidence in Chapman of overt bad feelings or tension. While there were Ku Klux Klan klaverns in Greenville and Georgiana, Mr. Greeley and later my father did not allow the KKK to operate in Chapman. My friend and employee Mate Montgomery remembered the community as a good place to be in those times. He told me that blacks who lived in Chapman were better off than many in other parts of the county.

The company's position in running the community was to structure things so that employees' and their families' basic needs were met, on the theory that healthy, happy people are the most productive and economical. Employees were charged 75 cents a month for medical services ($1.50 if they had a family), plus the cost of the medicines that the doctor sold them. The company painted and maintained their houses, which were rented at nominal cost and had large yards with shade trees, a garden plot, and usually a chicken coop, a barn, and a small pasture for a milk cow in the back. The company operated a "town crew" supervised by the police chief, which picked up garbage, clipped hedges, and maintained the parks, school yards, and streets. As an incorporated town with a mayor (at one time my father), Chapman had a police court to deal with minor infractions, saving the accused the lost time and money involved in going to Greenville for trial. Mate has told me that Mr. Greeley set the neighborhoods up with racial harmony in mind, with the lowest class of white workers housed farthest away from the plants up on Mill Hill (later called East Chapman) on the east side of town, where they had their own little school and branch of the Chapman Mercantile Company ("the Hill Store"). The purpose behind this, according to Mate, was to minimize contact and association between the lowest class of whites, who tended to have the most extreme racial views, and the black population, whose neighborhoods were closer to the center of things. He also told me that the company routinely gave jobs to people with physical infirmities, lost limbs, and so forth, so that they could make a living. I remember Herman Peagler telling me when I was in high school, "If a black man can't make it in Chapman, he can't make it nowhere."

Depression-era Chapman was a relatively safe haven for both white and black employees and their families in difficult times. Wages were low, and nobody had much money, but I recall that most people went about their lives with good cheer. There was little in the way of state or government safety nets as we know them today. People had to depend on their extended families, churches, and employers for most of what they got. In those days, drugs were almost nonexistent in the general society, liquor (often "bootleg") was always present but not much of a problem (Butler County didn't "go wet" until many years after World War II), and divorces were hard to get, looked down on, and infrequent. Doubtless there was plenty of sinning going on behind the scenes, but the consequences seemed much less far-reaching and more benign than is now the case. The prison population in Alabama comprised a tiny fraction of the state's population compared to the present, and whites made up a higher percentage of the inmates.

The schools were very basic facilities with little except teachers, textbooks, blackboards, erasers, and chalk to support their programs. The core curriculum emphasized reading, writing, and arithmetic and, in my opinion, furnished students with a better basic education than is now offered in the public schools. The company subsidized Chapman's schools and also had a hand in choosing and paying the teachers. My little white schoolhouse had three teachers and eight grades crammed into three rooms (first to third, fourth to sixth, and seventh and eighth). A large auditorium building across the street with a Masonic lodge on its second floor was used for school events and plays, PTA meetings, community functions, dinners, dances, and other entertainment.

My sense of the Chapman of my childhood is that it was a good, maybe even superior, place for its time. The early 1930s were hard times with down markets in all the company's sales areas. My father and his brothers Earl and Julian had their work cut out just to stay in business, and I believe they were at least partly motivated by a sense of loyalty to their employees. They considered the company stores and other infrastructure items they provided to be services necessary to accomplishing the larger goal of getting their products to market, and they operated these concerns to break even or make nominal profits rather than to exploit the employees. The houses and their maintenance were heavily subsidized, and there were no city taxes. The company embraced a philosophy later drilled into me as a budding Marine officer: take care of your men, and they will take care of you. Younger readers may recoil at the paternalistic nature of the times, but in my judgment this setup was fairly and responsibly administered and a healthy thing. It's also probably the only way a rural manufacturing business of consequence could operate at the time. Society evolves, and our little community would be out of place today, but at the time, people in Chapman enjoyed better, more comfortable lives than any of their ancestors—or most of their contemporaries for that matter.

WHEN MY MOTHER WAS pregnant with me, obstetrical facilities in and near Chapman were minimal, but her family in Birmingham had access to the best doctors in Alabama at that time. So they insisted she come home for the delivery, and I was born in Birmingham early in the morning of May 20, 1931. I was named for my father, who was thirty-one and working for the company under his father, Mr. Greeley. Though my grandfather died when I was only two and a half, I have a strong mental image of him holding me on his lap in a white rocking chair on the front porch of his faux-colonial mansion, Edgefield, which he built on his farm two miles northeast of Chapman in 1927. A well-groomed man with a strong, handsome face, he wears a dress shirt, tie, and suit in all the pictures I have seen of him. He had a reputation as both an astute businessman and a fair and ethical person regardless of the circumstances. Though not small-minded or mean, he could be tough when necessary; still, working people both white and black, as well as his peers, held him in high regard and liked (sometimes loved) him. He in turn admired and respected attractive women, often bringing them gifts when he returned from his business trips, and they liked him. He had a larger-than-life reputation in Butler County and south Alabama and the status of patron saint and cult figure in the little sawmill town of Chapman.

I knew my grandmother, Miss Essie, well and always held her in high regard. A strong-looking woman of medium height with rather severe regular features, she was a handsome rather than pretty older woman, substantial but not fat. She was sure of herself and looked people in the eye. Kind,

Edgefield.

generous, and well-liked by both sexes of every age, race, and station in life, she seemed at home in any place or situation. She enjoyed company and entertained a lot, both the steady stream of high-class visitors from all over and the locals, for whom she held an open house every year. Her good sense of humor helped her with people, but she was also very intelligent and a keen observer, which she concealed enough not to intimidate the simpler folk with whom she came into contact. She had a lifelong passion for music, loving to play the piano and violin and to sing, and was an expert in ornamental horticulture. She read a lot and liked to travel, even to offbeat, exotic locations in Mexico, as well as other parts of Central and South America. I was fascinated by the souvenirs she brought back from these trips and her descriptions of the people and places she had seen. She enjoyed swimming and fishing in the lake but did not play at any sports. She frequently "broke a sweat" working in the yard and enjoyed eliminating weeds and grasshoppers (which she called "Germans") with the hoe she usually carried. While I don't think she ever drove any of her cars, she was at home on the trains, ocean liners, and early airliners of the day. She wrote well and took some English and writing courses at Columbia University when she was in her sixties. She was the first of the family to suffer from Alzheimer's and was affected by it for several years before her death in 1960.

I frequently stayed with Miss Essie at Edgefield when my parents were away on trips, and I enjoyed being with her. She was warm and loving to me, and when I was a child, I used to get in bed with her early in the morning. She slept in a four-poster, canopied double bed with yellow satin up above, which I thought was exotic. She had plenty of help and kept the large, handsome mansion up in good style. She also had very good food and used to call me "the bottomless pit" due to my fondness for large portions and second helpings. The house was a tasteful reproduction of an antebellum plantation home with spacious rooms, very high ceilings, and a porch or gallery on the front (west) elevation with stately columns supporting a canopied roof at the top of the second floor. The third floor had a pool table and reading area where we spent a lot of time. It had attic storage rooms off each end filled with luggage, musical instruments, old books, pictures, and magazines: always an interesting place for a little boy. Designed by Frank Lockwood, the well-known architect responsible for some of the finest houses on Thomas Avenue, one of Montgomery's nicest streets, the house had white-painted yellow poplar siding cut at the mill in Chapman, green shutters, and a red slate roof. It stands today as elegant as ever.

My father and his siblings were obviously raised by loving parents who worked to provide them with constructive advantages and to ensure that they were well-educated and exposed to travel. It was understood that the boys were destined to enter management of the family business, and they all did except for the youngest, Nick, who didn't feel he was needed and went to Harvard Law after his postgraduate years at Oxford. He did meaningful legal work for the company in later years and was always close to his brothers and the business.

EARL, THE SECOND OLDEST after my father, was handsome in a dark, eastern Mediterranean way, with black curly hair and a mustache. He was outgoing and extroverted, athletic (he played tennis and rowed for Oxford), musical (he played a fair jazz piano as well as the cello in the family string quartet), and a natural ladies' man of formidable ability. He had style, dressing well in English clothes to show off his looks, and came across as an urbane, cosmopolitan Southern aristocrat. Though never burdened by false modesty, he presented his considerable ego smoothly and didn't offend most people. On his last trip to England before his marriage in the last days of 1937, he buddied with Errol Flynn (they vaguely resembled each other), and the pair must have cut a wide swath through their female shipmates on the *Queen Mary*.

Earl was at ease with all kinds of people and consequently well-liked by most, a useful talent in his sales activities with the company and later his political and business dealings. He represented Butler County for twenty years in the state legislature, where he was Governor Frank Dixon's floor leader. He was a member of the cabinets of governors Gordon Persons and John Patterson as director of conservation (forestry and parks) and the state docks, respectively, and he did a creditable job in both posts. He was one of the founders and guiding lights of the Alabama Forestry Association in the late 1940s and was instrumental in forming and running the Southern Pine Inspection Bureau, which continuously policed quality standards in the pine lumber industry in the South, doing much to overcome the bad name that had been caused by greedy, unscrupulous manufacturers during and after World War II. He was heavily involved in this work from about 1960 until the early 1970s, and it did a lot of good. He sat on many boards, and much of his time and hard work went to trade groups such as the Southern Pine Association (he served a term as its president) and the American Lumber Standards Committee. Earl's most prestigious board was the Business Advisory Council, a quasi-governmental body made up of a hundred of the heaviest hitters in U.S. industry that met several times a year and advised the U.S. president on economic matters. Earl may have been a little light on credentials to be part of this august group, but he was well-accepted, respected, and liked by many of the members, such as Henry Ford, C. R. Smith (American Airlines) and Juan Trippe (Pan American).

Once I asked Earl why he continued to live in Chapman instead of using his obvious talents to seek high office in politics or business. He replied, "I would rather be a big fish in a little pond than a little fish in a big pond," which made good sense to me and pointed me in a like direction. I believe that Earl was a good, if not great, thinker who understood the tactics of political and business dealings and how to use people to get things done. I would liken him to a talented field general like George Patton, good at winning battles but not cut out to be commander-in-chief. He once quoted to me the adage that "politics is the art of compromise," useful advice since I tended to think in absolutes. He was a little selfish at times but was always nice to me when I was little. As I got older, he tended to look out for me and helped bring me along. He put me on some minor boards to gain experience (a radio station, an insurance company, and the state forestry association). I often went to New Orleans with him on association work, and we had some good times eating, drinking, and listening to real jazz in some of the good little joints that used to be in the French Quarter.

Before his wedding, he lived with Julian and his mother at Edgefield. He had a valet/chauffeur, Isaiah Rudolph, to take care of his personal needs and travel with him in a trusted capacity. Isaiah was a sort of black protégé and resembled his boss in many ways. He had a smooth, very black complexion, fine Arabic features, blue gums, and white teeth. Intelligent and well-mannered, he had a keen sense of humor, a ready smile, and a quick wit. We kids called him "Dumb Mustard" after one of Popeye's running mates in the comic strip of the time, and I think he enjoyed the name. In later life, after a career in the civil service, Isaiah used to take grand trips around the country as the butler on Earl's private railroad car, *The Finest Hour*, and it would have been difficult to say which of them enjoyed these jaunts the most. A guest on the car once quoted Isaiah as saying, "When Mr. Earl passes, St. Peter going to tell him he ain't going to find nothing new in Heaven 'cause he's already had it all on earth."

JULIAN, THE NEXT BROTHER, was the most abstruse of his generation. Physically, he was unprepossessing, standing about five eight or nine and weighing about 150 pounds. Wiry, with erect posture, he was an expert horseman; he also liked to play hard at pickup baseball and was good at shagging flies. He had a receding hairline even as a young man and brushed his wavy hair straight back, which did nothing to soften his lean, cruelly patrician visage, reminiscent of images of Brutus I have seen. His eyes had an Asian cast, and he had been called "Chink" at the University of Alabama.

Energetic and hard-working, he was focused on the forestry business. He loved pine trees and was passionate about the potential they represented. He was a serious person without much of a sense of humor, and while he could be kind and generous in one-to-one situations, he was generally cold and unfeeling to those outside his immediate circle. People who knew his work respected his drive and knowledge, but most who worked for him feared more than loved him. He enforced his standards strictly and didn't hesitate to get rid of those who did not adhere to them or who crossed him. He was the brother who made the most enemies as he went through life, although he may have been technically in the right in many of the underlying situations. He was very intelligent along narrow tracks, knew how to "follow the money," and achieved considerable success in his chosen field, pioneering and developing forest-inventory techniques widely used in a long succession of lucrative jobs for the rapidly expanding pulp and paper industry in the Southeast.

Julian ran the woodlands side of the business with an iron hand, but his brothers seemed to take his recommendations with unanimity and respect. For years, they ran the company as a three-man executive committee, a triumvirate that gave the appearance of a close-knit, happy working relationship until seeds of discord started sprouting in the late 1950s. Julian was an extremely strong-willed man, and I know of no occasion when he ever acknowledged being wrong about anything. When his relationship with his brothers and close family began to fall apart in later years, he may have believed he was right and taking a high road to the truth, not withstanding underlying problems with personal jealousies and a conflict of interest.

His jealousy may have had its roots in an event during his formative years. Julian had a deformed kneecap on his right leg, the result, I believe, of a childhood injury. Mate Montgomery and Louise Solomon Davis, my former nurse, both told me that Julian lived apart from his family with an old black man in a log cabin on Mr. Greeley's farm for one or two years when he was a boy, supposedly at his own election to protect himself from further injuring his knee in the rough and tumble of the household routine with his siblings. James Peavy, who was in charge of electrical services for the company and remains bright and attractive at eighty-two, tells a different story: he is positive that Julian was isolated from the family because it was thought that he had contracted tuberculosis. James said that the first screen porch he ever saw was the one built onto the cabin for Julian's sleeping area, as fresh air was the recommended treatment for TB in those days. At the suggestion of one of his doctors, he was sent to Atlanta, where he boarded with a family for two years while completing his secondary education at a private school. I believe that this circumstance, possibly along with other defining events in early childhood, planted deep hurts and jealousies in Julian, and these came to the fore many years later with profound effect.

When I was a child, growing boy, and young man, Julian always took an interest in my development and seemed to like me. He saw to it that I learned to ride. My father probably paid for the expense involved, but Julian got a spirited, little black mare for me when I was about ten and arranged for a fine horseman, Ben Bowen, an old half-black/half-Indian man who ran a livery stable in Greenville, to instruct me in the finer points of caring for and riding horses using the English saddle. Julian and I took many rides on the trails through the woods on the family place, and I enjoyed the time with him. He was not a pilot, but he shared my interest in aviation, and we liked to talk about it. I think he saw some potential in me at an early age and resolved to do his part in bringing me along.

ESTELLE, THE ONLY DAUGHTER in the family, was attractive and intelligent, small and pretty. She had gone to a private school in Montgomery for high school before attending and graduating from Vassar College. She spent one summer studying piano at the École des Beaux Arts in Fontainebleau, France, and was an apt pupil. She loved her mother and father and her brothers and was proud of them. A kind person with a sense of humor, she was well-read and articulate and liked the arts. The best musician in the family, she played the grand piano in her living room to a semipro standard. She kept a neat, attractive, and happy house, liked people and games, and often entertained family, friends, and business associates of her husband, Keve. She and Keve lived in the New York bedroom community of Douglaston, located on the Long Island Railroad between Bay Side and Little Neck. Their house, now owned by their son Stallworth, is one of the oldest surviving residences in the New York area, having been built by a Dutchman in 1735. It had been taken over by W. T. Smith in partial payment on a lumber debt after the crash of 1929, and the young couple subsequently acquired it. It is a large, good-looking house with three levels and a big basement on a landscaped lot of an acre or more that slopes down to Long Island Sound in the rear. I first visited Estelle and Keve when I was nine during a trip with Greeley to the 1940 World's Fair. Later, I spent a great deal of time with them during prep school and college on weekends and short breaks, and I came to know them very well. Always kind and supportive, they really acted as foster parents. When my wife, Rosa, and I were courting, they adopted her, too, and we were all fast friends into their old age after they built a house here on the family place. Estelle and Keve made frequent visits to Chapman and always stayed at Edgefield, maintaining a close relationship with their extended family.

I saw the least of the youngest brother, Nick, when I was small because he was either in school or working away from home. He stood about five foot ten and had a lean, aristocratic look. He was good at tennis and played every chance he got all his life. A laid-back, thoroughly nice man, kindly, intelligent, very proper, and never a rounder, Nick was always pleasant with me and went out of his way to know and talk to me. When he was packing up to leave for the Navy in 1942, he gave me a ten-inch, 78 RPM record that featured Fats Waller and His Rhythm. One of the sides was "S'posin'," a 1929 tune by Andy Razaf and Paul Denniker. Waller's piano playing, backed by his tight five-piece band, was the most exciting music I had ever heard, and something like a big spotlight turned on in my head when I played it the first time, then over and over again. From that time on, I reveled in hearing bits of his playing on the radio and later on other records. Waller died young (at age thirty-nine) at the end of 1943, so I never got to see him, but I owe Fats and Nick a debt of gratitude for igniting in me an enduring love of real jazz.

Nick spent the war as an intelligence officer with VP-52, a patrol and bombing squadron flying Catalina (Consolidated PBY-5A) amphibious flying boats. I was very interested in military matters in general, airplanes in particular, and the progress of the war, and he and I corresponded during his service years. He joined the squadron in Bermuda in 1942 where it was searching for German U-boats and went on to the Southwest Pacific for extended operations against the Japanese. He enjoyed this, and I am sure he did a good job. He had enormous respect for the pilots and aircrew and went on some combat missions to better understand the unit's operations. The squadron pioneered night-bombing attacks on Japanese shipping. The planes were painted flat black for concealment, which gave rise to the term "Black Cats" to describe PBYs employed in this role. His squadron suffered combat losses and earned several Navy Crosses. When he came back from the Pacific near the end of the war, Nick married Elizabeth Smith, a young woman who had been working for American Airlines in New York. She was from South Carolina, but her grandfather, Hamlet (Ham) Tatum, was from Greenville, Alabama, where he ran the First National Bank. Nick practiced law in Mobile after the war and stayed there the rest of his life. He was competent and well-liked, highly ethical, and a gentleman. I don't think he was as driven as his brothers to stick his neck out and make it big. He was impressed with high society and its beautiful people. He liked to spend time around them, a trait he shared with his brothers, but for Nick it was an innocent part-time activity for his own diversion rather than for any personal or financial gain. To some he showed more style than substance, but all who knew him considered him well-meaning, responsible in his work, and a good citizen whose word was his bond.

MY BROTHER GREELEY AND I lived with our parents on the front street in Chapman in the second of four large, two-story houses located just north of the town center, bounded by the offices, store, post office, hotel, and doctor's office. The first house had been Mr. Greeley's before he moved into Edgefield in 1927 and was subsequently occupied by Mrs. Stallworth, the school principal, and her husband Bill, who ran the grocery department in the store. Miss Essie's older unmarried sister, Stella, boarded with them

Downtown Chapman, with McGowin houses, in the 1940s.

and operated a small kindergarten in her apartment, which I attended. She had previously been a teacher (the first one for my father, his brothers, and their cousins) and was the postmistress for many years. Miss Essie's younger half-brother, Fred Stallworth, who ran the store, lived with his wife and their son in a one-story house down the street.

It was the nicest section of town, with lots of trees in the big yards and neatly trimmed hedges. It was a pleasant atmosphere with a lot of space and greenery. Coal-burning locomotives pulling the frequent express and local trains sometimes shook the house, and the soot and cinders were bad when the wind blew from the northwest, but we never tired of watching the trains and hanging around the depot watching Mr. Chesley Price send and receive telegraph messages in Morse code.

Our house had wood siding painted white and green shutters by the windows. It was neat and attractive but not fancy. We had a screened porch

next to the driveway and an open porch off the living room. A long, wide front entrance hall passed a large, comfortable living room on the right and ended in French doors at the dining room. We had a breakfast room, butler's pantry, and kitchen with wood and electric stoves, a refrigerator, sinks, cabinets, and a table with chairs. The servants ate their meals there, as we did on Sunday nights when they were off. Our bedrooms were upstairs; Greeley and I each had our own, separated by a shared bath. My parents' bedroom was across the hall and opened onto a screened-in sleeping porch on the back of the house. There was another room on the southwest corner, reached through the hall to their bathroom and also from the upstairs hall. At that time it was used as a combination office and sewing room and for my father's clothes closets and chest of drawers. He installed a small bed and started sleeping there when I was about ten. Almost all the rooms had fireplaces, although a furnace for central heat was added later. Residential air-conditioning was off in the future, but my father put a powerful exhaust fan in the stairwell on the second floor to pull hot air out of the house and create a pleasant breeze. My mother had good taste in all things, and the house, while not really fine, was very comfortable and pleasant. Most of the rooms were wallpapered and had oriental or plain rugs over wood floors, pretty curtains, good furniture, mirrors, and tasteful artwork. There were many books and good magazines. Mother usually placed prettily arranged vases of fresh flowers throughout the house.

We also had plenty of help. Will Richburg, an experienced dairyman, took care of the yard, milk cows, and chickens and did all the heavy chores around the place, including coming in early on winter mornings to lay and light coal or wood fires in most of the rooms. Solemn, polite, and intelligent, Will had Caucasian features, a light complexion, and a Creole look. He owned his two-story home "cross the creek," an area of a couple of hundred acres where fifteen or twenty black families owned houses on small plots. Just north of a small section of company quarters called Hickory Hill, it was reached by a dirt road through the company land that surrounded the little enclave. Most of the people who lived there worked in Chapman but wanted their own places, regardless of how humble and remote they were. They had a small Holiness Church, and as a kid I often fell asleep lying in bed by the open window, listening to the rhythm of drums beaten in some ritual over there, in between the sounds of trains passing by.

Our cook at that time was Donnie Trawick, a large woman, tall and big-boned, with very black hair and a reddish complexion—she was obviously part Indian. She was a fine cook in her own right, and my mother had taught her many recipes. The *Boston Cooking School Cookbook* was their Bible, and we ate very well. Donnie lived in one of the newest company houses next door to the main colored church and near their school. Mattie Lou Mathews was our maid, a pleasant, pretty young woman who later worked for other family members before moving to Niagara Falls.

Doll Monroe, our washwoman, came to the house several times a week to return clean items and pick up the soiled. She "toted" everything in a big wicker basket balanced on her head, which was always covered by a white kerchief. She lived near the company livery stable about a quarter mile southeast of our home and kept a very neat and clean house, which I was in more than a few times. Doll was intelligent, and she and my mother were close. She was a conjure woman with occult powers and could see things unknown to ordinary people. Her granddaughter, a big girl appropriately named Hercules, was normally a nice teenager but got carried away one time and in a fit of anger bit Doll on the thumb. This was bad enough in itself, but was further complicated by the fact that she was blue-gummed, which to the older blacks meant she was "pizzen as a rattlesnake." Bites by such people were definitely to be avoided, and despite Doll's own formidable powers, plus help from Dr. Johnson, the thumb had to be amputated. As I recall, the two made up and got along well after this unfortunate incident.

Next to my parents and brother, Louise Solomon was the most important person in our house for my development. She came to work and live in our home as Greeley and my nurse in 1934 when she was eighteen and a recent high school graduate. She liked both of us children and gave me support and guidance in my developing personality. According to her, I always went at things head on with little regard for authority or what people thought about me as long as I believed I was right, which often led to scenes with my father and temper tantrums on my part that were quieted by putting me in a tub of cold water. Conversely, my brother always needed parental and public approval and acceptance and worked hard at pleasing whomever he came into contact with. Louise recalled that she and I started off eating at the family dining table, where my father insisted on polished manners and deportment and constantly corrected any lapses, which led to enough unpleasantness that we were banished to the breakfast room, where we enjoyed eating together for several years. Greeley always kept his emotions pent up and stuck it out, although he was sometimes reduced to tears at the table. Intelligent, well-read and well-traveled, Louise kept her eye on me until her passing in 2003 and was a valuable source of information, particularly on the personality and characteristics of various family members and others mentioned here.

OF THE MEMBERS OF my immediate family, I was closest to my mother, a good and beautiful woman with a lovely figure; an expert seamstress, she made many of her own fashionable clothes. She stood about five eight and had red hair and a fair complexion, which she passed on to me and my

Floyd, above, 1931; at right, with his mother, Mary Alice McGowin.

daughter Lucy. Outgoing and with an impish sense of humor, she was a lifelong Episcopalian with an eye for art and a sense of the theatrical. She was well-liked by men and women from all walks of life. She had a knack for getting the best out of servants, architects, decorators, artists, and painters by tailoring her approach to the individual's personality. She kept a well-appointed, comfortable, and spotless house. She was a formidable cook and routinely produced lavish dinner parties for the steady stream of family and out-of-town friends and business personalities often in our home, there being no first-class commercial accommodations and restaurants closer than Montgomery in the 1930s. She had an innate feel for medical problems and remedies and was always comfortable talking to doctors about herself or anyone else. She was stoic and brave about serious physical problems.

My mother came from a fine family in Birmingham, and the Chapman McGowins liked and appreciated her people, which resulted in a lot of visiting and tight friendships over the years. She was liked and accepted by my father's parents, Mr. Greeley and Miss Essie, and his siblings. My father's brothers married when they were well into their thirties, and their wives liked my mother and informally treated her as their leader in the local family framework. She and my father had different personalities, although they shared common values and tastes. They had many mutual friends in Birmingham, Montgomery, and Mobile and seemed to enjoy the same sort of people and social events. They also liked to travel together. I believe they loved each other and got along well and were happy together, at least in the first years of their marriage.

My mother had her own set of problems, which must have stressed and worried her over the years. Her father, Arthur Eastwood, had invented the electromagnet still used to move heavy loads of iron and steel. He was a millionaire by the time he was thirty, but he died at age thirty-six. Afterwards, my grandmother came back to Birmingham with her three small children. A vivacious woman who had enjoyed studying art in Paris before her marriage, she had what was called a "nervous breakdown" and lived the rest of her life an invalid in her nice home, cared for by a former nun, Miss Kelly, and a staff of servants. My mother and her siblings were raised by their grandmother, Mrs. Sharpe, and their aunts and uncles and went away to boarding and finishing schools. Her brother, George, and his wife had problems with alcohol, although they eventually joined AA, kicked their habit, and had many good years together. Her sister, Lucy, was married and raising her own family but suffered badly from depression from time to time. Lucy was close to my mother and was an attractive, thoroughly nice person. I liked all of my mother's family members and enjoyed their company. My mother acted responsibly in doing all she could for her mother, brother, and sister. While my father was supportive, I am sure these matters put a strain on their relationship. He was big on control and appearances and had little tolerance for personal weaknesses. My mother was not a problem drinker, but she liked cocktails at dinner parties and dances, and I believe my father was always uptight about this and afraid she might fall off the wagon. She smoked cigarettes (a pack or more a day of Old Gold and later Phillip Morris) and was also addicted to the old-style Coca-Cola that came

Floyd Sr. and Mary Alice with Greeley and Floyd Jr. at Edgefield, 1931.

in a green glass bottle. She always had one poured over ice in a tall glass at about 10 A.M. and another in the middle of the afternoon.

GROWING UP, I FELT my mother loved and appreciated me for who I was. Caring, affectionate, and considerate of me, she was tolerant of my errors and temperament and recognized that I had considerable potential. I adored her and liked to be near her. I wanted the same kind of warm relationship with my father, a good, well-meaning, complicated, reserved, and serious man who evidenced little sense of humor. He stood about five foot ten, had a medium build, and at times was a little chubby. Still, he was good-looking and always wore a mustache. A fastidious dresser, he wore tailor-made shirts and had most of his clothes and shoes made in London's Savile Row. He was health-conscious in his lifestyle and eating habits. He had smoked as a young man but gave it up, though he occasionally sneaked cigarettes when under stress. He drank moderately and always seemed to be scared to let himself relax and have a good time. While he lived well, he was never ostentatious. He rode horses, swam, played tennis and golf, and shot birds and squirrels, but he never seemed particularly athletic or outdoorsy.

A good provider for his family, he had high principles and was honest to a fault. Strong in his beliefs, he was determined and fearless in standing up for what he thought was right. Intelligent, well-educated, and well-read, he appreciated music and the arts. He also carefully perused the *New York Times* and *Montgomery Advertiser* every day, followed politics and international affairs, and made his own analysis as to what was going on. He was usually reasoned and correct in his assessment of these matters, as well as in his various business activities. He was conservative in his politics and voted Republican in presidential elections at a time when the South was still solidly Democratic. He was not an obvious do-gooder, but was responsible in his treatment of employees and those of lesser status. He helped more than a few deserving young people attain their higher education, particularly in music. Besides the lumber company and his other business affairs, he had serious interests in playing chamber music (his instrument was the violin) and reading history. He was an expert on the lives of Dr. Samuel Johnson and his running mate and biographer, James Boswell, as well as on the Civil War. Once he told me that it was important that I develop to a professionally competent level in interests other than my principal work. It was good advice, and I have followed it.

Maybe he loved us, but he came across to me as remote, more interested in censuring and correcting than nurturing or providing understanding, positive direction. His grandfather Alexander, literate although he had little formal education, had insisted on correct grammar and pronunciation and good speech from the family juniors, an insistence apparently delivered in a tactful, good-natured manner. My father tried to emulate him, and as a very young child I was constantly being badgered about my speech. I had a hard time differentiating between "cavalry" and "Calvary" and mostly used the latter for the former when asking questions about military matters. This was always reason for a scolding instead of any reasonable explanation, and

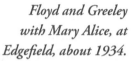

*Floyd and Greeley
with Mary Alice, at
Edgefield, about 1934.*

not exactly what I believe Christ intended from parents. I made the mistake more than once of placing Kansas City in Kansas (it is) in conversations with him, another serious no-no. He visited Kansas City, Missouri, several times a year to attend insurance company board meetings and only recognized the higher-class part of town on the east side of the Missouri River. Since he never showed me the geography of this situation on a map, I was left to my own devices to try to figure out the sense of why Kansas City wasn't in Kansas. Using any slang, especially "ain't," always provoked a spirited harangue—in retrospect, this is somewhat strange as he was a devoted Anglophile and "ain't" was commonly used in casual conversations by the English gentry and sporting set as least as far back as the early nineteenth century. I could give other examples, and perhaps he based his parenting style on the English customs and traditions he held in such regard. I can only say that in my case his constant criticisms came through as priggish mean-spiritedness rather than as constructive coaching.

I remember only two occasions when he spent any one-to-one time with me when I was little. He let me go quail hunting with him one bright fall Saturday afternoon at "the farm" (Mr. Greeley's estate) in a broom sage field west of Highway 31. He explained to me the tactics of the pointer bird dog that accompanied us, and he managed to shoot several birds. Another time he took me with him while he fished in the lake, and I thought the intimate companionship and closeness of these situations represented what a father-son relationship should be like. Later, when I was off at camp and school, homesick and missing my parents, I would dream about these times with a sense of profound loss when I realized that they were neither genuine nor likely to be repeated.

I HAD A COMPLICATED relationship with my brother from the beginning. Greeley was a handsome, well-built, athletic boy with black hair. He had one of his kidneys removed at Johns Hopkins as an infant due to a nonmalignant tumor and must have come close to losing his life. He came through this with no lasting effect and was strong and healthy. He was neither musically nor artistically inclined, but he was intelligent and quick with mathematics. He liked to scheme at games and with people and always seemed to know the

Floyd and Greeley with their mother, 1933.

angles and how to practice gamesmanship and one-upmanship. He followed sports in the papers and on the radio and seemed to know all the statistics relative to big league baseball and to understand the strategies involved in team sports, as well as cards and games. He was the firstborn and seemed to live a charmed life in the household, never getting in trouble or at least never getting caught. He did not talk back to my parents and was always at pains to please them. It seemed to me that he always had their interest and approval and could do no wrong. At the time and for long afterwards, I looked up to and trusted him.

He was a little over four years older than I, and his close buddy Max Spann, who lived on our street, was a year older than he. Max, blond, with good features, well-built, and aggressively glib, was a precocious boy who was in our home a great deal, as we were in his. Living as we did, I had little exposure to other kids my own age, so it was natural for me to look to Greeley and Max as both companions and role models. Four or five years make a tremendous age difference in children, but nobody ever explained this to me, and I didn't really understand the consequences until years later. I didn't know that, being younger, I wasn't supposed to be as smart, as knowledgeable, or as strong as they were. I couldn't understand why I always came up short in competitive situations, mental or physical, and after repeated failings, I became convinced of my inferiority, which complicated my life for the next few years. Along with my friend Howard Goodlett Olive (Max's first cousin), I followed their lead and tried to keep up with them, which led to constant frustrations. They naturally resented us dogging along behind them, and there was also probably some deeper sibling rivalry developing, but as time went by, I believe it went further than that. Two early events set the pattern.

In 1936, I turned five, and that winter was extremely harsh and cold for south Alabama. A severe early freeze killed all the trees in my grandmother's satsuma (tangerine) orchard when the trees were still in leaf and loaded with ripe fruit. Some of us got sick from eating the frozen citrus. Later it got so cold that the lake froze over, which has happened only two or three times in my lifetime. One bright, cold Saturday morning, I went there with Greeley and Max, and we watched ducks and geese make awkward landings on the ice. We were near the boathouse just down the hill from Edgefield, and there was a lily pond nearby, twelve or fifteen feet long and about three feet wide and two feet deep. It was covered with ice and looked like a Christmas scene shining in the sun. Greeley suggested that we take positions side by side on one edge and jump across on his count of three, meanwhile giving Max a high sign. I hunkered down between them, grateful to be included in the sport, and on the count of three launched myself as strongly as I could in a sort of standing broad jump, while they stood stock-still, enjoying their game. Naturally I landed short of the far bank, and my feet went right through the thin ice and deep down into the muddy bottom. I had on a new pair of brown leather Boy Scout–type shoes, and one was lost for good in the frigid muck. I got out by myself, covered with mud, freezing cold, wet all over, and deeply hurt and humiliated. I ran sobbing the quarter mile up the hill to the warm kitchen at the big house, where someone called my mother to come get me. Max Spann remained my brother's friend and close associate for many years, and I slowly came to understand just what sort of character he actually possessed. It took a long time, but eventually so did Greeley.

Several years later, a similar incident reminded me of the complex nature of my relationship with Greeley. I had been riding several times a week since I was ten, usually under my uncle Julian's supervision, and by the time I was thirteen in the early summer of 1944, I had confidence in my ability. Greeley had just graduated from Episcopal High School and was back home before starting college at Princeton. Our friend Hugh Thompson, then eighteen, was home on leave from the navy, and one day the three of us decided to go horseback riding. I saddled up my little mare, and Greeley and Hugh prepared Fox and Beauty, both large, well-behaved, gentle horses. We set off through the woods on one of the trails leading away from the barn and after a time came out of the timber stand and onto the long flat ridge we called "the landing field" just southeast of the lake. It had been used by occasional visiting airplanes since being prepared in 1930 and was about two thousand feet long. The steep slopes on the sides and ends were marked by terraces put in by my grandfather to control erosion on his farm. When we had walked the horses out into the broom sage covering the field, Greeley proposed that we have a race, one lap around the field. He communicated a silent message to Hugh to lag behind him after counting off a one-two-three-go standing start for our horses, which were lined up neck to neck. We started on the east side of the field near the south end and had a long, straight shot to the north. I was riding my spirited little horse in a fair imitation of a jockey (I was that size at the time) and got her going in a full gallop and pulled well ahead. Greeley and Hugh reined up well short of the north end so as to enjoy the predicament that had been created for me. I found myself trying to make the short radius turn at the north end before I realized that I was going way too fast for my horse to get all the way around. She got headed northwest before going off the field and down the slope toward the lake, jumping the terraces. I came off on the second jump and was catapulted head over heels to land on the back of my neck and shoulders on the grassy clay of the turned-out farm field. I was unhurt save for having my breath knocked out, but I was lucky not to be dragged by a foot caught in a stirrup, killed from a broken skull, or worst of all paralyzed for life. I had been naive and gullible and shown poor judgment in setting myself up for yet another example of brotherly love, but I was young and unschooled. I had then, and for a long time to come, the expectation of unconditional fealty in such a relationship.

I WAS A DECENT-LOOKING little boy with red hair, freckles, and a temper to match. I was bright and interested in the world around me and how it worked. Even as a young boy, I had definite ideas and tastes. When I was three or four, I was given a well-made sweater knitted for me by someone who went to a lot of care and trouble. It was bright red, and I wouldn't wear it because I didn't like the color. When I was older and thought back on this, I was ashamed. It was a perfectly good sweater, which many less fortunate children would have been proud to own. I also knew that I didn't like shrimp and oysters and would never touch them. I missed a lot of superior eating until I got older and finally actually tasted them.

As a young child, I obviously knew little and sometimes got into trouble by making rash assumptions based on incomplete knowledge. I also took people at their word and assumed that they were well-intentioned and truthful and that they had the best interests of the people they touched, such as myself, at heart.

Floyd, about 1937.

The McGowins at Edgefield; Greeley, Floyd, and their parents are at left, and the others are his uncles, aunts, and grandparents.

My nature was, and still is, to say what I think and not to play games with people. I was not an artful dodger, and as I got older I never adopted the smoke-and-mirrors or bait-and-switch styles of negotiation favored by many corporate con artists. I think I was laying a foundation for the honest and forthright person I wanted to become in later life. I believe that my willingness to state what I think up front, to speak plainly and directly, has generally served me well through the years, although it has caused me problems in dealing with some people. I favor the notion that "how you play the game, not whether you win or lose" is the ultimate winning strategy, as opposed to Bear Bryant's "nice guys finish last" style.

Growing up, I liked my home and the town of Chapman. As a small boy, I formed positive impressions of my parents, family, the townspeople, and our visitors. At that age, a child has no frame of reference, and I was in a privileged, protected circumstance with no physical wants or needs. I saw my family with an aura of goodness and believed that they were generally omnipotent in terms of brains, ability, and the rightness of their conduct and lifestyles. Any flaws had to result from some frailty, mistake, or character defect of mine. I very much wanted the security that real closeness with my parents and brother would have provided, and I was not a particularly happy preadolescent or teenager, which slowed my progress and threatened to send me down some bad roads. Getting from my starting point as a little kid to where I wanted to be in terms of character and values as an adult was not a straight line, and I am thankful to have done as well as I have. Over the long years that have intervened, with manifold experiences with the players, ranging from comic to tragic and including a lot of hardball personal and business dealings, I have formed the opinions I relate in this book. I realize that these are colored by my own character and personality and that one can understand only parts of others. I worked very closely with my father, uncles, and brother through years fraught with what amounted to momentous problems, possibilities, and opportunities—some pleasant but many stressful, unpleasant, and disappointing. The formal education that ultimately prepared me to meet and surmount the various challenges I have faced began right next door to our home in Chapman.

2

A Chapman Town Childhood

I started the five, second-best learning years of my life attending my great aunt's kindergarten, which was next door to our house. Miss Stella Stallworth was three years older than my grandmother, Miss Essie, and the sisters had been close since childhood. Miss Stella never married and spent most of her adult life in Chapman teaching school and running the post office. Her apartment occupied the southeast quarter of the second floor of the big, old sawmill house where Mr. Greeley had raised his family before moving into Edgefield, and she devoted one corner of her living space to the kindergarten. I enjoyed the little classes and quickly learned my numbers, the alphabet, and a little simple reading while socializing with the little boys and girls who attended with me.

After Miss Stella's kindergarten, it was easy to get started on my formal education at the public school. My teacher taught the first, second, and third grades in one big room with about eight or nine boys and girls in each class. Windows along the north side of the building kept the room ventilated in warm weather, and a big kerosene-fired space heater kept it warm when it was cold. The teacher's desk was in the front center of the room between the blackboard and the students. Most of the teachers during my seven years at the school were women of good to excellent ability. What they lacked in teaching aids and fancy educational material, they made up for in commitment and talent. They almost always maintained good order and discipline, and I don't recall that having several grades in the same room presented much hindrance to learning. The teachers were handpicked, and the company supplemented their regular state salary. The worst teacher we had was an older man named Mr. Bone, who lacked the strength of character necessary to maintain discipline. Kids can be mean, and we intuitively understood his weaknesses, which led to some cruel tricks that embarrassed him and disrupted the classroom on more than a few occasions. I believe he was replaced around the middle of my first grade school year.

I learned basic arithmetic easily and was reading without difficulty and for my own pleasure soon after I started the first grade. My teacher soon decided that I was way ahead of the other first graders and jumped me up to the second grade, where I had no difficulty keeping up. I was developing a serious interest in reading, which was a big help in school. I had access to a lot more material at home than any of the other kids and took advantage of it. I was a big fan of *Life* magazine, the *Saturday Evening Post*, and *The New York Times Magazine* and read them fairly thoroughly on a regular basis. I read my first novel, Bram Stoker's *Dracula*, when I was seven. As a result of having skipped first grade, I was barely thirteen when I finished school in Chapman. Still, my academic training was good. Mrs. Bill Stallworth, the principal and a distant relation of Miss Stella's, taught the seventh and eighth grades. With her black hair and rigid posture, she seemed to me a stern and imposing old woman, although she was probably only in her forties. A disciplinarian, she challenged, shamed, and sometimes punished pupils into doing their best. When I arrived at prep school in Virginia, I

Above, a Floyd school photo;
right, Floyd and Greeley.

was equipped to compete successfully with boys from all over the country, most of whom had attended good public and private elementary schools. The academic difficulties I sometimes experienced were of my own making owing to my age and immaturity rather than any lack of basic foundation.

As a young boy, I was keen to grow up so as to have more freedom, and I wanted to look the part. I didn't get my first pair of long pants until I was

Chapman's AC interdenominational Community Church during a flood; right, the interior of the church.

eight, so I used to wear a leather belt and sweater over my Duck Head bib overalls to make it look like I had on long pants. I got along well enough with the other kids, although I felt somewhat self-conscious because I was the boss's son. I certainly wasn't ashamed of who I was or of my family, but I was careful not to brag or otherwise make anything of my fortunate status. On a few occasions, other kids would remind me that their fathers had to work hard all the time, while my father presumably lived a life of ease in the office, which always made me feel awkward and bad. I got into one or two brief fistfights with other boys my age during my time at the school, which is about average for little boys. I believe I was accepted by the others and had my fair share of casual friends. Occasionally, I was in the front of the group and showed some signs of leadership and thinking ability.

The Chapman school years went by agreeably. I enjoyed them and liked the little weekly paper we got by subscription that had articles and facts of interest to children our age. We always had a Christmas pageant and a big operetta or play at the end of the year, and everyone had to participate in some way. I did my part but was always ill at ease on stage, something I didn't overcome completely until well along in my business life. On Saturdays, when the weather was good, a group of us would usually walk to Georgiana, four miles south down the railroad track, to see the movie with its accompanying serial, short subjects, newsreel, and comedy at the newly built Ga-Ana Theater, which seemed very modern and grand to us. On Sundays we walked to the interdenominational Community Church, which all of the McGowins supported and attended, for Sunday school and the service. The program was usually conducted by senior members of the congregation, like Mr. D. G. Campbell, who ran the supply house at the mill, but once a month the Universalist minister came from Brewton to hold forth and always stayed for lunch with the family. I always enjoyed the little wooden church for its peace, serenity, and sense of community, as well as for the singing, and this helped form my values. I took comfort from the simple services in a larger measure than I did from the more refined and ritualistic services presented by most of the Episcopal churches I attended sporadically in later life. I didn't understand the theology aspect very well, but I did learn the Lord's Prayer, the Ten Commandments, and the Twenty-third Psalm, all of which remain the strongest parts of my religious beliefs.

After church, the extended family always ate lunch together at one of our homes on a rotating basis. After the meal, normally capped off with rich, delicious ice cream freshly churned by one of the menservants, the family string quartet would crank up for an hour or two, always playing classical music, which I generally found dreary and depressing, an unfortunate prejudice since attendance was mandatory. I have a real love for some kinds of music and have always profoundly regretted not taking full advantage of the opportunities given to me as a child. At the age of seven, I started taking violin lessons from Christine McCann of Montgomery, who came to both instruct and play with the quartet. An old maid then of about fifty, she was an accomplished musician and a good teacher. I learned the scales and something of reading music well enough to get by, but I was never fully fluent in the intricacies and subtleties of the charts. I had a good sense of time and an innate ability to play by ear, which was useful in faking some of the pieces, and I made sufficient progress to win the regional contest for young violinists from the central part of the state held at Huntingdon College in Montgomery when I was nine. I was supposed to go on to Birmingham to compete for the state championship, but I used my youthful problems with motion sickness as an excuse to balk at taking the trip to the finals, which effectively ended my fiddle playing career. In truth I had stage fright, and though quitting was probably a big mistake, I was very headstrong, and grownups found it very difficult to make me do things I didn't want to do. I'm sorry that my parents, family, or teacher did not take the trouble to counsel me effectively to help me overcome my immature response to this challenge—it might have made a meaningful difference in my life. I have come to be very much against children and young people quitting things they have started before giving them their best shot. Taking the easy way out often sets up a self-defeating behavior pattern for subsequent undertakings, a lesson I learned and had to overcome the hard way.

I subsequently played at learning the piano for a couple of years but never got past the beginning stage. My teachers were good enough, but I didn't much like the music we played and didn't have the motivation to pay the price in dedication, hard work, and practice it takes to learn any discipline.

Perhaps if I had been started on simple versions of Fats Waller's tunes, a spark would have ignited my considerable latent feeling for music and my talent would have kicked in, possibly pushing my playing to a professional level. I have always regretted not capturing this opportunity, but it took years working through early adolescence to appreciate the folly of self-inflicted failure and to gain the focus and motivation necessary to really succeed in learning complex new activities. Instead, I experienced boom-and-bust cycles in which my sometimes considerable successes were canceled out by my trying to just get by and failing in the process. My brother purported to espouse the philosophy that a "gentleman's C" was the preferred achievement level for real men who were also cool guys, and my immature eyes associated this attitude with the sort of glamorous lifestyle he and his prep school and college friends exhibited and that I hoped to emulate. In actuality, Greeley was intelligent and never had any real trouble with courses in school, but I bought into the decadent façade hook, line, and sinker. This lack of high standards and commitment was merely an extension of my failure to apply myself with music lessons and caused me considerable trouble. I didn't learn to apply myself consistently as my abilities allowed, to be what we called a "hard charger" in the Marines, until I was about twenty. I had to work through this depressing era of my life, to see the truth and overcome my problems, almost entirely on my own, which I think made me a much stronger, albeit somewhat scarred, person in the long run.

A LOT HAPPENED IN Chapman during the late 1930s, the events being a sort of microcosm of goings-on throughout America and to some extent the wider world. Franklin D. Roosevelt and his Democratic administration took firm control of the federal government just as Adolph Hitler was rising to absolute power in Germany. Both men were charismatic personalities who took office at the cusp of economic travail in their countries. Both offered the hope of restoring order, prosperity, and national pride to their respective peoples through the implementation of bold new programs that were widely supported. Both had more effect on their countries and the world than other leaders of the twentieth century, effects still noticeable today, especially in the United States.

In Chapman, the brothers had digested and adopted Julian's business partner Les Pomeroy's recommendations for improving logging and forestry practices and actively acquiring more land, and W. T. Smith was growing, despite the Depression. The brothers had also made many friends in Europe during their Oxford days, including highly placed people in England, Belgium, and Czechoslovakia. Between contacts with them and their own appreciation of events, they properly concluded that another war in Europe was inevitable and that the United States would be involved in some fashion. They had committed to a plan to generate a constantly improving, long-range timber supply and in 1938 turned their energies toward modernizing and expanding the plant facilities in Chapman and the satellite mills at Greenville and Linden to make them more productive and efficient. The cost of the 1938 mill improvements at Chapman totaled some $500,000, which was borrowed from the Merchants National Bank of Mobile, where my father was a director. This was a lot of money at the time, the equivalent of a good many millions in today's dollars, but it was a prudent investment.

I watched the upgrading of the mill facilities with great interest—it was something like having your own circus every day with constantly changing acts. Several tall smokestacks were erected to service a new boiler plant and these, along with two new water tanks, were painted by a traveling troupe of specialists who did their work sitting on little swing seats or bosun's chairs, which were suspended by pulleys from the top of the stacks and tanks. This work seemed even more daring and exotic in that several of the painters were good-looking women, a very unusual sight in those days, making it seem all the more like entertainment. The paint was hardly dry on the tanks before some of us boys led by Greeley and Max climbed the one adjacent to the mill late one Sunday afternoon when nobody was around. We went all the way up individually and sat on the ball at the very top to qualify as real risk takers. In retrospect, it seems a wonder that one of us was not killed or seriously injured in this or some of the other unsupervised, highly dangerous shenanigans we got up to.

Besides the construction at the mill, there was a lot of activity in the town and surrounding countryside that seemed very grand and wonderful to me. President Roosevelt started many new "alphabet" programs (over forty in all) as part of his New Deal intended to ameliorate the effects of the Depression and improve many Americans' quality of life. Some of these were well-designed, much-needed reform measures, such as the Federal Deposit Insurance Corporation (1933) established to insure deposits and restore confidence in the banking system, the Securities and Exchange Commission (1934) established to regulate and increase public confidence in the stock market, the Federal Housing Administration (1937) established to regulate and improve mortgage availability for housing, and the Soil Conservation Service (1935) that sought to improve agricultural practices and protect the nation's farmland and water supply by introducing better farming methods and techniques like terracing fields and planting kudzu (a bizarre and ultimately disastrous idea) to control erosion.

One of the better New Deal programs, the Civilian Conservation Corps (CCC) established in 1933, effectively employed young men across the land in work useful to the public good, and unlike many of Roosevelt's ideas, it had the added benefit of disappearing when the need for it passed. The CCC, or "Three Cs," worked in state and national parks and made improvements in public facilities in rural areas. A camp housing about two hundred young men was built on the high ground west of Highway 31 just south of the main entrance to Chapman on company land. The buildings, long low-frame structures covered with tar paper, comprised a mess hall, dormitories, an auditorium, and offices. They were not luxurious in any way but perfectly adequate for the job. The young men recruited to the CCC, mostly working-class boys who faced unemployment in the job-scarce civil sector, received room and board, clothing, and a little pocket money for doing useful work until the economy improved. They wore uniforms: blue denim utilities and hats for work and a green semimilitary dress uniform like park rangers for more formal occasions. Supervised by a professional staff, many of whom were reserve officers in the military, they built bridges on the country roads around Chapman and fire towers for the Forestry Commission, linking them together by installing a dedicated system of phone lines. In the beginning, the camp housed only whites, but its occupants were all blacks for the last year or so that it operated. The economy started to pick up in the late 1930s, and the camp closed near the end of the decade. Like many other important parts of Chapman and its infrastructure, all vestiges of the CCC camp have disappeared. From everything I know about this program, it was well run and a good thing.

A less respected scheme put in by FDR was the Works Progress Administration (the WPA, or "We Piddle Around" in the vernacular) established in 1935, which offered temporary jobs to older unemployed men in public work projects and seemed to be marked with considerable mismanagement and graft. From what I saw, the work ethic was lax to nonexistent as compared to the CCCs and private employment. The WPA surveyed the low-lying ground on which Chapman was built and constructed a well-built system of long, straight, deep ditches joined with good-quality, permanent culverts and sewers, which effectively drained storm water and reduced flooding in the town. I used to pass the workmen digging these ditches every day on the way to and from school and observed a lot of standing around and talking. Still, the end results were positive for Chapman, and this program also faded away at the end of the 1930s. At this time the main roads linking Chapman to the highway, as well as the main streets in the town, had been paved, and concrete sidewalks had been constructed in the central part of town. I am not sure if the WPA had anything to do with these improvements, but it was probably involved in some way.

I MADE SOLID ACADEMIC progress throughout the seven years in the school at Chapman, always making good grades without much effort, attended by a little boredom since I wasn't really challenged. Outside of my immediate family, my socialization, with respect to my relatives in Chapman and Birmingham and the various adults I came into contact with, developed well enough. The grownups, many very intelligent and cultured business and professional people, were usually nice to me. A lot of them took enough interest to devote considerable time talking to me. In retrospect I think they saw some spark of potential that they wanted to encourage. I liked dealing with adults and was more at ease with many of them than with a lot of kids my own age.

Two men who meant a lot to me in my young years were Jake Lehmann and Stanley Horn. Mr. Lehmann lived in Birmingham and operated a very busy and successful accounting firm with his nephew Joe Ullman. Their more than six hundred clients included most of the major lumber companies in Alabama. They were the first Jewish people I knew, and both had played professional baseball, Mr. Lehmann in the Class A Southern League and Joe Ullman as a big league relief catcher with the St. Louis Cardinals. Tough guys with the rough edges knocked off and overlaid with a patina that reflected their more genteel second profession, they looked like characters out of a Humphrey Bogart movie. Mr. Lehman was muscular, short, and squat with a wizened face, while Joe was tall and lanky with very black shiny hair, eyebrows, and eyes, an olive complexion resembling a perpetual deep tan, and a slightly Asian look. They smoked Picayune and Home Run cigarettes, respectively, unfiltered and made with harsh, black tobacco. Smoking these was the weed equivalent of drinking straight medicinal alcohol, and they made me choke when I later tried them. Mr. Lehmann started working for W. T. Smith in 1917 and did the company's audits and financial statements, as well as the family's personal tax returns. My parents liked him and Joe well, and the two always stayed at our house when working in Chapman. Very intelligent, witty, and kind, Mr. Lehmann always brought a little present when he came and made room for some one-on-one time with me. His Birmingham offices were down the hall from my dentist, Dr. Edmund Wood, and I always looked forward to seeing Mr. Lehmann when I went there to have my teeth worked on. He had my picture hanging on the wall of his personal office.

Mr. Horn published the Southern Lumberman in Nashville and knew everybody worth knowing in the business. A tall, spare man with a lean, stern face, handsome and very dignified, he was an authority on Samuel Johnson, Civil War history, baseball, and the lumber industry, as well as a formidable writer who had authored several books in addition to pieces for the *Atlantic Monthly* and *Saturday Evening Post*. He and my father had a lot of common interests and mutual respect. Unlike my father, Mr. Horn was one of the funniest men I have been privileged to know. His high intelligence took in everything around him, and he often related wonderful stories with droll humor and a straight face. He had played a little semipro baseball, and while not on par with Mr. Lehmann and Joe Ullman as an athlete, he had a masterful understanding of the game and its human side. Having owned the Southern League's Nashville club and known all the major figures in the game, he produced a steady stream of side-splitting tales in the vein of Ring Lardner about the players and other characters around professional ball. He was equally at home talking about some of the more colorful people in the lumber business, especially the japes and knaves who had made it big despite their ignorance. I knew Mr. Horn from the times he used to stay at our house when I was little until his death in the late 1970s. In the later years of our relationship, when we attended association meetings, I never missed an opportunity to sit at his knee at breakfast (he used to order the "bud end" of the grapefruit, supposedly sweeter, which always had the desired effect of confounding the waiter) or in the bar at the Roosevelt Hotel in New Orleans, and I would get him to retell some of my favorite stories. One of these involved a badly run yo-yo factory he had invested in. Mr. Horn thought he would kill two birds with one stone by having this business make bats for his ball club at a considerable savings over the Louisville Sluggers they used. All went well until his star hitter's bat broke on what would have been a game-winning home run ball after poling three fouls off fastballs high into the stands behind home plate. The disgusted player stormed back to the dugout deeply frustrated and loudly announced that either the God damned yo-yo wood bats had to go (they did) or he had to be traded. Another involved a countryman from the hills of Tennessee who made a lot of money in the hardwood lumber business during World War I and finally visited Memphis, where that trade was centered. In telling Mr. Horn about the wonderful sights he had seen there, he mentioned being particularly impressed by a theater he had attended and talked at length about it. Curious, Mr. Horn pressed him for the name of this place, which the rube had forgotten. He finally dredged it up out of his memory and remarked, "Yeah, I remember now—I seen it over the door. It was the E-X-I-T theater."

IN THE SUMMER OF 1940, my brother, Greeley, went off for two months to Camp Carolina near Brevard, North Carolina. An established, well-run place, the camp drew boys from all over the South, and many of the senior counselors were prep school and college teachers. One of these was Ramsay D. Potts Jr., a tall, lanky, and handsome economics professor with yellow hair from Tennessee, who organized a weeklong trip to the New York World's Fair at the end of camp for a group of ten or so boys. Greeley was enrolled, and Potts agreed to take me as the youngest (I was nine) and only noncamper. We rode a day coach to New York and sat up all night. It was a fun adventure with a lot of interesting new sights and sounds. I remember pulling into the Baltimore Station early in the morning and buying a breakfast of bananas and oranges from the "news butcher," who passed through the car selling eats and papers out of the large baskets he carried. We stayed in one of the big commercial hotels in midtown Manhattan, four boys to a room, and everybody behaved surprisingly well. We went to the fair as a group every day, riding the Long Island Railroad from nearby Penn Station to Flushing Meadows near the location of the Forest Hills tennis complex. The fair seemed unbelievably large with interesting modern architecture, and I never got tired of it. I especially enjoyed two of its thrilling rides. The Parachute Jump hoisted you about five hundred feet in the air swinging under a chute attached to guidance cables, then released you to float down—it was exhilarating and provided an excellent view of the whole place but was not dangerous. The roller coaster was world-class and very scary. We saw the beautiful, buxom, and statuesque Eleanor Holm and erstwhile ape-man Johnny "Tarzan" Weissmuller swim in Billy Rose's *Aquacade*, as well as several very impressive divers and clowns who were fun to watch going off the high board. Some extremely interesting exhibits included General Motors' *World of Tomorrow*, which anticipated the interstate highway system, and General Electric's show, which exhibited the first television set and man-made lightning. The hot dogs were the best I had ever eaten.

Even as a little kid, I was interested in the war, which had started the year before in Europe, and I found it more than a little strange that the British and Germans were running exhibits in close proximity to each other. The Battle of Britain was in full swing at the time, and the papers and radio were full of war news. The United States was still technically neutral, but it seemed obvious that at some point we would join the war on the British side. I admired the German military machine but not its politics. Three years later on August 1, 1943, Ramsay Potts, by then a major, was one of the principal leaders of the first big raid on the Ploesti oil refineries in Romania, flying a four-engine B-24 named The Duchess from a base in Libya in that extremely dangerous and costly low-level strike. His B-24, with its ten-man crew, carried 3,100 gallons of high-octane gas and 4,300 pounds of bombs. It grossed over 64,000 pounds on takeoff on this flight across the Mediterranean, a 2,000 mile round trip that lasted over thirteen hours. This early exercise in strategic bombing did considerable damage to the objective despite some screw-ups in execution. Potts accounted himself very well in the action and was soon a highly decorated boy colonel. He ended the war with a distinguished record as a combat leader and went on to become a general in the Air Force Reserve and a prominent Washington lawyer.

After Ramsay's tour, our group of boys dispersed. Greeley and I went a few miles past the fair to Douglaston, Long Island, to spend a few days with our aunt Estelle and her husband, Keve Larson, the first of many visits for me. Estelle took us to Coney Island to see the boardwalk and swim and drove us all over the area in her sporty 1936 Ford convertible. One day we drove to Port Washington a few miles to the east of Douglaston to see one of Pan American's four-engine Boeing 314 Clippers take off from their base on Long Island Sound for a long Atlantic crossing. At this time, Pan Am's services ran to Foynes in southwestern Ireland (the northern route) and Lisbon in Portugal, both neutral ports. Charles Lindbergh had taken off from a nearby field to go to Paris only thirteen years before, and seeing and hearing the great flying boat was heady stuff that served to whet my already considerable appetite for all things aeronautical. Estelle also took us to LaGuardia Airport, which was five or six miles from Douglaston on the way to the city, where I feasted my eyes on the most planes I had ever seen in one place, mostly airline Douglas DC-3s and Lockheed Lodestars. Greeley was too interested in all this to bother me much, and we enjoyed the trip together.

The balance of my preteen growing up wasn't particularly happy, and I don't look back on this period with much satisfaction. I exhibited many bad traits in the years between ages ten and thirteen, when I was trying to grow up. It was mostly trial and error with a lot of the latter. I wanted to leave childhood behind but didn't know how to emotionally, and I received few clues from my parents, who took very good care of me in the physical sense but provided little in the way of constructive coaching and guidance. My father meant well in his fashion but didn't know how to communicate or express love and affection or to let anyone get close to him. His constant criticisms had the effect of robbing me of confidence. Kids require discipline to grow up healthily, and it is the parent's or teacher's responsibility to communicate a sense of fairness and reasonable purpose in its administration; otherwise, it comes across as misplaced and mean-spirited, which leads to resentment and more bad conduct. My mother showed more warmth and love but never gave me much strong direction or advice either. I was rebellious and justified some of my sorry ways thinking that since I wasn't cut out to be a good boy, I would skate by as the best bad boy I could manage, which wasn't very satisfying. I didn't get into any really serious trouble, but I didn't have an easy time. I was prone to making excuses and lying about things I had done and sometimes feigned sickness to stay home from school. I stole a few things like packages of BBs and chewing gum. My male hormones started to kick in strongly, leaving me frustrated and to a large degree ignorant as to what was going on. When I was twelve, my parents gave me a little book entitled *Growing Up*, which explained where babies came from in very general terms and not much else. I think they were embarrassed to talk about sexual matters with me, although I was cautioned against masturbation and sex outside of marriage in broad terms and was left to my own devices to fill in the blanks of my sexual ignorance.

Not withstanding my difficulties in getting along with my parents and brother, I had both deep feelings for them, our home, and our little town and a profound belief in their goodness. When away from them for extended periods, I felt great sorrow. Christmas was especially meaningful to me in those years. Aside from the excitement of the presents, the season's Christmas tree, decorations, hymns, and carols always made me do some profound thinking for a young boy. I deeply appreciated what I had and was largely able to ignore the lack of family closeness. I felt for the poor children I knew, white and black, and admired their families' ability to hold their heads up

Floyd, Floyd, Sr., and Greeley when Greeley was a student at Episcopal High School.

and make it with far fewer material things than we had.

Greeley went off to Episcopal High School in Alexandria, Virginia, in the fall of 1941. He had also skipped a grade and entered the tenth there at age fourteen. I don't know that he wanted to go, but he had no choice. My father had strong feelings about our education, and my mother always backed him up. He may have been the only boy in the county to go off to high school at that time. On December 7 of that year, a Sunday afternoon, I was playing football on the lot behind the Spann house up the street, when one of the Spann girls came out to tell us that the Japs had bombed Pearl Harbor in the Hawaiian Islands. That stopped the game, and I ran home to join the grownups in the living room in front of the radio, exited and anxious.

I went off to Camp Carolina with Greeley for two months the next summer. I was homesick the whole time, which kept me from enjoying the experience much. We were separated into four groups by ages and supervised by junior counselors, who were college boys. We got instruction every day in sports ranging from golf and tennis to boxing and wrestling, archery and riflery. The camp overlooked a good-sized man-made lake where we swam and canoed. We lived in rustic wood-framed cabins that were comfortable enough and ate together in the big mess hall, which served good food. We didn't get away from the camp property much, but I remember going into Brevard with a group one Saturday in August to have lunch and go to the movies. I bought a paper that headlined the Marines' unopposed landing on Guadalcanal in the Solomon Islands northeast of Australia, which made a considerable impression on me. Everyone back home, including kids like me and our parents and grandparents, was united in support of our forces and avidly followed the news. The naval battles of the Coral Sea and Midway had recently been concluded with heavy losses on both sides. The U.S. Navy lost two of its precious carriers, the *Lexington* in the Coral Sea and the *Yorktown* at Midway, but many of the pilots and aircrew had been saved to fight again. The Japs lost one small carrier in the Coral Sea but four of their big ones at Midway, along with a large number of their most highly trained and experienced naval airman. These actions were among the first major naval engagements fought solely by aircraft (the surface units never saw one another), and Midway dealt the Jap fleet a decisive blow from which it never recovered.

Camp held two more adventures for me, the first being a spectacular departure from the canned program. Two of my favorite comic strips were *The Katzenjammer Kids* and *The Captain and the Kids*, which sprang from the former. These strips revolved around a portly old retired Teutonic sea captain raising his twin nephews, Hans and Fritz, smartass blond boys about my age who played an unending series of practical jokes on the captain and other authority figures without really hurting anyone. On more than one occasion, they had crept up to a hornet nest and inserted a plug in the small entrance hole at the bottom so as to remove the hive of enraged insects without harm to themselves for use as the main prop in their trick of the moment. Hornets are native to South Alabama, but their population is small. Reclusive and secretive, they usually build their large papier-mâché nests (a little larger than a rugby football and wider at the top) in hardwood trees whose leaves aid concealment. Their very potent sting is much more painful than that of wasps or bees. At that time, I had never seen one of their nests in the wild and had gleaned my knowledge of their ways from the funnies and movie cartoons. One night in the cabin, when we were talking just before lights out, one of the boys mentioned that he had spotted a fine hornet nest built in a mountain laurel overhanging the lake on the far bank in an isolated area easily accessible only by water. I was intensely interested and asked for precise directions to the location, while simultaneously starting to form a plan leading to the mother of all Camp Carolina practical jokes.

Late the next morning, during a free period, I checked out a canoe for a reconnaissance of the hornet nest. I was not committed to any action unless conditions looked very favorable, but I had armed myself with the plug from my small flashlight, which looked to be perfect for stopping up the nest if conditions permitted. I spotted it without any difficulty and, eager and curious, eased the canoe to a point about thirty feet away for a really good look. I didn't know that hornets employ scouts as a sort of combat air patrol to protect their turf. They had seen me and divined my intentions and notified higher headquarters back at the nest. They formed their attack plan with dispatch and got it in motion. One minute I was drifting in the canoe, fat, dumb, and happy, and the next thing I knew, I was being attacked from head to toe by thirty or so flying warriors adept at sinking their stingers into my tender hide. The only smart thing I did that day was to dive overboard instantly and swim away under water as quickly and as far as possible. I finally had to surface and dragged myself up on the dam with my eyes swelling shut, in intense pain and probably going into shock. The hornet headquarters recalled the attacking force and gave me no more trouble.

The next thing I remember is waking up in the small infirmary the camp maintained and talking to a doctor who had been called from town. I lay in the bathtub a lot, then was covered with calamine lotion and spent four or five days recovering. If I had had a weak heart or allergy, this might have been fatal instead of merely serious business. I didn't get into any trouble over it as I maintained that I had been minding my own business, which was correct as far as it went. It was a harsh introduction to the truism "you can't believe everything you read in the papers," which taught me to be more respectful of nature and its wild creatures.

The end of the camp experience was celebrated with a two-day canoe trip down the French Broad River. We put in near Brevard, four to a canoe, and traveled with the aid of the current and some paddling along the small river through largely unpopulated country. We made a camp in a field alongside the stream, where a party of camp employees met us with a kitchen on wheels, food for supper and breakfast, and tents that we erected in short order. It was a pretty ride and an adventure for most of us. The next day we made it to the outskirts of Asheville by midmorning, where the river part of the trip terminated. We got on buses for the short ride to the Biltmore Estate, the gigantic country home of George W. Vanderbilt, a sort of transplanted French Renaissance chateau set among beautiful woods and gardens. At that time, the estate still operated its own dairy, and our tour ended there, where we were given all the ice cream we could eat.

Camp was good for me, even if I didn't enjoy it a lot. I was bothered by homesickness, shyness, and a lack of confidence, which made me self-conscious when learning to play some of the sports, like golf and tennis. I did fairly well in boxing and wrestling and enjoyed shooting .22s in the riflery class. I wish I had participated in sports more—I think I might have had some success in athletics later on if I had made a better start.

BACK HOME IN CHAPMAN, the war touched our lives on a daily basis. Though commodities like meat, sugar, coffee, shoes, tires, and gasoline were rationed, ostensibly to conserve supplies, there were no real shortages. The intent was probably to dramatize the war effort by exacting token sacrifices on the home front as well as to save a stock of scarce items. All able-bodied men under thirty-five, except a few in essential civil occupations supporting the war effort, were in uniform. Earl followed Nick into the navy and received a direct-line officer commission as a full lieutenant. He served as a 42-year-old volunteer based in New Orleans using his expertise to procure lumber and get it overseas for the forces. The work took him to North Africa and Europe; his job was useful, and he enjoyed it. Julian talked the Army Air Corps into reactivating his commission and making him an intelligence officer. A big party was held at the Forestry Commission's McGowin Tower (a ranger station Julian helped establish in the 1930s to detect forest fires and dispatch equipment to put them out) on a cool night in the fall of 1942. I attended with my parents and a large crowd of W. T. Smith and state forestry people who came to eat barbequed chicken and honor their 39-year-old boss and benefactor. Word came the next day that he had been rejected on account of his kneecap, so he stayed on running the forestry and logging operations and expanding his consulting business with Les Pomeroy.

By this point, I had developed a serious interest in following the progress of the war and read everything I could about it, in addition to listening to the radio and getting a visual feel from pictures in *Life* magazine, newsreels, and movies. The Battle of Britain, where the Royal Air Force (RAF) turned back the Luftwaffe in the summer of 1940, had made a deep impression, as did the Afrika Korps operations in North Africa under Erwin Rommel, sparking a lifelong fascination with these events. I painted a fair watercolor likeness of Rommel at this time, which I kept in my bedroom. I now have a similar professionally done portrait of him on my office wall.

That fall, the forces of the British Empire under Bernard Montgomery turned back Rommel's panzers at the Second Battle of El Alamein, just west of Alexandria and Cairo in Egypt. Within a week an Anglo-American force under the command of Dwight Eisenhower landed in Morocco and Algeria to conduct the very successful "Operation Torch." Rommel's forces, caught between Allied forces to the west and east, were at the end of a long, interdicted supply line across the Mediterranean. In February 1943 Rommel dealt the U.S. II Corps a blow at the Kasserine Pass, but the Germans failed to capitalize on their success due to shortages of fuel and supplies and (according to Rommel) because he was ordered to exploit his penetration in the wrong direction. Soon after, he hit the British Eighth Army at the Battle of Medenine but couldn't do much damage. Rommel then left Africa in March 1943 to undertake an important role in the defense of Nazi-occupied Europe. When most of the fighting ended that spring, 238,000 Germans and Italians had been taken prisoner in North Africa, which proved fortuitous for both W. T. Smith and some of the prisoners.

W. T. Smith was pumping out lumber at a high rate, thanks to the brothers' foresight in modernizing the production facilities in 1938. In September 1943, James Forrestal, then undersecretary of the navy, awarded the company the coveted Army-Navy "E" Award "for outstanding production of war materials," and a grand celebration was held in Chapman later in the fall for the presentation. W. T. Smith was the largest lumber producer in Alabama, and its products were sent over most of the world during the war. Many homesick soldiers in places like England, Italy, and New Guinea wrote home about feeling heartened by seeing the company's locomotive trademark (Old 14) stamped on lumber used at their facilities. Labor was scarce, and women were employed for the first time to do some of the lighter jobs in the plants.

At this time, a large contingent of Afrika Korps troops had been shipped to the southeastern United States, and many made their first stop at a big, hastily constructed master POW camp at Aliceville in western Alabama. Julian negotiated with the army to get two hundred of these men to work at W. T. Smith for the balance of the war. A Highway Department camp located on old U.S. 31 (now AL-185) just north of Greenville, which had housed state prisoners used for road maintenance, was made available for the German POWs, who arrived in the fall of 1943. Most worked with the logging crews in the woods to fell trees with "gator tail" saws and cut them into log lengths. Power saws, invented in 1930 by Andreas Stihl in Stuttgart, Germany, were widely used by Hitler's armies. They were not seen much in southern logging until the early 1950s. The prisoners were good at this work and seemed to enjoy it. A few of them worked at the machine shop in Chapman, where one of their first jobs was cutting up twelve retired company locomotives with acetylene torches into scrap metal for the war effort. These steam engines would have become very valuable as functional antiques from the 1880s and 1890s, but no one had the foresight to preserve them.

I saw the POWs on an almost daily basis. The Afrika Korps comprised some of Germany's best troops, most of whom were veterans of the campaigns in Poland and France at the start of the war. Fine-looking young men with deep tans, a lot of them had blond hair and looked exactly like the "Germans" in the war movies of the day. Mostly handsome and tough looking, they compared very favorably in demeanor and appearance with their scruffy, sad-sack American guards, who sat in the shade or slouched around smoking cigarettes and looking bored. The guards, one for each working party of Germans, were armed with M1 carbines, mostly symbolic, as the Germans were well behaved and had nowhere to go, hence no reason to escape. I think most of them realized that they were well off and safely out of the brutal fight for what was by then a lost cause. Even so, they remained loyal to their country, and those among them who criticized it often met with unfortunate, fatal "accidents." One died like that in the Greenville camp from hanging, officially a suicide but almost certainly of the assisted variety. I have read that there were a good many such deaths at the big Aliceville cage.

Under the Geneva Convention, POWs are entitled to humane treatment and must be paid if put to labor. To his credit, Julian saw that our prisoners received excellent treatment in their camp and at work. He took me there in early 1944 when I was almost thirteen for a detailed look around. The Germans, using their ingenuity, had turned the convict camp into a neat, pleasant spot. In fact, it compared favorably to the living conditions I experienced in a couple of places as a young Marine a few years later. The clean and airy barracks had cots and footlockers on each side of a center aisle. The mess hall, with its red-and-white checked tablecloths, had a cheerful atmosphere. The Germans had excavated cool cellars in the hard red clay under each barrack, screened them in, and floored and finished them with lumber, creating comfortable recreational spaces for reading, playing cards, smoking, and drinking their beer ration. They had their own cooks, one of whom once gave me some very good, hot, freshly baked cookies. They also had their own officers and doctor. Besides the good food and conditions in their camp, they were given unusual recreation opportunities. On weekend afternoons, small groups occasionally got to go to the movies at the Ritz Theater in Greenville where they sat in the balcony. In warm weather, large groups of the prisoners were trucked to the lake at Edgefield for swimming parties on the site where my house now stands. I watched them enjoying themselves swimming and horsing around and even trying to catch snakes (unsuccessfully) in the water.

Years later, my good friend and logging superintendent, Bill Parmer, told me about his experiences working the Germans who felled trees and sawed logs in support of our Greenville sawmill. Bill liked them and remembered them as good, smart workers with an eye for business. He told of an episode in which Willi, the German noncommissioned officer (NCO) in charge of one of the work parties, came to him in a huff one day over the timber they had been assigned to cut. At the prisoners' election, the company paid them on a piecework rather than hourly basis, so the more they produced the more they earned. Logs were measured then using the Doyle Log Scale (a calculation based on small-end diameter and log length), which favored big timber. In effect, the same amount of work cutting large wood yielded a lot more volume than cutting smaller-diameter trees. Willi told Bill that his men couldn't be bothered with cutting the trashy timber they had been assigned, adding, "Give us the big trees over there. Let the niggers cut the little trees!" Bill said that though he couldn't fault Willi's economic reasoning, he couldn't afford to give in easily. So, they worked out a compromise whereby Willi's men would finish the instant task, and in the future timber would be apportioned more carefully on the basis of size and quality, with the Germans and black Americans getting the same amount of bad and good. Everybody ended up satisfied with this fair and diplomatic solution.

My description of the prisoners' living and working conditions may come as a surprise to some readers, but it is absolutely true. It should be remembered that we were thousands of miles from the fighting in a land of relative plenty with respect to simple, basic necessities. The Germans performed good-quality work, efficiently and productively taking the place of our men, who were off fighting. It was good business to keep them as motivated, healthy, and happy as possible. I believe that this made a lot more sense than the inhuman, savage treatment afforded prisoners by many belligerents, and if carried out as a general rule in wars, this style would better serve all concerned in the long run. For several years after the war, Julian's office received many letters from former prisoners in Germany thanking the company for their treatment and sending their personal regards to various company employees with whom they had worked.

THE SUMMER OF 1944 started with the June 6 D-Day landing of a large Allied invasion force on the Normandy beaches along the French channel coast. I was visiting my first cousin George S. "Pete" Eastwood II at his home in Mountain Brook for a few days, and we heard the news after breakfast that morning on the radio. I remember well the bright cool day in the beautiful Birmingham suburb, just as I remember the days when I heard about the other defining events of the war. Later that morning, we rode bicycles past many of the attractive homes set back from the tree-lined streets in their neatly landscaped yards to the Mountain Brook Club. We swam in the pool and ate lunch in the grillroom, which embodied the club's posh, monied, and refined Southern WASP culture. The war with Germany had started almost five years before, and the invasion boosted everyone's morale tremendously. Most Americans felt confident that we would win, even in the darkest days of World War II, because we had goodness and righteousness on our side (and also because we were a long way from frontline death and terror). The invasion made this a certainty in our minds, and most felt that the assured victory would come sooner rather than later. Those who lost fathers, sons, or brothers understood the war for the meat grinder that it was. For kids like me, and probably a lot of grown-ups, it seemed a noble, grand adventure of good overcoming evil, which obscured the terrible pain and suffering overseas and our minor inconveniences at home. The war did have the positive effects of uniting the country in a way that younger people today may find difficult to understand; it ended the Depression once and for all with full employment at better wages; it caused a massive leap forward in all sorts of technologies such as automotive, aviation, and electronic design and production methods. Finally, it jump-started the South out of the malaise of second-class citizenship that had been its lot since the days of Reconstruction following the Civil War. Hundreds of airfields were built in the region, along with a heavy concentration of army and navy bases to take advantage of the favorable climate and easy living. Along with the concurrent development of air-conditioning for all manner of buildings, homes, and transportation, the wartime investment in military and production facilities with their related infrastructure was the opening shot in the South's rise again as the revitalized Sun Belt.

Back in Chapman, I went to work in the commissary's grocery department as a general-purpose flunky. I got a Social Security card and made twenty-five cents an hour. It was mostly light work with all manner of people to talk to, so the time passed pleasantly and rapidly. I stayed there for a month, then was sent back to Camp Carolina to attend the second half (four weeks) of that summer's program. I didn't want to go, and by mustering up all the resistance I could, I'd gotten out of the first half. One day I found myself alone on a Pullman car on the *Crescent Limited* watching the fields of north Georgia go past the window. My parents were determined to make something out of me whether I liked it or not. In the throes of beginning adolescence, I was not easy to discipline or control. Maybe they felt that a more structured environment around a lot of kids my age and social class would bring me along. My father, a devoted Anglophile, probably thought that sending me away from my home as a little boy, barely thirteen, was in keeping with the tried and proven upper-class English tradition.

When the train pulled into Greenville, South Carolina, at about four in the afternoon, someone met me for the two-hour drive to Brevard. The camp was just as I remembered with the exception that almost all of the counselors were either very young (under eighteen) or fairly old. I muddled through the month homesick and not very happy, but I was starting to acquire some of the toughness needed to cope with unpleasant situations beyond one's control. Pretty soon we did the traditional canoe trip, and my parents picked me up for a visit to High Hampton, a rustic resort in nearby Cashiers, where they were spending a few days with my mother's sister Lucy, her husband, and other relatives.

After we returned home, I had a couple of weeks in Chapman, which effectively ended my childhood there. On September 17, 1944, I boarded *The Southerner* at the big Terminal Station in Birmingham to start the trip to a new life away from home, and it would be eleven years before I would return permanently.

3

School Days

The *Southerner*, the train that carried me away from Alabama and my childhood there, was new, all coach, and streamlined, with shiny stainless steel cars, reserved seats (a new innovation), and a dining car. I rode with my cousins Pete Eastwood and Jim McVoy and a couple of other older boys. The seats got hard after a couple of hours, but we could get up and move around when we wanted to. Though not up to the Pullman car standard of service and comfort, the train was nice considering the wartime conditions, with everyone having a seat and access to hot food. I felt both apprehensive and excited about what I was getting into, more resigned than enthusiastic, and tried to act nonchalant and grown-up. By the time we pulled into the station in Alexandria, Virginia, the next morning, we were tired and grungy. We took a cab to the school a few miles west of the center of town and registered.

Episcopal High School (EHS) sits on top of a high hill on a large property with expanses of trees and fields. It borders the Virginia Episcopal Seminary attended by young churchmen pursuing a postgraduate degree in religion in preparation to be ordained in the Episcopal priesthood. When I started, the school had an enrollment of 216 with thirty-one seniors who would graduate. Mr. Archibald R. "Flick" Hoxton was principal with a staff of eighteen masters. Then sixty-nine, he had run the school since 1913 and taught there for fifteen years before that. Six of the masters, Messers. Reade, Daniels, Shackleford, Carter, Williams, and Whittle, had started teaching at EHS between 1893 (Reade) and 1910 (Whittle). The other masters, with the exception of Mr. Male and Mr. Clark, were getting on in middle age. Mr. Hoxton and his half dozen senior henchmen reminded me of overripe citrus left unpicked on the tree; they mostly had thick, blotchy, wrinkled skin and rheumy eyes and walked with the carriage of the elderly in their

Standing: Julian M., Floyd Sr., Miss Essie, and Earl M. Seated: Mason M., Florence M., Floyd, Greeley, Mary Alice, Ellen Pratt McGowin, Bettie M., Alec M., Eleanor, and Little Bettie at Edgefield in 1947.

threadbare, chalk-stained suits. Though all probably decent, well-intentioned, moral men with great depth of experience and teachers of adequate to superior ability, they were also considerably past their prime; some may thus have had difficulty empathizing with their students' needs for guidance and direction over and above discipline and quality lesson content.

At the time I attended EHS, most of the physical plant was old, plain, and well-worn with the exception of the gym, infirmary, and library, which had been built much more recently. The majority of the boys were housed in two large, three-story, brick dorms, Alumni and Memorial. A few seniors shared double rooms, but most boys lived in cubicles about five feet wide and ten feet deep; I have seen a picture of one of the cubicles taken in 1914, and they had not changed any thirty years later when I was assigned to one. Each contained a window over a radiator, a straight chair, a wardrobe with drawers and a small hanging closet, and a narrow cot. They contained no rugs, curtains, or other decoration and were open across the front, though canvas drapes hanging on each side of the hall end could be closed at night for a semblance of privacy. About thirty boys lived on each floor, sharing a communal head with open shower and toilet rooms on either side of a large room containing a number of washbasins and mirrors. There was no privacy in the head and very little anywhere else for most of the boys. On each corner of the dorm floor, two older boys shared a double cubicle, which was considered a slightly better standard of living than occupying a single. My cousin Jimmy McVoy, one of four senior monitors, and Tick Semmes, the head monitor, shared the double room across from the head in my dorm.

As EHS included grades nine to twelve, the students ranged in age from thirteen to eighteen, and each dorm was a duke's mixture of big and little boys, some relatively mature and worldly and others, like me, very small and naive. Life in the dorm gave me a box seat to observe how the older boys thought and acted, and maybe the idea was for the little guys to learn from watching the big boys. I rapidly caught up vicariously on the pleasures of sex, drinking and smoking, and other dark subjects.

The students were mostly Southerners, many from Virginia and the area around the District of Columbia and North and South Carolina. States like Georgia, Alabama, and Tennessee were also well represented. A sprinkling of boys came from all over the country and places like Cuba and Brazil. They were mostly from upper- and upper-middle-class WASP families, generally at least fairly smart and of good character. Some were the sons of congressmen and flag officers. Quentin Roosevelt attended the high school while his father, Teddy, was the sitting president of the United States, and Senator John McCain, himself the son of an admiral and later a presidential contender, is a graduate.

We all ate together in a large dining room on the first floor of the large building, which housed the kitchen, post office, principal's office, masters' lounge, study halls, and classrooms. The dining room contained ten tables on each side perpendicular to a wide central aisle running the length of the room. Each table seated fourteen boys and was presided over by a master, who sat at the head with his back against the wall. Senior boys sat nearest the master, and the youngest occupied the middle seats. The master served the generally good food on heavy china plates. Student waiters took care of two tables each and were paid for their work, in addition to receiving other privileges.

There were forty monitors in addition to the head monitor and his four senior assistants. All third- or fourth-year boys appointed by Mr. Hoxton to help maintain discipline and order, they represented a privileged elite comprising a little over 20 percent of the student body. They were generally nice, solid boys who fit into the school's ethic. Some of the smarter freethinkers, otherwise qualified, didn't make the cut.

New boys like me were called "rats," although this didn't mean much after the first month or so. I can say that I was never hazed or physically abused at any time and experienced very little unfair treatment from the monitors when I was a rat or during my subsequent two years at the school. At the same time, I came to despise the EHS system, which I believe provoked bad attitudes and conduct from the common students. A less repressive and more open school society would have been better for everybody. I strongly object to a system that puts one group of young people in a position of authority over their peers and think the hazing done at the service academies and college fraternities is gross and obscene. I later went through Parris Island as a young Marine and found the orchestrated harassment dealt out by the professional cadre of drill instructors a very effective, positive experience and quite different from one group of kids lording it over another.

The school dress code required neatness and a good appearance at all times, meaning a coat and tie, reasonably clean clothes, shined shoes, and neatly trimmed hair. The coat-and-tie requirement covered all meals, classes, and chapel services. Boys our age did not wear suits, except on infrequent, important occasions, and I mostly wore sport coats with gray flannel or khaki trousers. Members of my generation expected one another to look as good as possible, and peer pressure saw to it that we conformed. Back then it was fairly easy to accurately judge peoples' places in society by how they looked and dressed, before traditional values were trashed in the 1960s and 70s. I didn't have a lot of fancy clothes, and I wore a lot of hand-me-downs from Greeley, but I made a conscious effort to present myself as well as I could.

The school took great pride in its honor code—to wit: "I will not lie. I will not cheat. I will not steal. I will report any person who does so." Students inscribed exam papers with the following signed statement: "I hereby certify upon honor that I have neither given nor received assistance since the beginning of this examination." While much was made of the above and violations were rare, I question whether it meant a great deal unless the student had accepted these values on his own, making the platitudes window dressing. I later attended Lawrenceville, a much larger school, which had an unwritten rule that students were to act as gentlemen but no honor code as such, and I never heard of anyone cheating or stealing during the two years I was there. In four years at Yale (four thousand plus undergraduates at the time), I recall only one case of a student being caught cheating on an exam, and he was summarily kicked out. In the Marine Corps, lying, cheating, nonpayment of debts, and the like were not tolerated under the threat of severe penalty and dismissal. An officer's word was his bond. Like Lawrenceville, Yale and the Marines didn't fool with pious, feel-good pretensions to honor, but the cultures of these institutions were strong enough to produce a very high level of good conduct.

EHS had a sort of penal code comprising some two hundred odd rules and regulations, each carrying a stated penalty of so many demerits, varying according to the severity of the offense. In the lobby across from the mailboxes at the front of the post office, each master had a clipboard mounted on the wall where he posted notices and, more importantly, demerits. The punishment recipient usually only learned of the master's displeasure when he saw the demerit prescription publicly posted, and I don't recall that one of the masters ever discussed a punishment award with me. We were expected to accept with stoic equanimity whatever the gods threw down, even in cases that clearly involved poor judgment or patent injustice. Nietzsche said words to the effect that "anything that doesn't kill you is probably good for you," and at times this idea seemed part of the masters' plan.

A student who got four or more demerits in a week had to "walk them off" on the road circling the principal's residence and the academic buildings in full view of all and sundry on the next weekly holiday. These were usually on Mondays instead of Saturdays for some arcane reason. Everybody got a minimum of one holiday a month to go to Washington for the day, but those who had accumulated four or more demerits during the week just ended were permitted no leave. The masters all had encyclopedic knowledge of the rules and penalties and were empowered to "stick" violators for infractions against the code, and in some cases, they made up infractions and penalties according to their own sense of righteousness. The monitors could also "stick" other boys, and part of their job was to rat out lesser kids if they saw them breaking the rules.

Most of the boys seemed happy enough and well adapted to the school's *modus operandi*, but I never liked it much. I was part of a minority of kids who were not inherently bad but thought for themselves and, finding some of the school's methods outside the values they could reasonably accommodate, formed a negative attitude as a result. Many of this group went on to considerable success. Besides the one or two percent of born losers found in any group, the boys who shared my feeling that the place inhibited development of their full potential amounted, I would estimate, to about 15 percent of the students enrolled. Former student John Stewart Bryan III (1952–56) writes in his *Chronicles*,

> "Son," my grandfather is reported to have said to my uncle at his wedding in 1938, "I hope today will be the happiest day of your life."

"No, Father," he is supposed to have replied, "the happiest day of my life was when I left the Episcopal High School."

The students who did like the school, particularly natives of the Old Dominion, exhibited an almost comical snobbery about the place. They, along with their parents, referred to it as The High School. Most of them hoped to attend The University (UVA). The sacrosanct few who got their tickets punched at the first two and went on to matriculate at The Seminary were adjudged to have gone to The Trinity. My guess is that EHS and UVA were solidly ensconced in the bottom half of the top fifty schools and colleges then as now, certainly very good and with some notable alumni, but hardly up to the pretensions of some of the swelled heads who felt so good about themselves by virtue of their attendance.

On a recent visit, my first and only since leaving in 1947, I was favorably impressed by the changes in attitudes and methods that have taken place in the ensuing years, in addition to a much improved, expanded, and handsome physical plant. EHS is now a kinder, gentler place, virtually unrecognizable from my day. The people I talked to, including the headmaster and development officer Jeff Clark, himself an ex-head monitor, were young, intelligent, and eager. When I told them of some of my frustrations with the school, I had a strong sense that they had heard it all many times before, and things were much changed for the better. They are still big on the honor code, which seems to be the link that ties them to the school's past and, as such, is viewed as a sacred symbol, regardless of its merits.

MY STUDIES AND SOCIAL development started out well enough as I was too intimidated by the place to be anything but a conformist and felt compelled to do well enough to merge into the crowd. I took English, ancient history, Latin, algebra, and probably a fifth course.

The EHS academic year was divided into fall, winter, and spring sections, with a final exam at the end of each period in each subject, which counted heavily toward one's grade. I did well in all my subjects initially and scored a ninety-six for the fall term in Mr. Evan James "Bus" Male's algebra class. He was a young man of about twenty-six who had been classified 4F (unfit for military service) due to a shoulder injury, though he looked pretty healthy. Mr. Male looked very German with tight lips, an unsmiling face, and an icy, stern demeanor. He was always very correct, but distant and aloof, and seemed to look right through me. I was never comfortable talking to him and feared him.

I didn't find the schoolwork difficult due to the solid foundation I had gotten in Chapman in the simple little three-room school. I probably would have sailed through EHS in four years if I had attained a happy mental equilibrium, but this was not to be. I was acutely homesick to begin with and sort of a "lost ball in the high weeds," too insignificant for anyone to pay any attention to. I liked some of the teachers and at that stage didn't have any reason to think badly of any of them. Mr. Henry T. "The Rock Ape" Holladay taught me Latin. He was a good teacher and an upbeat, cheerful personality who knew his students. After a good start, my unhappiness started to manifest itself in a progressively more slovenly study pattern, and

I ended up failing the course and having to repeat it the following year. Mr. Holladay knew that I was smart enough and accurately diagnosed my problem to be the result of insufficient work, calling me "The Play Boy." He was never mean to me, and I wish he had seen fit to sit me down and give me some good advice and counsel, as I liked and respected him, but that sort of thing wasn't done at the time, at least with the lesser kids.

Mr. Robert E. The Hawk" Latham was another nice man who taught me history. He had known my aunt Estelle in his younger days and was personable and had more social graces than most of the masters. I think several of them were heavy drinkers or had other personal or personality problems, but the war had been going on for several years, and the school probably had the best it could get, given the prevailing low salaries and lack of people to draw from. It goes without saying that there were no women teachers; the only two females on campus were Miss Annie "Enema Annie" Glascock, who ran the infirmary, and Miss Doris Coates, the dietician in charge of the food service. Miss Glascock was stocky and seriously ugly, with black hair and a matching mustache. She looked like a white-clad troll but was a kind, capable nurse and a good administrator, and she was always nice to me in the considerable dealings I had with her. Miss Coates was short and plump with a pretty face. She was about thirty-five and did a first-class job with what she had to work with, and she liked me and went out of her way to help me in a meaningful way later on.

I played "cake football" with the smallest boys who weighed less than 130 pounds. I didn't have enough knowledge or confidence to fill one of the more skilled positions like playing end or in the backfield and was a guard. I did alright but never got any real coaching. I also played centennial basketball but never learned to like the game or play it well. I belonged to the Wilmer Literary Society and took a confirmation course, which led to my joining the Episcopal Church, something I did on my own without any prompting from the school or my family. A seminary student, Hugh White, taught this on Sunday afternoons to about a dozen of us. Religion was a big deal at EHS. We had chapel every day, including Sunday night, and walked to the seminary for services in its big church every Sunday morning. I enjoyed the hymns and singing and tried to appreciate the theology, but

I never learned to understand much more than I had already gotten in the little nondenominational Sunday school in Chapman.

The daily routine at EHS followed a standard pattern that varied little from day to day and month to month. We got up at six thirty and breakfasted at seven. This wasn't a bad meal except when (once a week) fried scrapple was served in place of bacon or sausage. Scrapple is a Yankee dish popular in Philadelphia made from recycled pigs' noses, ears, tails, and other marginal parts. It was probably good, but I never was able to eat it after I learned the ingredients. Another breakfast accessory peculiar to EHS was treacle, which was used on pancakes, French toast, biscuits, and the like. I think it was sweet corn syrup, probably favored because it was cheaper than maple or cane, and I never used it, preferring jam or jelly if I couldn't have the good stuff.

We had classes in the morning and a short chapel service, which mixed prayers, a hymn or two, and announcements read by Mr. Hoxton or one of his lieutenants. During periods when we had no class, we sat at our assigned desks in one of the big second- or third-floor study halls for fifty minutes at a time. Half way down the big room, one of the masters sat at a desk on a raised dais along one wall, from which he had a good, clear view of the entire room. Monitors could hold up five fingers and, after getting a nod from the master on duty, leave the study hall to go to the bathroom, get a drink of water, or just take a stretch to relieve their boredom. Common kids like me were required to sit mutely and study (reading papers, books, or magazines was prohibited). Classes ended at three, at which point we went to athletics. The gym seemed very large and fine inasmuch as I had never seen anything but the small and mean structures at the high schools at home, and I took some pride in using such a grand facility.

For some relief from the campus, we were allowed to walk to a large new grocery store, the Country Garden Market, not far from the edge of the school property. The store served a recently built subdivision called Fairlington, and we bought a lot of snacks like chocolate milk, raisins, and cupcakes, and, later on, cigarettes. Girls who lived nearby could occasionally be spotted and sometimes talked to. Some of the big boys were successful in sneaking off for liaisons, a dangerous practice for a number of reasons. I also liked to go to the library, which was relatively new, good-looking, and attractively decorated. Besides indulging my reading habit with books and magazines, I enjoyed being in surroundings much nicer than the rest of the school. A little island of comfort, culture, and civilization in the midst of the stern and ugly facilities where we spent most of our time, it was my favorite place at EHS.

Shortly after supper every night, we went back to our study hall desks for a couple of hours and were allowed to write letters or read for pleasure during the last thirty minutes before we returned to the dorms to get ready for bed at 10 A.M. We didn't have to work outside of our lessons except for dishwashing in the scullery off the kitchen, which we did on a rotating basis, and there were enough kids so that this chore was not onerous.

We had Sundays off, except for church in the morning and chapel, or "vespers," after dinner. Mondays were usually the weekly holiday, and boys entitled to leave the campus were free to go to Washington for the day. We walked to the stop near the market and caught one of the frequent buses for a ride of thirty minutes to the terminal near the middle of town, a couple of blocks from the movies and stores along F Street. I very much looked forward to these pleasurable, albeit brief, respites from school and had a routine, at least initially. I usually got a haircut at the barbershop in the basement of the Willard Hotel, shopped at Garfinkel's Department Store, and ate hamburgers at the Mayflower Donut Shop for lunch. I also always visited the Brentano's bookstore near the movies to look for books about airplanes (there weren't many in those days). The afternoon was devoted to catching a newsreel and movie, preceded by music from a huge pipe organ that rose up on a hydraulic lift on one side of the stage near the orchestra pit. Sometimes the theater also put on a vaudeville show before the films. O'Donnell's seafood restaurant, located between F Street and the bus terminal, was popular, and I had no trouble buying beer there by the time I was fifteen. The Gaity Burlesque Theater was nearby and had popular girlie shows, risqué for the times though very tame by today's standards. Some of the big boys and masters occasionally favored its matinees, but I never looked old enough to get in, scantily clad women being considered much more of a danger to kids than beer.

I got along well enough during that first term. I didn't make any close friends, but I think I was well enough accepted by most of the boys, big and little. On the other hand, I just didn't like EHS much. I resented the school's culture, which affected my enthusiasm and work ethic, and was developing a rebellious attitude that would lead me into academic difficulties and self-defeating behavior patterns that I would struggle for years to move beyond.

That November, I rode the train from Washington to Douglaston in New York to spend Thanksgiving with the Larsons, the first of many such visits while I was in school and college. Greeley was there, and his descriptions of life at Princeton made it sound sophisticated and wonderful in stark contrast to EHS. I anticipated these short holiday outings eagerly, but they were somewhat bittersweet as they were over almost before you could blink, and it was time to crawl back into the pumpkin that boarding school represented.

The long Christmas holiday came a few weeks later. Mr. Willoughby Reade read *A Christmas Carol* at the last vespers service, which by tradition signaled the beginning of the holiday respite. He was about seventy-three at the time, a tall, spare, white-haired Victorian figure who specialized in giving readings of Charles Dickens. I always thought this appropriate in that EHS reminded me of nothing so much as a sort of Dickensian reformatory for lonely, wayward boys, which became a pest house during the annual infectious disease epidemics that swept through the school two out of the three years I was there.

After we were finally released to return home for the holidays, those of us heading south couldn't get space on the *Crescent Limited* out of Washington and ended up riding a very crowded ACL or Seaboard train overnight to Atlanta. It was full of servicemen, and people stood or sat on suitcases in the aisles. I was reading Colonel John W. Thomason's —*and a Few Marines*, which provoked the curiosity of some of the military people, and I let them pass the book around. We got to Atlanta and had several hours to kill waiting for the *Crescent*. It was a bright, cool Sunday morning, and I walked around the center of town with Fred Wilkerson, Junius Smith, and John "Sleepy" Owens, all older boys from Montgomery whom I had known for years. After we boarded the train, I stood in the vestibule at the end of my car looking out the open window in the top half of the door as we crossed into Alabama west of LaGrange. I stayed there most of the way to Montgomery, soaking up familiar scenery, the verdant countryside, the pines, cotton fields, and farm houses. Even though it was early winter and most of the homes were rustic and poor, the landscape communicated to me a feeling of warmth, life, and better times to come. I felt a profound sense of homecoming, the first of many such instances when I understood plainly that I was bonded to my native Alabama for better or worse.

The Christmas season in Chapman was always a good time, especially as being away made me really appreciate my home and the society around it. I sampled a few cigarettes and drinks out of sight of the grownups at some of the parties, but I wasn't a real user at that point. Tobacco flourished without prejudice and was widely used across the entire spread of economic and gender lines. Little kids and most athletes didn't smoke as a rule, but something like over half of the rest of society did, including many doctors, actors, rich people, and others of high status. Our part of the South had many Bible Belt-induced restrictions on drinking, and most of the rural counties, including Butler, were legally dry. As far as I could tell, this never had much to do with restricting the large-scale consumption of spirits; it just made getting good booze more inconvenient and expensive and was especially repressive and sometimes dangerous for the poorest working-class people. In most of the movies, the stars smoked and drank throughout, and the advertising was high-quality stuff pitched at would-be sophisticates, way over Joe Camel's head. I was certainly convinced that smoking and drinking constituted visible merit badges attesting to one's couth and maturity, and I resolved to give both a go as soon as I got a little older.

I went up to Douglaston for another long weekend toward the end of January. My uncle Nick, by then a lieutenant commander, was also there, just back from two years in the South Pacific with his Catalina squadron and courting his future wife, Elizabeth, who worked in the city for American Airlines. We went shopping together, and I got a new pair of shoes at Abercrombie & Fitch at their superb original store on Madison Avenue. I started feeling a little strange that day, and by the time I got back to school late on Sunday afternoon, I knew I was really getting sick. I turned myself into the infirmary where Miss Glascock checked me over and put me in the isolation ward, where several of the eight beds were already occupied. I was one of the first to come down with scarlet fever in what was to become a major epidemic affecting a third or more of the boys. Scarlet fever can be a serious disease with lasting effects, such as heart murmur, but I was fortunate only to have to lie low, feeling bad for a couple of weeks. I was also lucky to be in the infirmary, which was soon filled to capacity, and several dorm sections were turned into temporary wards.

On the night of April 12, as we sat in study hall at twilight, someone came in with a note for the master on duty. He read it and stood up to tell us that President Roosevelt had just died at his "Little White House" in Warm Springs, Georgia. I wasn't particularly sad to hear this as FDR was not trusted or admired by my family, but it was a solemn occasion marking the passing of an individual whose adept use of political power made for many changes, good and bad, in the country and the world.

In early May, the war in Europe ended with Germany's unconditional surrender, an event much celebrated by most all Americans. For my birthday later that month, my parents sent me an Eastern Airlines ticket from Washington to New York. I got out of school one afternoon at the start of the weekend and boarded a 21-passenger DC-3 at National Airport for the flight to LaGuardia, which took just over an hour. The stewardess was a beautiful blonde who, a couple of weeks later, was featured wearing her uniform in a Parker Pen ad in the *Saturday Evening Post* using one of their deluxe "P-51" fountain pens. I was much impressed by her as well as the airplane and the exotic sights, sounds, and smells peculiar to it. I loved every minute of the experience, and it cemented my resolve to fly myself someday if at all possible.

That summer of 1945, I did my first work for W. T. Smith, performing minor common-labor jobs in the Forestry Department. I cut brush with a machete to clear the view for the compass in the surveying crew and pulled the chain measuring distances between sets. I also worked with the timber markers and began to learn some of the rudiments of sustained-yield forest management. I got more out of it than the company did, and it served to begin to open my eyes to the hard labor that many people did for a living and helped the maturing process I had begun by going off to school.

On August 10, we started out in my father's Pontiac on the long drive to Highlands, North Carolina, for a ten-day vacation at the Country Club. We left Chapman in midmorning and stopped in Montgomery for lunch at one of the downtown hotels. There, we learned that the Japs had surrendered following the second atomic bomb drop at Nagasaki, and we witnessed a giant party forming among a horde of young Army Air Force officers and men from Maxwell and Gunter air fields. Champagne and booze of all descriptions flowed freely in the bar and dining room as well as the lobby, and it was an emotional scene. Many of the participants were seasoned combat veterans working at training and instructor jobs as a rest from the war, and the relief in their faces that it was finally over was very real and plain.

IN SEPTEMBER, I BOARDED the *Crescent* in Greenville and made my way back to EHS. I returned to my same cubicle in the dorm and picked up where I had left off. While perhaps not as acutely homesick, I wasn't happy to be back.

That year my closest friends included Andy Kelley, Hugh Richardson, and Jack Rollins. We were all minor rebels operating outside Mr. Hoxton's value and behavior systems. We used to meet regularly in an out-of-the-way spot on the edge of the school's 80-acre property to smoke cigarettes and compare our philosophies. Andy was Black Irish from the Chicago area and looked like a budding Mafia soldier; we called him "Machine Gun" after the famous gangster George Kelley. He left EHS after our second year to go to Lawrenceville, where we graduated together. Hugh was from Atlanta, a smart, pleasant guy who left EHS when I did to go to the Hill School in Pottstown, Pennsylvania, Lawrenceville's big rival. Jack Rollins was from Houston, also smart with a sardonic sense of humor. Another friend, not a part of the above group of subversives, was Ernest Helfenstein III from Frederick, Maryland. Intelligent, laid-back, and funny, Ernie was a good student who never got into trouble and liked the school. Descended from a line of German nobility dating back to the ninth century, his family came to this country during the Revolutionary War, and his father claimed that he was the first Helfenstein not to be a priest or minister since about the year 800. He joined the EHS faculty in 1957 and stayed there forty years, winding up as associate headmaster.

I made it a point to cultivate Miss Coates when I saw her during my dish-washing stints, and she made me a subwaiter with the opportunity to learn the job and occasionally help out when one of the regular waiters was sick or away on a sports team. This proved very valuable to me as I became one of the regulars the following year, a highly coveted and prestigious position bringing some extra pocket money, but more importantly, an extra holiday every month.

During that second year at EHS, I had to walk demerits three times, which served only to harden my resolve that the school and I were in different orbits. While I was technically guilty of the offenses as charged in each case, I was setup in two of them with the instigators getting off totally and completely. The most blatant setup got started in the mid-morning study hall kept by Mr. John M. "The Wet Dream" Daniel. An older boy, Richard Bland Lee from Gainsville, Virginia, sat in the desk behind me. He was bigger than I, played varsity football and baseball, and generally smelled strongly of BO. While brash and tough and not very intellectual, he wasn't truly mean, just a minor bully. Bland had been made a monitor with all its privileges. One, which he exercised on a daily basis, was to "hold up five" during our period together to escape the tedium for a few minutes by making a head call and then loafing around the water fountain in the hall for a few minutes. He would always come back to his desk with a mouthful of water, which he would spray down my neck and back as he sat down. I had to sit there and take it as it violated the code to rat out other boys, he was much too big and strong for me to fight, and old man Daniel's eyesight and attention were not strong enough to take in what was going on. Finally, one day after study hall ended, I saw Bland passing as I was getting a drink at the fountain—an opportunity too good to miss. Without hesitation I came up with a large mouthful, which I sprayed on his neck and back, and to his credit, he just grinned and kept going. When classes let out at noon, I went down to the lobby to my mailbox, and one of the boys told me I had better check Mr. Daniel's clipboard. I went over and read the following:

McGowin—10 demerits

For spitting a mouthful of water on another. Such actions should be associated with guttersnipes, not gentlemen.

John M. Daniel

I don't know what Bland thought, probably just that it was funny, and he made no move to come forward and take any responsibility. Mr. Daniel had his head up and locked and surely thought he had scored a good lick against a bad kid.

On another occasion, I got into trouble in one of my classes. I was minding my own business when Fuller E. "Ears" Callaway III passed me an insulting note. Scion of the LaGrange, Georgia, textile family (a Pullman car named for his grandfather went through Chapman on the *Crescent* every few days), he was a grossly unattractive boy with lank, longish, greasy black hair. His ears stuck straight out from the sides of this head, and somebody said he looked like a taxicab going downhill with both doors open. He had vaguely oriental-looking squint eyes set in a round, pasty face always festooned with yellow-topped, inflamed zits. "Ears" was not a friend. I scribbled a short reply to the effect that he should stay out of my way and stick his note in the appropriate place. The master only saw my part of the transaction and posted five of the best demerits for me when he went downstairs, which "Ears" found highly amusing. In later life, he married Ingrid Bergman's daughter Pia and lived in San Francisco. Years later, I read that he had committed suicide, possibly due to too much booze, drugs, and money.

The third and last time I got punished that year was entirely my own fault, and even though I never felt any warmth for Mr. Male, I recognized that he could have made my situation much worse. One night I got tired of studying and surreptitiously, or so I thought, composed a letter to my friend Elisha Poole, who went to high school in Greenville. When I finished, I put it in an envelope, which I put in my jacket pocket. The next thing I knew, Mr. Male appeared beside my desk and with a piercing glare told me to give him the letter, which I did, knowing I would get into serious trouble if he read it. Poole was an aggressively intelligent boy who, like me, had begun to experiment with cigarettes and liquor, and both of us were eager to be sexually active with girls. In truth, the interest and desire were all we had as opposed to any real knowledge or successes, but that didn't keep us from concocting ongoing plans and stratagems to effect the desired eventuality. When I had last seen him, we had discussed the possibility that our parents might allow us to rent a cottage for a week at Tower Beach in Ft. Walton after school was out for the summer. We thought that they might possibly stake us to this (I am sure now they would not have) and that we could lure some hot high school girls into our pleasure palace to rock and roll with booze and sex. In my letter I laid out these possibilities clearly and explicitly. The whole thing was totally wishful thinking but made for an interesting exercise in make-believe. I knew that Mr. Male was no friend of mine in that I had ended up failing his algebra class after a strong start the year before, and I felt that he had me figured for a sorry punk. I believed that if he read the letter and took it to Mr. Hoxton, it would be strong evidence of my lack of purity and the end of my time at EHS. When study hall ended, I walked up to Mr. Male at his desk and asked for my letter, which he handed over to me, unopened. He didn't say anything but gave me a chilling look and later seven demerits to walk off the next Monday.

In late winter of that second year, an epidemic of red measles swept through the school. This is a truly bad illness (for me, even more unpleasant than scarlet fever), and by the time I got it, nearly half the school was sick or recovering. The infirmary was full, so I lay in a bed in a room in Blackford Hall with other boys, too sick to care. We couldn't read as light was bad for the eyes while the illness was acute, but we were able to listen to the radio to songs like "Don't Fence Me In" and "Choo Choo Ch' Boogie," which were hits at the time. EHS is the only place I have ever been that suffered these mass illnesses, and it must have had something to do with the close contact and poor sanitation in the dorms.

Toward the end of the session, I tried out for, and was selected to sing with, the upcoming year's choir, one of thirty-seven members. We principally sang at church at the seminary every Sunday morning. The main attraction for me was that it "paid" an extra holiday per month, but I did enjoy the music. Happily, Ernie Helfenstein and I put in for a double cubicle and got it, so we would be moving to a new dorm and slightly larger and more private accommodations in the fall.

My studies were still a problem due to lack of motivation. I was trying to get by with minimum work, content just to pass as opposed to wanting to do my best. I eased through every subject except first-year Spanish. It finally dawned on me that my poor performance was going to add an additional year to my prep school sentence, an obviously self-defeating behavior, and I resolved that one way or another I would turn my situation around.

That summer I worked for the company in a loading crew in the mill's shipping department. The work was not unpleasant, and much of it took place in a big, tall, unpainted shed built of weathered wood over a rail siding, which was dark, spacious, quiet, and cool. It was one of the oldest buildings in the plant and dated back to before the turn of the century. I worked around whites and blacks, many of whom were getting on past middle age. They taught me how to chew tobacco, which I never really liked and only used sparingly to try to look tough. I gained a better idea of the business and an added appreciation for the way the people thought and worked.

Having turned fifteen that May, I got my driver's license (the age had been lowered during the war and was later raised back to sixteen). While I had the motor skills and reflexes to be a good driver, I lacked the maturity to exercise consistent good judgment, often driving too fast. I was a sort of infant Mr. Toad, enraptured by motorcars and the potential for speed they represented. My aunt Estelle got a new '47 Ford convertible, and Greeley and I were given her old '36, a classic in perfect shape and still very classy and handsome, with a V-8 engine and mechanical brakes. Besides the Ford, I sometimes got to drive my mother's Buick Special and a large Oldsmobile that belonged to Miss Essie. I may not have had any wrecks, but I did have some narrow escapes on the narrow streets and highways. I also started dating girls that summer, in Birmingham as well as at home—just enough to break the ice and gain a little confidence around them. I was at a very awkward, gawky age, and it would be another year before I became more successful in these affairs.

THE FOLLOWING SEPTEMBER, I got back to school early one day. Feeling lonesome, I stood looking out the window at the end of the hall just outside the entrance to the semiprivate double cubicle Ernie and I would share, thinking, there I was, in for another year—a depressing prospect considering that I probably faced two more on top of that with no time off for good behavior. Putting these thoughts out of my mind and managing to adopt a somewhat more positive attitude, I resolved to stay out of trouble and not fail any more subjects.

Both of my jobs that year brought me some pleasure. I enjoyed singing with the choir—especially the extra day off that came with it—and as the seminary represented the High Church, I got a nine-month behind-the-scenes look at the pomp, ceremony, and ritual of big-time religion. The waiter job was far more demanding and entailed covering two tables, three meals a day, every other week. We wore clean white aprons and coats for every meal and worked in a highly disciplined, rapid, and coordinated fashion. As I remember it, we carried oval aluminum trays—large enough to hold a service for twenty-eight—of thick china dinner plates, butter plates, knives, forks, and spoons. We stacked this heavy load in a prescribed pattern, then hoisted the tray, balanced it on our upturned palms over our right shoulders, and double-timed down the center aisle to the kitchen, pumping the heavy tray up and down in the air, like dancers in a professional stage revue. I lost control of one loaded tray during the course of the year, but this was no big deal as just about all the waiters had done it once or more to the amusement of the assembled students and masters. I gained a sense of belonging and satisfaction from becoming skilled at a difficult and unusual task, as well as from the close association and working relationship with the other waiters, almost all of whom were seniors, jocks, and/or monitors and represented the student power structure. I was one of their group mostly because Miss Coates liked and had faith in me, but they accepted me as a peer, which made me feel good. Plus, in addition to our pay and extra day off, we ate in an informal, relaxed atmosphere after the meal service, we could eat as much as we wanted of the good food, and we got double "bosses," as the desserts were called. The school served only Breyers Ice Cream, which was premium-grade stuff. I especially liked the vanilla, which had little black specks of the real bean in it.

By this time, I knew my way around the school as well as the District of Columbia. I had become hardened, streetwise, and smart enough too avoid trouble and the accompanying demerits and flack. My two jobs and small circle of outlaw friends gave me a sense of belonging, and I was happier than I had been previously, but I also realized that EHS was never going to do much for me. The only thing I failed that year was football. I went out for the junior varsity team and played guard in the line. By this time, I was five foot ten with an average build and weighed about 140 pounds. Still lacking confidence and ignorant of the fine points of playing my position as well as the overall game, I wound up as a sort of blocking dummy for the more aggressive and adept boys to use in perfecting their moves and plays. This wasn't any fun, and midway through the season, I decided that I wasn't going to subject myself to this unpleasant punishment anymore. One day at lunch while waiting tables, I screwed up my courage and walked up to our coach, Mr. "Young Flick" Hoxton (the headmaster's son, who had played end on the Yale football team opposite "Ship Wreck" Kelly in the late 1930s) and told him respectfully that I was quitting his team. This was very hard for me, but he accepted my resignation without any emotion, just nodded and said okay, and I felt relieved.

My only "illegal" activities that year were smoking on a daily basis with my circle of friends at school and in Washington, as well as drinking the occasional beer. My cousin Billy McVoy, Jimmy's brother, had started at EHS, and he accompanied me to the District frequently. Both of us had discovered jazz music and were developing a serious, lifelong love of it. We went as often as we could to the Howard Theater in the heart of the black section of Washington to hear live big band performances. We saw Count Basie, Lionel Hampton, Duke Ellington, and Louis Armstrong and their bands in person and enjoyed the shows immensely. As some of the few whites among the huge crowds of blacks in attendance, we must have stood out, but all accepted us as fellow enthusiasts. Jazz musicians were among the first free thinkers to disregard the color line and accept people for themselves and their talent, and I think our acceptance was a tacit extension of this mentality.

One day in the early spring, my father came up to the school where he had made an appointment to see Mr. Hoxton with me. At the appointed time, we were ushered into "Old Flick's" private office, where he sat stern and expressionless. At seventy-three, he'd seen it all by then, I guess, and he listened impassively. My father told him that he and my mother had decided that changing schools might be a good thing for me, as obviously my full potential had never been activated at EHS for whatever reason. Various relatives of my mother and in-laws from Birmingham had attended Lawrenceville in New Jersey, and they hoped that it might prove a better place for me. Mr. Hoxton listened to this carefully, agreed that this might be so, and offered to do what he could to make it happen. We were like two sides in a friendly divorce, eager to effect an amicable breakup, to declare peace with honor and get on with it. I certainly didn't want to stay, and I am sure that Mr. Hoxton, having given up on me some time before, was happy to free up a place for a more tractable boy. He gave me permission to accompany my father to National Airport, where one of International Paper's D-18 Twin Beeches was waiting to fly him back to Alabama, his business in the nation's capital being finished. My father knew that I had a budding fascination for aviation, and when we got to the airport, he took me out to the airplane, where he introduced me to the pilots and told them of my interest. They showed me the airplane, which was like a little airliner (I later flew them), and let me use the wobble pump by the copilot's seat to raise the fuel pressure necessary for engine start. This was fascinating stuff to me. I appreciated my father's kindness, understanding, and confidence and went back to school feeling much better.

I was let out of school early on a Friday a couple of weeks later and caught the train to Trenton, New Jersey, four miles south of Lawrenceville. I got to the school in the early afternoon on a beautiful, bright, warm spring day. The large campus, mostly around the "Circle," had extensive greenery, trees, and shrubs and was very neat and tidy. I made my way to the administration building, a very handsome structure that looked like a larger version of the EHS library, where Fred Eichelberger, the director of admissions, had his office. Boxwood hedges, clumps of rhododendrons, some magnolias, and big elms in full leaf surrounded the building. Bumblebees did their thing in the flowers, and birds called in the trees. There was a strong, good smell of newly mowed grass, freshly trimmed boxwood, and other flora. Even though it was north of the Mason-Dixon Line and populated mostly by Yankees, the place, at least on that day, had a Southern feel and seemed warm, comfortable, and genteel in a tasteful, laid-back way. I entered the well-furnished and tastefully decorated building, which smelled of furniture polish like my great-aunt Ethel's fine house in Mountain Brook. I knew before I got any further that I was in a good place that would work out for me—the vibrations were strong and unmistakable. Meeting Mr. Eichelberger, a trim, studious-looking fellow in his mid-thirties with horn-rimmed glasses and a casual, button-downed, Ivy League look, was sort of an anticlimax. He went over my transcripts and asked a few questions that evidenced considerable homework on his part. I told him that I really wanted to come to Lawrenceville and nothing so much as to succeed and go on to college. He told me matter-of-factly that they would be glad to have me as a fourth former in the fall and that he expected me to do well. I felt a great sense of relief as I left his office and made my way to Princeton, four miles north of the school, to spend the weekend with Greeley.

Back at EHS I felt good about my new direction and had sense enough to keep a low profile for the rest of the session. I had begun to understand my failings as a student and felt confident that I would succeed in the future if I knuckled down and applied myself. I was heartily sick of prep school and wanted very much to grow up and move on to more mature pursuits. EHS had given me a lot of experience, both positive and negative. It had toughened me emotionally, and my failures had made me recognize the importance of self-discipline, goal setting, and above all motivation. I was well enough socialized, though still shy, lacking in confidence around outgoing young people, and something of a loner in large groups. I knew my way around, and my values were sound enough, although maybe too advanced for my age.

On my last holiday in Washington, I went to Garfinkel's and bought a gorgeous tie, rich green with small yellow and red rosettes, to wear with my new white-linen suit to the prom, which was held in the gym on the night of June 3, 1947. The tie cost about $11, a lot of money in those days, and I caught some minor grief from my father over this extravagance when he saw it on the bill from the store after I got home. It was a conscious symbol celebrating my deliverance, and I went to the dance looking like an adolescent Tom Wolfe in my fancy threads. I wasn't advanced enough to have a date, but I enjoyed being a fly on the wall, ogling the older boys' girls and listening to the good big band music, high on the knowledge that I was leaving the place the next day for good.

After being home for a couple of weeks, I started my summer job as the office boy and junior clerk in the forestry office where my uncle Julian made his headquarters. One day in late June, my father kept me at the breakfast table after my mother and Greeley had finished, as he needed to discuss a serious issue with me. During the several weeks I had been home from school, he had received reports that I drove too fast and was possibly endangering myself and others. Accordingly, he stated matter-of-factly, his solution was to ground me for one year. I was not to drive any car under any circumstances until a month after I had turned seventeen. This was a carefully considered, sound step on his part, and I took it as such in a mute, resigned way as I had little conversational rapport with him and realized that any counterargument on my part would certainly prove futile. Though humiliating and inconvenient, this was probably a good thing, and it did make a strong impression on me. Since I didn't have the means to do much else, I worked diligently at my job and saved most of the money I got from my pay of fifty cents an hour. I put the money away to fund the fulfillment of a much hoped for dream.

IN THE TWO YEARS immediately following World War II, there was a general belief that the Air Age had arrived in America, evidenced by the superb manufacturing and training facilities that had cranked out high-quality airplanes and the pilots to fly them by the hundreds of thousands during the war. Many assumed that this know-how could be channeled into the production of a wide range of modern designs to fill the needs of individuals, businesses, and new airline companies. The new planes, for the most part, were touted to be sexy and efficient, easy to operate, safe, and above all affordable. It was thought that many of the wartime pilots would want to own or have access to personal airplanes and that vast numbers of ordinary citizens were itching for the opportunity to learn to fly. This combination would create a big base of eager customers for the planes that the new peacetime aviation plants were cranking out in large quantities, often for sale at below-cost prices.

An important part of all this was the GI Bill, which Congress had enacted at the end of the war providing generous educational benefits for all veterans. This was generally a fine thing that provided college educations for millions of ex-servicemen and helped round out one of the highest-achieving generations in our country's history. In addition to college, the GI Bill funded any number of vocational training programs. Some were legitimate, but many put cash into the pockets of vets and the schools they attended with little lasting benefit in practical terms. Flight training was one such program: it genuinely helped many to gain professional licenses and later jobs in aviation, but the majority dropped out when their eligibility (money) and interest ran low. From the end of 1945 until 1949, almost every small town had a GI Bill flying school operated by pilots who had usually been working in military flight training. They sought to stay involved with flying while making some easy money. The whole postwar Air Age bubble broke after two or three years, but in the summer of 1947, it was very much a reality and tantalizingly close.

Hearing that one of these flying schools was in operation at the Greenville Airport located off Highway 10 a few miles northwest of town, I decided to find out if they would teach a sixteen-year-old. One day in July, my uncle Julian took me with him on a trip to the mill at Linden, and we stopped by the airport that afternoon on the way home. I entered the little office, a small, crude lean-to grafted onto the side of the ramshackle hangar, and presented myself to the owner, a tough-looking Yankee named Bill Seymour. He listened to me for a minute or so, then told me that I would need a signed parental permission form since I wasn't eighteen. Lessons costs $10 an hour in his Cub, and the plane rented for $7 for each solo hour. He told me to come back when I had the form signed and my money lined up. I rejoined Julian, who had been looking around outside, and we talked about flying, something he was interested in as well, on the way home. I did not tell him exactly what I had in mind, but I think he understood and was prepared to be supportive.

When I got home, I talked to my mother privately, and she signed the slip. She and my father were going to Europe on a trip in August. I told her that I would have enough money to fly past solo by then; if I succeeded, maybe my father would be willing to back me further when they returned.

Soon afterward, my parents left on their two-week trip to Europe, flying over on Pan American from New York. I had saved up a little over $150 and got a ride to the airport for my first lesson on August 9, 1947. Bill Seymour sold me a thin logbook and introduced me to my instructor, Ethel Jones, a plain and businesslike blond woman of about twenty-five wearing shorts and a sleeveless cotton shirt. She spoke clearly and directly, which made her orders and suggestions easy to understand and follow, and I always listened to her with rapt attention. She took me out to the airplane we would be flying, a well-worn and somewhat shabby prewar Piper J-3 Cub. I think it had been used for CPT training (a government program started before the war to train college students and others in basic flying), and its fabric covering had faded from bright yellow to orange. It was an early model without brakes but with a steerable tail wheel, which helped on the ground. It had no radio or electrical system and employed an "Armstrong starter;" in other words, someone had to hand-prop it to start the engine. Powered by a four-cylinder, air-cooled Franklin engine, which developed 60 hp and turned a wooden propeller, it was a very basic airplane, really little more than a powered glider, but it was simple, tough, and virtually foolproof if flown properly. Being so light, however, its handling demanded constant attention, particularly on landings and takeoffs. It was very well suited for economical initial training to produce good pilots.

Ethel walked me around the airplane and explained how the flight controls worked as she physically moved the ailerons, rudder, and elevator through their limits of travel. These surfaces controlled the plane in roll, yaw, and pitch and were usually used in concert with each other to produce smooth, stable flying, either straight and level or in various maneuvers. We checked the oil level in the little engine and the fuel in a tank in back of it. The fuel gauge consisted of a wire mounted on a cork float, which stuck up vertically just ahead of the front windshield.

Ethel had me sit in the rear seat (J-3 Cubs had to be flown solo from the back for weight and balance considerations) and explained the use of the throttle, which I held with my left hand while holding the stick back with my right. She put a chock under the right wheel and, after having me verify her challenge of "switch off," carefully pulled the little prop through several turns to prime the engine. When she called "contact," I turned the magneto switch to both, cracked the throttle, then called "contact" back to her, and she flipped the prop through, starting the engine. It began emitting pleasant little sounds, and the plane came to life with vibrations and quivers. Ethel came around the right side, kicked the chock out of the way, and got in the front seat. She left the split door open with the top half held up by a retainer under the wing and the bottom half hanging down vertically against the lower fuselage, which made for maximum ventilation as well as some noise in the heat. She told me to "follow through" on the controls by holding the stick loosely with the fingers of my right hand and resting my feet very lightly on the rudder pedals. She taxied out to the threshold of one of the three grass runways, checking the magnetos as we went as there were no brakes to hold the plane still for engine run up on the ground (real checks were done with the wheels chocked). She looked around for traffic, then lined up and opened the throttle. The little plane leisurely gathered speed, and the tail came up off the ground to briefly assume a straight and level altitude rolling over the grass on the front wheels. In a twinkling, I felt the stick move slightly back, and we were flying in a straight, shallow climb with the little engine barking manfully at maximum power and a pleasant wind going by the open right side of the tandem cockpit. That first lesson lasted only thirty minutes, during which Ethel demonstrated the proper attitude for the plane in climbs and descents, as well as various turns, straight and level and in the landing pattern. Thrilled, I gave every minute my undivided attention.

I won't go into the nuts and bolts of my lessons through solo except to give some general impressions. Ethel was military trained and had been a WASP pilot in the war, winding up as a test pilot flying Stearmans, BT-13s, and AT-6s as they came out of maintenance at Gunter Field in Montgomery. She had done exacting professional work in serious airplanes. She was dedicated and intelligent about what she was doing. The course had very little to do with navigation and regulations and included nothing at all about radios or instruments as the plane had none. We focused heavily on safe handling of the airplane, and I had to be able to do precision spins (e.g., recover on a precise heading after doing two or three turns while pointing straight at the ground) before solo. We did a lot of stalls in various flight altitudes and a great many landings and takeoffs. When Ethel finished with me, I was a safe and predictable stick-and-rudder pilot. I may not have known much about the fancy stuff that came later in bigger, faster, and more sophisticated airplanes, but I had gained an excellent foundation that gave me the moves to transition to other planes without any problems. I soloed after eight hours and fifty minutes on August 22. Because of my job, some of my dual flights lasted only thirty minutes late in the afternoon, but I managed to fly on twelve of the fourteen days between beginning and soloing, and the most difficult part for me was cadging rides to and from the airport since I wasn't allowed to drive. This was the first time I had ever applied myself to my full measure from start to finish on a serious project, and it proved to me that this sort of approach guaranteed success. As I write this almost sixty years later, I can look back on a life in which airplanes, flying, and association with real pilots have always played an integral part.

I was staying at Edgefield with Miss Essie and Betty and Julian while my parents were away. Every night I told them about my experiences at the airport, which they followed with interest and encouragement. I loved the lessons and had no difficultly in following Ethel's directions through practice to an acceptable level. The day I soloed, she rode with me while I went around the pattern and landed a couple of times. She then turned around in her seat and told me to pull over by the runway intersection to let her out so she could watch me do three takeoffs and landings by myself from a central point on the airport. I made these without difficulty and noticed that the plane flew with more ease and pep without the 130 pounds that she represented. I was proud and happy to be flying alone finally and felt no fear or apprehension, which spoke well for Ethel's brand of instruction. When I got back down and we went into the little office to sign my logbook, Seymour cut off my shirttail and wrote my name and the date on it to add to the collection tacked to the wall marking this rite of passage.

When I came back to fly again the next day, Seymour told me that Ethel was gone, headed to South America to fly DC-3s for Montgomery Ward. She hadn't said anything about this to me, but our relationship had been strictly professional. She was an excellent teacher but was all business, and I knew little about her background at that time. While she taught at Greenville, she lived with Seymour and his wife in a small, unpainted frame tenant farmer's house fronting on the dirt lane leading into the airport from the paved farm-to-market road. Their physical possessions were scanty, and I had the feeling that the most important thing they had was their love for and dedication to flying. I didn't see Ethel for forty years but finally located her in Bloomington, Illinois, where, well up in her seventies and pushing twenty-five thousand hours of flight time, she still taught basic flying as the chief instructor for a large flying club.

When they got home a couple of days later, my parents supported what I had accomplished. In retrospect I am sure my mother told my father about my plans before they left and received a tacit okay from him. He told me that he would give me some modest support in the form of a little cash for flying after I depleted the rest of my money. Getting to know something about flying was good therapy for my driving habits as safety is an integral part of the discipline and those who disregard this truism don't last long. Some airplanes like the Cub have attained cult status as lovable, forgiving machines, but those who treat them as such do so at their peril. They can kill you just as effectively as their heavier, faster, and more complex relatives—as more than a few highly experienced and respected pilots have learned over the years. Flying also boosted my self-esteem, which added to my self-confidence and probably helped me to succeed in my subsequent schooling and other activities.

I flew every day except four until I left for Lawrenceville in the middle of September. After riding with me for forty-five minutes the day after I soloed, Bill Seymour was satisfied with my flying. Over the next three weeks, I had a total of five hours more of dual and twelve of solo. He checked me out for cross-country flying in short hops to Evergreen and Luverne and also introduced me to a new plane, the Aeronca 7AC. Toward the end of this period, I flew down over Chapman by myself a couple of times and got my first aerial views of the town, mill, and Edgefield. I did a lot of circling and dropped a tennis ball in front of the big house for Julian and Greeley to try to catch. It was the beginning of a lifelong fascination with looking at nature, the sky, and the earth's beauty from the airborne perspective, which smoothes out the trash and imperfections that ground-bound people have to look at.

I ARRIVED AT LAWRENCEVILLE strongly resolved to have a positive experience. I was determined to mind my own business, keep a low profile, and stay out of trouble so as to move on to college when I was eighteen. I had applied for a single room to keep to myself as much as possible and decided not to play football or other team sports to avoid my previous frustrations as a scrub player. While my goal to have a positive experience worked out, the other goals didn't, which was just as well.

I registered and found that I was assigned to room with Thom Blackwell in Hamill House. My parents, friends of his mother and father, had agreed to their request that Thom room with me so that I could look after him on his first break with home. I hardly knew Thom and resented the situation being forced on me. He was the only child of Miss Myra and Mr. Billy (Mr. Blackwell had an older son and daughter by his first wife, who had died), well-to-do, respected people in Greenville. Tall and blond, a gangly, awkward-looking adolescent but potentially good-looking, Thom was the apple of their eye, a little spoiled, not challenged or motivated, and not overly bright. On the positive side, he was bighearted and honest with a good sense of humor. At first, he was homesick and did not like being jerked out of Greenville High School, where he could coast along without any stress. At Lawrenceville, he was thrust into a sophisticated, fast-track educational environment that he was ill equipped to cope with, but he did the best he could. I liked him and helped him adjust to his new circumstances, and we became good friends despite being very different.

Hamill was one of eight "Circle" dorms, which housed the third- and fourth-form boys (tenth and eleventh grades), enough to form a strong intramural league for competitive sports with three hundred or so potential players. Our house master, William R. "Wimp" Wyman, a rotund, red-faced math teacher possessed of a quick wit and a strong, outspoken personality, lived with his wife and young son in a private apartment in the house, and they took their meals with us in the dining room on the first floor. Mr.

Wyman was very intelligent and ran a tight ship without being obtrusive about it. He was assisted by Jack Karpoe, a science teacher who coached the house teams and had his bachelor quarters in the house. Thom and I had a large, pleasant room with dormer windows on the third floor of the house, which was one of the oldest surviving buildings at the school, dating back to the 1830s (the school was established in 1810). Our room overlooked the main street , which connected Trenton and Princeton. The Jigger Shop, a good-sized student hangout with a soda fountain, dining area (the pancakes and hamburgers were good), and magazines and funny books, was directly across the street and very convenient. It was owned by a middle-aged man named Ray Arrowsmith, who ran a good business and was popular with his main customers, the students. Thom and I got some comfortable secondhand easy chairs, good reading lamps, and a rug to finish out our room. The school supplied us each with a single bed, chest of drawers, desk, and chair, and we had a clothes' closet. We shared a head with several boys on the top floor. It was a good living situation with a homey feel, and we did most of our homework and studying in our room, as well as having other boys come by for bull sessions and socializing.

Lawrenceville was an old, successful high-quality school with a lot of money behind it donated by wealthy patrons and alumni. It was, then as now, one of the top five preparatory schools in the country and placed a large number of its graduates in Ivy League colleges. The first-class facilities, teaching material, library, staff, administration, and student body made for a very pleasant working climate and comfortable atmosphere reflective of the sense of renewal that succeeded the war years. The school had a strong faculty totaling eighty-two when I was there for about 580 boys, or one working teacher for every seven or eight students. It was as good a place as there was for those who wanted to teach at the secondary level, and the school employed sound screening to pick successful applicants as there were very few duds and many stars. The headmaster, Allan V. Heely, had graduated from Yale in 1919. I never really knew him, but the school did well under him. The assistant headmaster, Alton R. Hyatt, also a Yalie, Class of '18, seemed to have much closer contact with the faculty and students. I came to know him very well, and he became a mentor and a strong friend.

The rest of the faculty were about equally divided between middle-aged men like Heely and Hyatt and the younger teachers, most back from the war. They were usually easily approachable with good personalities and commonly provided aid and counsel to the boys who needed it. Most preferred teaching at Lawrenceville as opposed to a college because students were still young enough to be positively influenced by their guidance, and they got much satisfaction from seeing young people energized constructively to reach their full potential. Many were genuine characters unafraid to display their disparate, independent styles. In a group as large as the faculty, some were obviously abler, smarter, or more agreeable than others, but I never perceived any of them as incompetent, unfair, or hard to deal with.

The students were broken into three distinct groups. The Lower School was off to itself on one side of the campus away from the Circle houses, classrooms, chapel, and administrative offices. Its four houses accommodated one hundred boys, enough to form their own little league of sports teams and other types of competition. The first- and second-form boys lived in cubicles just a little nicer than the ones at EHS and had the most disciplined and controlled environment at the school because of their young age.

The three hundred boys of the third and fourth forms lived in the Circle houses and comprised a sizable community in which everybody had the chance to join athletic and other teams and groups. As a junior living in a Circle house, I quickly sensed a new freedom to live my life in a grown-up, responsible way, unencumbered by formal rules or a disciplinary apparatus, save the few punishments reserved for the direst sins. Absence without leave, cheating, drinking, stealing, and lying were cause for being shipped home without a second chance. From the time we arrived, we knew that we were expected to police our own conduct, behave responsibly, and act like gentlemen. Each house had a president and small council for administrative purposes to help the masters, but this very low-key arrangement bore no resemblance to EHS's monitor system. I found it a healthy, refreshing atmosphere that worked well, with formal discipline having to be applied only rarely. The only rule I broke that first year was to smoke on the sly since I didn't have the required parental permission to do it openly in the designated places. I never smoked in the house, but some of us used to go down a side street past Petronne's Market where we sat on a fence by the railroad track and puffed away while engaging in pleasant bull sessions. I don't think anyone in authority cared one way or the other about this as long as we were discrete.

The fifth form, or seniors, numbered 178 boys, who lived a privileged life apart from the younger students. They had their own quarters and dining facility, as well as an even freer, more relaxed lifestyle.

The student body was diverse. Half or more came from the northeast quarter of the country, with the balance from literally all over. The Cuban dictator Batista's son Ruben was there, and we had a Greek shipowner's son, Elias Kulukundis, in Hamill. There were a lot of Southern boys, as well as many from California and the Pacific Northwest. About fifty day students commuted from Princeton, Trenton, and the local countryside, and around fifty boys, or 10 percent, attended on scholarship. The boys at Lawrenceville were much like the men I met later at Yale, although the bar for admission was slightly lower. Lawrenceville would take a chance on a boy if the school thought it could help him hit his stride and cope with the scholastic program, knowing that some, probably less than 10 percent, would end up leaving before graduation because they couldn't hack it. Students were required to keep up with their classmates, and those who couldn't or wouldn't did not return the next year.

I SPENT MY FIRST week at Lawrenceville getting organized and adjusted. I was not homesick, and what I saw confirmed my earlier impression that I was in a good place. I declined to go out for the Hamill football team and held out for a week before yielding to considerable pressure. My housemates knew that I had played before and understood more about the game than some of them, and at five foot eleven and 145 pounds, I was also bigger than a lot of them. They made me an offensive guard and defensive end, and I wound up playing both positions creditably for most of every game, and found that I enjoyed it.

Every morning we got up at six thirty, had breakfast, and cleaned our rooms before going to chapel at eight. The whole school attended this brief service together. We had assigned seats by houses and a prescribed, efficient way of entering and leaving. After we sang a hymn or two and said a prayer, these weekday services were used for announcements and anything else the administration wanted to talk to us about. Attendance was also required at a regular church service every Sunday morning. Lawrenceville was a nondenominational school, and though the faculty and students were predominately WASPs, a good number of Catholics and Jews attended, who had access to priests and rabbis for their special services. Catholics and Jews were scarce in the rural South, and I had known very few before going to Lawrenceville. I found no discrimination or prejudice there or later at Yale, and that kind of thing never entered the interpersonal equation.

Classes were usually over by lunchtime. I enjoyed all of them, applied myself, and made consistent good grades the entire time I was there. The atmosphere and culture were conducive to learning, and going to that school was fun, at least for me. In later years I met graduates, some related to me, who had ambivalent feelings about the school. I think their problem was that they didn't have anything to compare it with, hence did not fully appreciate the opportunity they had. Something good can usually be gained from any experience, including negative ones. I found Lawrenceville to be so different from Episcopal that I thought I had landed in the prep school promised land, and I appreciated it and was glad to give it my best.

That fall I settled in as a solid rear-ranks guy. I had an adequate number of friends much like myself—basically good guys but not highly visible or big men on the campus. I read a lot and was influenced by the characters in books by Ernest Hemingway, F. Scott Fitzgerald, William Faulkner, James M. Cain, and some others writing about pilots and military people in the recent war. I was still somewhat immature and lacking in discipline, a little awkward in some social situations, and wrestling with an inferiority complex. I tried to be my own person and was not afraid to try to find my own way as opposed to strictly following the popular norms of the herd.

My parents had told the school about my flying and that they wanted me to be able to keep it up. There was a small field called Twin Pines about four miles west of Lawrenceville, near Pennington, which had a short 2,200-foot grass runway, with the approach to the northwest over tall trees. Norman Delker and his attractive, blonde wife, Sue, ran the operation out of a small, ramshackle office, offering flight instruction, rental airplanes, maintenance, fuel, and tie downs for local and transient small planes. It was very basic, not as nice as many Southern fields, but it served my purpose very well. A handsome young man with neatly trimmed brown hair and a mustache, Norm had become a pilot during the war. He was a good instructor, dressed well, and had a more polished appearance then Bill Seymour. I presented myself to him on September 24, ten days after my last flight in Greenville, and he soloed me in a J-3 Cub after a 25-minute evaluation. I flew a little every month that fall to keep my hand in, but I was busy with my school-work, football, and weekend activities. I always hitchhiked to and from the field, which was easy to do in those days, especially since it was obvious that I was a schoolboy. Aviation was still in its postwar boom, and I followed this closely, avidly reading *Flying* cover to cover and anything else I could find about airplanes. Lawrenceville had an attractive, comfortable library that looked like a much larger version of the one at Episcopal, and I spent many hours there with the books and magazines, especially on Saturdays and Sundays when the weather was bad. I never bragged or tried to make a big deal about my interest in flying, but it was unusual, and as far as I know, I was the only kid in school who was doing it.

I was also increasing my familiarity with the wonderful jazz music of the time. New York was home for many of the really good musicians, and I soon became familiar with a number of the joints and clubs where they played. The liquor laws in the city were very loose, and sixteen-year-olds were legal to drink, so I was a welcome customer in these places. I was learning about booze on a trial-and-error basis and occasionally drank too much, but I never got into any trouble as a result, only sick and hungover occasion-ally. Like most of my friends, I had little knowledge of the finer points of civilized drinking, and the stuff we started out quaffing was bad enough to make anybody sick: Cuba Libres (rum and coke), Moscow Mules (vodka and ginger ale), and Sea Breezes (gin and grapefruit juice), sweet, insidious stuff all the worse because of the cheap liquor the bars used.

I had the opportunity to see and hear at very close range many of the jazz masters. My favorite places were Eddie Condon's on West Third Street in Greenwich Village and Jimmy Ryan's uptown jazz joint on West

Fifty-Second Street. Condon's was a fairly large, well-decorated place with a small, elevated bandstand at the end and a narrow, horseshoe balcony that accommodated overflow crowds. Ryan's was smaller, long and narrow, with a little bandstand at the end that I liked to sit near, often with a date. These establishments catered to a mixed crowd, including a few prep school kids like me, a good many college students, and others of all ages who were drawn to, almost hypnotized by, the superb music. An evening looking and listening produced an intense high for me—much more so than the booze. Condon's especially attracted a mixed crowd apart from the hardcore music lovers—beautiful high-society people, Broadway and Hollywood actors and actresses, prominent writers and professional athletes, and always a few high-rolling businessmen doing the town, often with women who were not their wives. Some of these people knew and loved the music, but a lot of them just wanted to be seen. I saw Tallulah Bankhead on more than one occasion, and Rita Hayworth, Robert Mitchum, Henry Fonda, and John Houston were also fond of Condon and his music. The kind of gawking tourists one sees nowadays at jazz places in New Orleans and San Antonio were notably absent. Most of the customers were well behaved and kept quiet while the musicians were playing, and there was rarely any trouble, although these places did employ bouncers. Occasionally one of the out-of-town visiting firemen, usually a self-important, arrogant type ignorant of the music, would commit the gaffe of loudly demanding that the band play a favorite song. The musicians didn't make a lot of money, but they were highly talented and fiercely independent. They played what they wanted and brooked no interference. They usually either pointedly ignored these types or got pissed off enough to put them down. I heard Wild Bill Davison tell more than one to "hire his own band" if he wanted his requests played.

The music was pure jazz that originated in New Orleans at the turn of the century and moved north in the 1920s, where it was refined into the "Chicago Style" played by blacks and whites alike. Besides the standards from the teens and twenties, they played their versions of later blues, ballads, and show tunes. The complex interplay between the musicians resembled a symphony at times. They played many of the same pieces as swing bands led by musicians like Benny Goodman and Artie Shaw, but without scored music and with a more direct, forceful beat and instrumental presentation, often communicating much emotion and feeling. Many of the great players were born in the first quarter of the century, and they were in their prime when I first saw them. I liked the purists who found bop and modern jazz repulsive, and that kind of music was never heard in Condon's or Ryan's, where the jazz played was as good as it got and timeless to those who appreciate it.

It didn't seem long before the fall term was over and Thom and I were boarding the *Crescent Limited* in mid-afternoon in Trenton for the pleasant journey home. We shared a compartment and enjoyed the ride in comfort, getting to Greenville after lunch the next day. The *Crescent* was a great train, and I made thirty odd trips back and forth on it over the years with a lot of good times. All the Pullman porters, conductors, and dining car people recognized me and knew my father and family. Besides having very good food in the diner, the train had a club car at its rear, which in later years became a great place to socialize with friends, chat up girls, and indulge in drinking and smoking. This kind of travel was very civilized and a pleasure in itself, now gone but not forgotten.

The Christmas season was a happy time at the end of 1947. It was good to be back home in Alabama with its crisp, clear weather. My parents gave me some money for flying—my main present and one that I appreciated. I went back to Bill Seymour at the Greenville Airport; he rode with me in his almost-new Aeronca Champ to be sure I hadn't forgotten how to fly. He turned me loose after half an hour, and I flew by myself on ten days, including Christmas, during the two and a half weeks I was home, logging a little over eight hours flying time. I passed over Chapman and Edgefield on four of these short flights and was again impressed with the natural beauty of the mostly forested area.

I attended the traditional family parties in Chapman, and we always went to Brewton for the progressive cocktail and dinner evening that the Millers and McMillans put on every year in their fine houses. There were enough young people at these affairs for me to socialize and enjoy myself, and it was easy to sneak a few drinks without calling any attention to myself. I had an occasional date in Greenville and on our visits to Birmingham.

I hadn't had any serious relations with girls at that point, although I was eager to make what I could out of the opportunities I had.

I was glad to be reunited with the people I had grown up around, especially my childhood pal Howard Goodlett Olive, my brother Greeley, and his best buddy Max Spann. Howard Goodlett, always called by the two names, was a senior at Georgiana High School where he was a serious, solid, hardworking student. He didn't smoke or drink, but we were congenial and had a good time catching up on each other's happenings. We took our traditional walk around Chapman after supper on Christmas Eve under a clear sky lit by bright stars. We used these strolls to discuss our respective philosophies and try to make sense of our progress through adolescence. We were still very young, naive, and untried in a lot of things, and sex was very much a mystery. In our ignorance, we found it hard to reconcile the libido constantly aroused by our overactive male hormones with the prevailing moral code.

Max Spann, Howard Goodlett's cousin, was a very complex individual and unique in my experience. He was twenty-one and attending the University of Alabama on the GI Bill. He had been drafted into the army when he finished high school in 1944 and was in the Philippines when the war in the Pacific ended. He claimed that he had witnessed an elaborate reenactment of MacArthur's initial landing, purporting to show his triumphant return to Manila after a resounding defeat three years previously. The general was pictured in many still photographs and newsreels wading resolutely through the water to the beach from a small landing craft, wearing his trademark gold-trimmed field marshal's service cap and smoking his corncob pipe. Max himself was a consummate con artist and appreciated the general as a fellow expert who had the wisdom to record this scene of great public relations value in perfect safety—as the area had been secured, no Japs were anywhere about—and under ideal conditions for getting the best camera angles to picture himself in a heroic light.

Max stood about five-foot-ten and weighed a solid 185 pounds. He had closely trimmed blond hair, strong, regular features, blue eyes, and a mouthful of perfectly shaped, large, white teeth. With wide shoulders, strong arms, a narrow waist, and muscular legs, he was a handsome, strong-looking young man who resembled a youthful Charles Atlas, the famous bodybuilder. By this time he had come up with the macho sobriquet "The Blond Bomber" when referring to himself in the third person, a bastardization of the great heavyweight Joe Louis's colloquial handle "The Brown Bomber." He had a quick mind and sharp wit, always exuded confidence, and could talk easily with anybody, gaining that person's trust and approval. He had parlayed these assets into the grade of master sergeant, the highest enlisted rank, while still eighteen, less than a year after entering the army. He wound up in Korea in the army of occupation after V-J Day, where he was a big-time operator who exploited many opportunities to use his position and unit's assets for fun and profit. After getting into trouble over his black-market commercial activities and a liaison with a Red Cross nurse, he was busted but had managed to climb back to technical sergeant (one stripe below master sergeant) by the time he was sent home and released. I know this to be a fact as I saw his honorable discharge papers.

Max played an important part in my life when I was a child, adolescent, and young man. He fooled me for a long time, just as he did my brother, family, and a lot of the people whose lives he touched. He was given to outrageous, larger-than-life, and frequently comic statements and deeds, which endeared him to many, and he used this quality to ingratiate himself with those who could help him achieve his objective of the moment. He was an inveterate liar, often telling untruths about inconsequential matters apparently just to stay in practice. His attractive facade masked the dark and roguish personality of a self-styled outlaw. Back then, I looked up to him and thought him a talented eccentric destined for great things.

The Christmas break ended quickly, and it was back to New Jersey for the winter. The school year was divided into two parts punctuated by big exams, which I did well on at the end of January. I was comfortable with the academic and social sides of Lawrenceville and knew how to study and take tests, partially as a result of my very poor showing at Episcopal. I participated in a couple of elective, noncredit activities since the weather was too bad to do any flying. Herbert "Herb" Harwood, a good friend in Hamill House, and I took an auto engine course given after supper several times a week by Frank Birch, who taught industrial arts and supervised some

Floyd in middle age playing a trombone.

of the maintenance activities at the school. Working with a couple of other boys, we disassembled a Ford V-8 while Mr. Birch plied us with the parts' nomenclature and the theory of the internal combustion engine, along with the function of each component and how it related to the others. After we had everything cleaned and laid out neatly on the workbench, we put the engine back together and got a passing grade. I don't know how good a job we did, but at least we didn't have any parts left over. I've never considered myself as having more than an average hands-on mechanical ability based on this experience and later military training in field- and detail-stripping various weapons, but I've always had a strong love for good equipment and its proper operation and maintenance. At the time, Herb and I were very interested in cars and could instantly identify and rattle off the comparative merits of each model.

I also took trumpet lessons most of the year but dropped them as I could never get comfortable with the geometry of the mouthpiece in relation to my lips and the structure of my mouth. My embouchure was never effective, so I had to hold the instrument down at a pronounced angle to blow. I liked the straight-ahead, direct execution of the melody line that trumpets play in jazz bands and felt that the instrument fit my style and personality, so I was disappointed when it turned out to be a physical mismatch. In later years I found that the trombone mouthpiece suited me much better.

During spring vacation in March, I renewed my flying. I got an hour of dual at the Birmingham Municipal Airport in a Fairchild PT-23, a version of the PT-19 with an uncowled 220 hp Continental radial engine. I'd never flown a military airplane and a round engine before, and I liked it. Used as a primary trainer for Air Corps cadets, the Fairchild was bigger and a little more complicated than the light planes I was used to, but it was well designed, easy to operate and land, and a pleasure to fly. I flew on nine days during the two weeks I was home and had accumulated a total of forty-five hours and fifty minutes by the time I got back to school. This was more than enough time to qualify for a private pilot's license, which I was anxious to get as soon as possible after turning seventeen, the minimum age.

I went to see Norm Delker at Twin Pines Airport when the weather got nice at the end of April and talked to him about prepping me for the private pilot's written exam and flight test. He gave me some dual totaling an hour and fifty minutes in his J-3 Cub on April 23 and 25, and I flew solo for an hour to get comfortable in the plane since I had been flying Seymour's Aeronca Champion during my vacations in Alabama. Norm told me to lay out a triangular course on a sectional chart with stops at Morristown and Woodbine and back to Pennington, which would satisfy the solo cross-country requirement for the private license.

The next Saturday, May 1, I got to the airport by midmorning, pre-flighted the Cub, and took off northbound for the short 45-minute flight to Morristown. It was cool and bright, like a late winter day, with a brisk west wind following a frontal passage, not too rough but strong enough to affect the navigation. I was using pilotage to find my way, which entailed following the compass course plotted on my map with appropriate corrections for magnetic variation and the crosswind component to keep from being blown off course. Morristown and Woodbine, located on the southern tip of New Jersey, were both large World War II vintage fields, each with several hard-surface runways. My objective was to shut down, refuel, get my log book signed by an instructor at each stop, and return to Twin Pines by early afternoon.

The first leg went well as that part of New Jersey is well populated, and there were plenty of prominent landmarks, roads, and towns to make eyeball navigation easy without much concern for holding a precise compass heading adjusted to compensate for the drift caused by the strong wind. I got my book signed and a quick turnaround at Morristown and took off on a southerly heading down the length of the state. Pretty soon the populated area gave way to a large expanse of pine barrens on flat, sandy land that stretched as far as I could see, a million-acre area called the Pinelands. The forest had only a few dirt roads and no other cultural features that I could relate to my charted course on the map. I pressed on hoping to recognize something while starting to play "what-if" games in my mind related to the wind speed and direction. After twenty or thirty minutes, my confidence in my navigation had eroded seriously, and I started to take stock of my options. At that point, I came to a railroad track running northeast-southwest through the woods, and I made a snap decision. I had read in *Flying* that railroads invariably led to towns, and if lost one could emulate the old barnstormer's trick of reading the sign on the station to find out where you were when you arrived. After making a half right turn and following the track to the southwest, I was soon gratified to see the outskirts of a town on the horizon. When I got a little closer, I spotted a small airport on the edge of the small city and decided to stop and sort things out. I landed and taxied up to a hangar with "Camden, N.J." painted in large letters over the doors. I got out and nonchalantly ambled into the office, where I used the restroom and got a cup of coffee, normal actions for transients that aroused no interest. When I got the plane propped and started, I took a couple of minutes to identify the railroad running from Camden to Cape May on my chart and resolved to substitute the IFR (I Follow Railroads) method of navigation for the less-reliable pilotage and had an easy flight to Woodbine. I logged it in my book as a nonstop, one hour and forty-five minute flight from Morristown and had the fixed base operator, who was doing business in one of the big ex-navy hangars, sign off on it.

In over 17,000 flights, this is the only time I have ever been lost or unsure of my position in an airplane, and the experience made a lasting and constructive impression, resulting in much more careful planning and disciplined adherence to navigation. When I got back to Pennington after an hour and twenty minutes, I told Norm and Sue Delker that I had had a good, uneventful day of flying, and he signed me off for a job well done, which it probably was, but in a more convoluted way then he knew. In reconstructing the flight on the chart when I got back to school late that afternoon, I found that I had been almost exactly on track and would have been fine if I had held my course to Woodbine, which gave me confidence in an ironic way.

Late in the spring term, Mr. Wyman, our housemaster, counseled Thom and me individually to review our academic situations. Thom was failing in some areas and needed to make up two courses to return in the fall. I was doing well in all of my subjects but needed two additional credits to enter the fifth form, another reminder of the opportunities I had wasted at Episcopal. The school had been in touch with our parents, who had agreed to our attending a six-week session at Long Lake Lodge, a tutoring camp in Maine, to remedy these deficiencies. Wyman and some of the other Lawrenceville masters taught there, and he told us that we would have to pass exams supplied by the school at the end of the session. Thom and I were hardly overjoyed by the prospect of spending the peak of the summer studying, but we were resigned to the situation and determined to make the best of it. Herb Harwood and I elected to room together senior year and drew a room assignment in Kinnan House, a small, two-story, stone house a short distance up the street from Hamill that housed about twenty fifth formers.

Soon after returning home, I went to the Greenville Airport to arrange to take the private pilot's test and found that a big change had taken place. Bill Seymour and his wife had skipped town early one morning with their airplanes and meager possessions to make a new start in Florida, leaving behind a large unpaid bill for aviation fuel obtained from John Byrd, the Standard Oil dealer in Greenville. Seymour covered his tracks well and shortly sent back word that he had been killed in a crash, stymieing his creditors. As far as I know, he lived to a ripe old age in the Sunshine State, where he must have fit right in. His place had been taken by C. D. Beerman, a bur-ley, red-faced, sandy-haired man and former navy primary instructor, who had moved to Greenville and set up another flying service at the airport. I introduced myself and told him what I wanted, which suited him since he was a designated examiner empowered by the Civil Aviation Authority to give tests and issue certificates. He was satisfied with my flying after giving me an hour and thirty-five minutes of dual on June 14 and 15, covering stalls, spins, 720° turns, slow flight, and the entire range of flight maneuvers comprising the test. It was hot in the little Aeronca bumping along in the summer thermals. Beerman chewed tobacco and spat frequently in a coffee can he kept on the floor by his right foot in the back seat, and I felt queasy at times during the flights. I went back a couple of times to review the maneuvers by myself and take the written test, which was short and simple in those days, and I scored 100 percent. I flew with him for an hour on June 27, and he issued my license. I had a total of fifty-eight hours and fifty minutes flying time logged.

At the same time I got my pilot's license, my driving privileges were reinstated, simplifying life and restoring my personal freedom of movement. Beerman had a couple of ragged ex–Air Corps Stearman PT-17s and checked me out in one a couple of days later after two 30-minute dual rides. This big, rugged biplane powered by a 220 hp Continental radial engine was most certainly the best primary trainer ever built. It was a serious airplane that demanded good technique to land safely, but I liked it and had no dif-ficulty in satisfying Beerman that I could fly it. During the next few days, I took my first passengers for joy rides: Max Spann, Thom Blackwell, and Kay Harrigan, a precocious 14-year-old who looked and acted a good deal older. Her father, Bill, was the power behind Scotch Lumber Company and one of my father's best friends. We dated off and on during the next several years, though not seriously as she was very popular and played the field aggressively, often with suitors a good deal older than I was.

We went to the Grand Hotel for a long family weekend over the Fourth of July, and I left from Mobile that Sunday afternoon for Maine. This involved riding an Eastern Airlines DC-3 through the night all the way to Boston with stops every hundred miles or so. Thom boarded in Montgomery, and we ate a small dinner and breakfast handed out in boxes by the steward and slept a little in our seats with a pillow and blanket. At Boston we transferred to a four-engine Northeast DC-4 for the short ride to Portland, where we were picked up and driven thirty miles northwest to the camp, just south of Bridgton on the west side of a big lake.

Long Lake Lodge was a pleasant, well-run place. The main building housed a common room, dining room, kitchen, and the classrooms. There were ten or twelve masters and about eighty boys. The main recreational activities were swimming and canoeing. Thom and I shared a snug two-man cabin with a lot of screened window area, which was very pleasant during the cool nights. The food was good, as was the instruction. Mr. Wyman taught me solid geometry and calculus, and I made high marks all along and on the subsequent school tests. The boys were a good lot, mostly seniors, some of whom were going to take a postgraduate year at one of the major prep schools so as to increase their competitiveness for admission to one of the better colleges. The group was generally smart and attractive, almost everybody took the camp seriously and did good work, and we had a good time. I enjoyed the six weeks in Maine and gained another measure of confidence in my ability to do the work properly and relate well with the other boys.

We had a good bit of freedom and usually walked the three or four miles to Bridgton on Saturdays to look around and shop. One night we walked to a small town south of camp to a carnival where we went on some of the rides and looked at the concession stands. We came across a tent show toward the back of the midway that promised exotic dancers and bought tickets for the next show. The star turned out to be a beautiful brunette girl with a perfect figure. She seemed about sixteen and combined her chaste,

clean attractiveness with an act that wound up with total nudity and powerful, lewd sexuality, a sort of whore/Madonna combination, which had us
blissfully gaping with total concentration before it was over. This was the
first time I ever saw anything of the sort, and in its way it was the best. I
have often wondered who the girl was and how she came to be there in that
raunchy setting, as well as where she went from there.

Thom failed his school exams, but I believe he meant to do this, at
least subconsciously, as he had never wished to go off to school in the first
place. He wanted nothing so much as to return to his comfortable niche at
Greenville High School. He seemed happy and healthy enough, but deep
down something else may have been influencing him to get back home as
he was dead six months later, the victim of a painful and fast-moving attack of leukemia.

After getting home in the middle of August, I spent a few days in Birmingham at Aunt Ethel's house going to the dentist, getting some clothes,
and visiting with my cousins. I asked Jimmy and Billy's sister, Betty McVoy,
if she knew a pretty teenager named Joan McCullough, whose picture I had
seen in the Birmingham paper. Betty laughed and told me that Joan's sister
Shirley was one of her best friends and offered to arrange a date, which I
accepted with alacrity. Joanie turned out to be a year younger than I was,
and we hit it off pretty well. She was the first young woman I cared a lot
about, and she liked me. We dated frequently for the next couple of years
and got to know each other well enough to establish a real bond without
making a lasting commitment, and we both went out with other people
during this time.

I got in seven more flights during the first part of September before leaving for school, three in the Aeronca Champ and four in the Stearman, one
of which was my first "job." Beerman asked me to ferry one of the biplanes
to Tuscaloosa for maintenance, which was both free flying time and good
experience. I took James Alexander, a war veteran in his late twenties who
was taking a commercial course under the GI Bill, with me to pick up his
new Cessna 140, which was undergoing an inspection. We both enjoyed the
uneventful trip over on a bright, cool afternoon. James's plane wasn't ready
when we arrived, so we didn't head home until very late in the day. I was

enjoying watching him fly and looking over his nice little plane as this was the first of what would be many good hours in Cessna tail draggers. When we were just northwest of Selma, the sun dipped below the horizon on our right, signaling that only a few more minutes of twilight remained before full darkness. James looked around at me and said, "Floyd, I don't know how to fly at night, so you take us the rest of the way home." I appreciated his confidence in assuming that I had mastered advanced aeronautical skills but quickly told him that I didn't know anymore about night flying than he did and that we'd best get on the ground as soon as possible. Sky Harbor, a grass strip paralleling the river, was just over our nose, and James made a nice landing just before black dark. He called up Beerman, who came to get us in his four-place Stinson Voyager, and we were on our way back to Greenville under a starlit sky an hour later.

A WEEK LATER, I was back at Lawrenceville for my senior year. Herb and I had a nice corner room on the ground floor of Kinnan House. Our house master, Hans Rastede, an aging bachelor pushing fifty and a Phi Beta Kappa graduate of Harvard with a master's degree, was stern, aloof, and somewhat of a disciplinarian. He taught German, so I never had him in class. All of us in the house were well behaved, so he never had any occasion to boss us around, which seemed to frustrate him. Once he burst into our room and angrily accused me of smoking there, which was against the rules. I kept my cool and told him that I had never done this (true) and would never take such a stupid risk when all I had to do to smoke legally was walk a few steps to the front porch or upstairs to our lounge. I told him that I had been going to school for a long time and knew how to behave, that he was barking up the wrong tree and had best leave me alone. He beat a retreat, and I never had any further trouble with him. I never figured out what got him started after me in the first place.

Our small group in Kinnan was congenial and lived in a very pleasant atmosphere, somewhat like that at a junior college. We ate with the rest of the senior class in Upper House about a quarter of a mile across the campus. The Jigger Shop was just across the street. We had to attend all classes and chapel services and study as we saw fit, but we were free to do what we wanted the rest of the time. Mr. Alton "Red" Hyatt, the assistant headmaster, lived in an attractive, two-story house next door, and he and his wife adopted the Kinnan boys. They had us over for cake and coffee once or twice a week and got to know us in what was almost a family situation in the best sense.

I was very happy that year. I got along well with a number of the other seniors and had an attractive girlfriend back in Alabama. Joan and I corresponded regularly. I had several weekends and longer holidays each term during which I visited the Larsons in New York and hung out in the jazz joints. Once or twice Herb took me to visit his family in Washington D.C. I had time to read a lot and went to the library whenever I had a chance. My life was coming together, and by this time I had progressed from an awkward, rebellious adolescent to a more mature teenager with his act together. Prep school had been a drag in earlier years, but I had finally taken to it and perhaps learned more about myself and life by successfully working through earlier difficulties than would have been the case had my progress been smooth from the start.

While I was home during Christmas vacation that year, my father took me aside one day and asked me where I wanted to go to college. He and my uncles, as well as various cousins, had gone to Alabama, where my friend Elisha Poole was now in attendance and giving me glowing reports of the no-strain scholastics and assorted debauchery he was encountering, so I told my father that Alabama would suit me fine. Looking at me sternly, he told me that this was out of the question and that I could go to any college I wanted as long as it was Harvard, Princeton, or Yale. I sensed that his edict was nonnegotiable, so I picked Princeton, which I had become familiar with over the past five years. It was only four miles away from Lawrenceville, and I had visited Greeley on a good many weekends during his time there. My observations had confirmed its reputation as a party school, and it was attractive and prestigious in its way. A lot of Southern boys attended, as did many Lawrenceville graduates, and it was much favored by my classmates. While ranked as one of the best colleges, it did not carry as intimidating a reputation for academic excellence as Harvard or Yale, a fact that gave me some comfort.

One day in February, I got a message that Mr. Hyatt wanted to see me in his office. I had gotten to know and like him and wondered what he wanted. When I visited him that afternoon, he told me to sit down and tell him where I wanted to go to college. When I said that I planned to put Princeton first, he asked me why, and I mentioned that my brother was a graduate and that I had seen enough of the place to be familiar with it. He shook his head, looked me in the eye, and said, "Floyd, you don't want to go there. You are going to Yale." I liked and respected Mr. Hyatt a lot and placed much confidence in him, so I agreed, "Yes, sir," then asked why. He told me it was a better school based on his experience as both a student and teacher at Yale, and since my family was in the timber business and Yale had a graduate forestry school, it was the proper place for me. Accordingly, I put Yale down as my first choice and was accepted without a problem, doubtless with the help of his recommendation. Mr. Hyatt was one of the older people who recognized some good qualities and potential in me and gave me unsolicited advice and help that proved very valuable at critical junctures in my life. I was touched by the fact that he wanted me to go to his alma mater when I thought about it, as he was a very solid, competent, good man.

Three World War II veterans in my class were taking a postgraduate senior year. These young men lived apart in rooms in the town. I got to know one of them, Bill Albrecht, in a couple of my classes. Small, dark, and intense, trim and strong, Bill had graduated from a military school in Pennsylvania in 1944 and gone straight to Yale, where he lasted about six months. I never knew exactly what had happened as he was a smart guy, but he left Yale for the army, where he attended the Officer Candidate School and joined MacArthur's forces in Japan as a lieutenant for a year or so at the end of the war. He was determined to do things right the second time around, which accounted for his elaborate preparation. We decided to room together at Yale and signed up to do so after we were both accepted. We ended up rooming together all four years.

The rest of the spring at Lawrenceville passed rapidly and pleasantly. I kept my flying up by taking a number of interested classmates along, who shared the cost. One day I had Hal Erwin, a friend of Herb's from Washington, in the back seat of a Piper PA-11, and we were sightseeing in the warm sunshine near the school. He asked me to show him a loop, so I put the nose down and eased in full power. When the airspeed passed a hundred miles an hour, I came back smoothly on the stick and held constant back pressure as the nose came up and over the top, then down the backside. I didn't mention that I had never done a loop before, not wanting to alarm him, and congratulated myself on the fact that the maneuver had seemed to go smoothly and in the manner of the written explanations I had seen. In later years when I got into serious acrobatics, I realized that I had flown what we called a "little e" loop after its elongated, elliptical shape—not dangerous but not pretty. To get one to come out perfectly round, like the letter o, you have to relax back pressure so as to float over the top in a nearly weightless, or "zero G," state, a subtlety in execution far past my understanding at the time.

Pretty soon we were taking our final exams during the last few days at school. The weather was perfect almost every day in early June—warm but not too hot, clear and bright. The campus had a ripe, good smell and was very attractive with spring flowers in bloom, pretty trees of many varieties everywhere, and large expanses of well-tended lawn. Suddenly, it was all over, except for a slightly tense couple of days waiting for the final grades to be posted. I had reason to believe that I had been successful, but it was still a mighty relief when I finally knew that I was well and truly done with prep school, the longest five years of my life. My mother and father came for the graduation, and while they didn't say so, I am sure they were as glad as I was about my successful finish and acceptance at a good college.

The summer also passed quickly and agreeably. Soon after I got home, I went to Birmingham, where Dr. Jim Mason, a friend of my mother's and an interesting, nice man, operated on my right knee to repair a sandlot football injury. The procedure, my first experience with surgery, was done under a spinal anesthetic, meaning that I was fully conscious and followed along with interest. Having been with a MASH unit in North Africa, Dr. Mason had massive experience with trauma surgery, and he got a good result on me. I stayed in St. Vincent's, a well-run place controlled by an order of nuns, old-fashioned but pleasant, with my leg in a cast from hip to toe for a little over a week. Joan and some other girls paid me a good bit of attention and brought in beer concealed in their pocketbooks, leading to some impromptu good times. We drank the beer and listened to Stick McGhee's "'Drinkin' Wine Spo-Dee-O-Dee" on the radio. While not the jazz I knew, the song really rocked, and I loved it. We used to put the empty beer cans on a ledge outside on either side of the window, out of sight from inside, and I think the "dead soldiers" stayed there in full view of passersby until the hospital was remodeled some years later.

I spent the rest of the summer working in the forestry department. One week I served as guide for three Austrian foresters who were visiting the States under a government program to see how the Americans went about the wood business, and I found the time with them interesting and educational. All had been officers during the war, and one, who had piloted a Focke Wulf 200 Condor long-range maritime reconnaissance plane that had been shot down while shadowing a convoy over the Atlantic, had spent time as a POW picking sugar beets in New Mexico. I showed them the entire W. T. Smith mill and woodlands operations and drove them to the Montgomery Airport for an hour-long flight in a brand-new, rented Piper Pacer. They enjoyed the opportunity to see the forests and countryside from the air. The pilot especially seemed to like it, and I let him handle the controls during part of the flight. If they found it strange to be flying over what had recently been enemy territory with an eighteen-year-old as pilot in command, they didn't show it. In fact, they seemed to find it just a normal part of the way Americans operated.

Joan came down to visit for a few days and got along well with my parents. We swam in the lake at Edgefield and were around Greeley and his girlfriends some at night. We also visited the sawmill to observe the surreal scene of big logs being broken down into timbers, dimension, and boards under bright lights amid the steam and dark shadows. It was high drama amid exotic sounds and smells that was never boring. I drove her back to Birmingham and stayed a few days getting my teeth checked and preparing to leave for college.

One day I had a serious and defining run-in with my brother, Greeley, who was about to depart for his second year at Oxford. We were alone on the screened porch of our old house in Chapman, this being just before my parents moved into their new house overlooking the lake on the Edgefield property. Greeley was fooling around with a powerful air pistol that I had bought in New York, a pellet gun with the heft and shape of a German Luger. He made a serious, overt threat with it over some now forgotten issue, which got to me very forcefully as the culmination of the degrading physical bullying that had been going on for as long as I could remember. I wasn't as heavy as he was, but I stood six feet, weighed about 165 pounds, and was in good shape. I got up in his face and told him that if he ever so much as touched me in the future, I would hurt him badly, and I meant every word. He understood me and confined his negative moves in our relationship to more subtle manipulations from that point on.

While never a confrontational person, I could honestly say I was no longer as easily intimidated or abused as I had been as a boy growing up in Chapman. Clearly, I was gaining confidence, learning to stand up for myself, and coming into my own. After a long and difficult adolescence, I now prepared to embark on the next phase of my life, one that would test, mold, and cement my character and the man I was becoming.

Part II

Wild Fire

"Courage is of two kinds: first, physical courage, or courage in the presence of danger to the person; and next, moral courage, or courage before responsibility; whether it be before the judgement-seat of external authority, or of the inner power, the conscience."

— CARL VON CLAUSEWITZ, *On War*

Floyd at Yale.

4

An Innocent at Yale

In June 1950, I was coming off an inauspicious freshman year at Yale. After five years of boarding school restrictions, I reveled in the personal liberty New Haven's liberal college atmosphere offered, including the overpowering temptations of wine, women, and song. If the local pleasure possibilities palled, numerous women's colleges and the Big Apple were close at hand. I was figuratively and literally drunk with almost unlimited freedom, inhibited only by the rules that women had to be out of our rooms by ten at night during the week and by midnight on weekends, and freshmen could not have cars. I have never shown signs of having alcoholic tendencies, but I consumed more hard liquor during this year than during any comparable period in my life.

The results of my libertine lifestyle were predictable, and my studies suffered. I dropped one course (chemistry) and failed another (a math course dealing in esoteric number theory like why calculus works). I made the "Dean's Team," a euphemism for scholastic probation, meaning real trouble since Yale didn't allow you to fall behind—you either came up with the requisite credits or went home for good. One day in May, Hal Whiteman, the dean of freshmen, called me into his office on the Old Campus where all the first-year students lived. An imposing man who had served as captain of the 1940 Yale football team and as an army major in World War II, he advised me to attend summer school to replace the academic credit lost when I dropped chemistry and to repeat the math the following year in addition to my regular course load. When I asked where he wanted me to go to summer school, Dean Whiteman said that since I was from Alabama, the university at Tuscaloosa would be a logical choice.

I returned home in June and worked in the woods on a forestry crew for a month, waiting for the summer school term to begin. The start of the

Korean War galvanized me to mend my academic fences as it soon became evident that the combat was going against us, possibly leading to a protracted national emergency. Draft boards were activated under the Selective Service Act, and it looked like one either had to be a better student than I had been or join some military component to stay in school and avoid being classified as 1A and inducted into the army as a private.

After the Fourth of July, I rode a bus to Tuscaloosa, got a single room in a dorm, and walked down to the quadrangle in the center of the campus to register. I got a rude awakening from the academics, who said I lacked the prerequisites to sign up for any of the meaty, core subjects that I considered helpful to my education. I made a desperate analysis of my options, which boiled down to taking a course called "The Economic Geography of Latin America" or going home. Skeptical as to whether Yale would give me credit for something so crip sounding, I placed a call to Dean Whiteman, who told me that if I passed geography, he would give me the credit, and I could come back as agreed. I got a ninety-six in the course, my highest grade in college.

The summer school at Alabama was different from any educational experience I had had to date—not altogether unpleasant but hard to take seriously. Fred Wilkerson, a friend from Montgomery residing at the Phi Delta Theta fraternity house, arranged for me to take my meals there and use it as a social base. Fred had graduated from Episcopal High School, gone into the navy as a hospital corpsman near the end of the war, and started college at Princeton where he stayed about a year before flunking out. He was a nice guy, and we drank and dated coeds together to while away the time.

School was something altogether different. The geography teacher, a man who had been employed in the oil industry in Venezuela and some of the Central American countries, was fluent in Spanish, knew his subject as only someone who has worked in it can, gave interesting lectures, and in general presented a worthwhile, well-structured course. The problem was his students, in the main middle-aged or older public school teachers who attended summer school to earn advanced degrees. Their interest in furthering their education was practical since teachers' pay in Alabama was, and probably still is, based on the highest degree held by the teacher rather than any objective measurement of ability as an educator. The first Friday of the course, the teacher chalked questions for a 10-minute quiz on the blackboard and went out into the hall for a smoke. I got to work answering the relatively easy questions, when I was disturbed by the sensation of someone breathing on the back of my neck and pressing on my shoulders. I turned my head and was startled to find the old blue-haired woman who sat behind me leaning on my back, attempting to copy my answers—a rude shock to my young and tender sensibilities as I had never seen anybody cheat before. The test results also presented a problem for the teacher as a good majority of these so-called students failed to meet the minimum passing score. He solved this problem the only way he could—by making the tests and written projects easier and easier until most of the class was passing.

I returned to New Haven in September as a sophomore in good standing in the class of 1953. My main order of business, besides getting the academics squared away, was resolving my status with regard to military service, a matter of urgency. My thoughts turned directly to the Marine Corps and its Platoon Leaders Class (PLC). I had first become interested in the Marine Corps as a small boy of six after my cousin Wayne McGowin Brown from Andalusia, Alabama, graduated from the Naval Academy in 1937 to become the youngest officer in the Corps. Wayne's main instructor at The Basic School (TBS), then held at the Philadelphia Navy Yard, was Lewis B. "Chesty" Puller, one of the ultimate Marine legends and five-time winner of the Navy Cross. Puller's combat career stretched from Haiti and the Banana Wars in Central America, to Guadalcanal and Peleliu in the Pacific, then to Inchon and Chosin in Korea. I have several friends who served at his side as officers in combat. Once, in 1952, he inspected our company while we were on the pistol range at Quantico, and I vividly remember him getting right up in my face, looking tough but giving me a word of encouragement. He seemed a short man (actually he was five foot ten inches, but most of us were over six feet) with a big chest and long arms and a face that looked like he opened beer bottles with his teeth. Tough as he was, Puller was not without a sense of humor when it was needed to lighten up desperate times.

The second event that defined and focused my interest in the Marine Corps and caused me to explore the possibility of becoming a part of it was reading —and a Few Marines, written and illustrated by Colonel John W.

Thomason Jr., USMC. I was only twelve when I got the collection of stories, some true and some fiction, but all based on the author's life and experiences. One of the true stories, titled "Hanneken," told of Herman Henry Hanneken, one of Puller's contemporaries, who devised and implemented an elaborate scheme to trap and kill rebel Haitian leader Charlemagne Peralte. Five months after that escapade, he shot and killed Charlemagne's successor, Osaris Joseph, a lesser Haitian bandit chieftain. In Nicaragua in early 1929, Hannekan brought in alive another notorious bandit leader, Sandino's chief of staff General Jiron. In addition to the Medal of Honor, he received every award the Marine Corps gives for bravery: the Navy Cross (twice), the Silver Star, the Legion of Merit, and the Bronze Star. He retired as a brigadier general in 1948 after a thirty-four-year career. Interestingly, he attended Kendrick Seminary in St. Louis with the idea of becoming a Jesuit priest before joining the Corps in 1914 at age twenty-one. There are similarities between Jesuit and Marine ethics.

In the Old Corps medals were sparsely given and well deserved. The big ones, in order of importance, were the Medal of Honor, our nation's top award for bravery under fire; the Navy Cross, almost as rare and prestigious; and the Silver Star. As mentioned earlier, Puller earned a record five Navy Crosses, and Colonel Thomason was decorated with both the Navy Cross and Silver Star for his service in France. I can recall that the first time I met Marion Carl, then a lieutenant colonel commanding VMJ-1 in Korea; he wore only the Navy Cross ribbon under his wings. This kind of understatement has always seemed more classy and powerful than the current practice of awarding numerous meaningless ribbons, medals, and badges to military people who are just performing their jobs.

In —and a Few Marines, Thompson describes people and places vividly, and I was much impressed with the work ethic and spirit of the Marine officers and NCOs, as well as with the classy way they conducted themselves in fighting, loving, or just doing their duty. Thompson's wonderful drawings and watercolors further projected this image, especially meaningful to me since I draw a little myself. At the time I had never heard of Thompson and did not know that he was considered the James Boswell of the Marine Corps or that Ernest Hemingway thought him the greatest authority on warfare of his time. I did have enough sense, even as a raw kid, to know that I was reading the right stuff, and it made a powerful impression on me. So, when it came time for me to sort out my military status, the Marine Corps' PLC was the only solution I seriously considered.

The Corps has always been picky in selecting its officers and wants most to be college graduates. The PLC was established in 1935 to attract good-quality young men from the colleges to supplement the trickle of officers obtained from Annapolis and college Naval Reserve Officer Training Corps (NROTC) units, as well as "mustangs" commissioned from the ranks. I am not sure just how many got in each year, but except in wartime, the program was pretty small. The selection process involved an initial overall evaluation of the candidate. The criteria were not discussed, but I am sure they involved some mix of physical toughness, motivation, emotional stability, and the ability to think on one's feet. After candidates passed the initial screening and started the program, additional IQ and psychological testing was done, and most had a one-to-one session with a navy psychiatrist, a "talking doc." The program involved junior and senior six-week training periods in the summers at Parris Island and Quantico and, in my time, an additional 21-week attendance at The Basic School for further infantry and supporting arms training after graduation and commissioning. No time at college was taken up by any military classes or activity, and recruits were free to quit at any time before commissioning.

Soon after the fall term started, I went to the senior Marine, a lieutenant colonel, in the NROTC Department and told him that I wanted to join the PLC program. I don't remember the specifics of the interview except that I tried to show my interest as best I could. The colonel was noncommittal about my chances, saying that in time I would learn whether I had gotten in or not. Several weeks passed before a letter came saying that the program had no room for me. About this time I also received a letter from my draft board at home to the effect that I was 1A and would probably be called up at the end of the school year. Things looked bleak for a few weeks until another letter came from the Marine Corps. They had reevaluated their need for officers and told me to report to the colonel's office to be sworn in. The carnage among junior officers with the Chinese coming into

Floyd at the Yale Flying Club in the 1950s.

the war in November 1950 was very high, and somebody at Headquarters Marine Corps had rethought the whole matter.

I reported to the colonel's office, where I was sworn in, issued a temporary ID card, and set up for a physical at the Yale Health Department. While this may seem a backward sequence of events, the "Marine Corps way," if a little odd, was sound. Once they swore their candidates in, the draft was legally blocked, and the details could be handled later, which turned out to be right on in my case. The army had suffered badly in the recent North Korean and Chinese offensives and was pulling out all the stops to step up its input of raw manpower. Despite ample documentation, the draft board in Greenville, Alabama, ignored my new status as a budding Marine and scheduled me almost immediately after I had passed the PLC physical to report to the federal building in New Haven, where I took the preinduction physical as part of a motley group of Yalies and townies. The competition for my body culminated that summer when I got notice to report for induction into the army during the middle of boot camp at Parris Island. I passed this on to my senior drill instructor, who seemed unusually eager to take care of it. Both formally and informally, Marine Corps culture looked down on the army and considered screwing them out of men, weapons, and supplies—or engaging in a bar fight or two—as good fun.

After being sworn in, I vividly recollect looking at myself in the mirror on top of my bedroom bureau. While glad and a little proud, I realized that I had made a commitment that one way or another would change my life—it wouldn't be easy, but there was no turning back. My exact thought was that I had put myself in the position of someone who had jumped off the top of the Empire State Building and hadn't hit the ground yet. It occurred to me that my sophomoric view of the Corps was strongly influenced by romantic thoughts based on books like *From Here to Eternity*, *The Caine Mutiny*, *Battle Cry*, and *Mister Roberts*. There was likely to be a hell of a lot more challenge to this than lying around slop chutes and grog shops with my friends, immaculately turned out in our good-looking uniforms.

Being a young Marine officer in wartime was not a protected situation. There was no guarantee of meriting a Navy Cross but a good chance of earning a white one. The most likely military occupational specialty (MOS) for people like me was 0300, or infantry officer field, referred to as "Oh Three Oh Shit" in the black humor of The Basic School. I was resigned to starting out as a platoon leader if my hopes for going to flight training at Pensacola and becoming a Marine pilot didn't work out. Like most, I had joined for the challenge, a need for discipline, and a desire to be with the best. I was nineteen years old and feeling a lot of self-imposed pressure to clean up my act and amount to something, to grow up and be a man, and I didn't feel like I had done much so far. I had graduated from one fine school and advanced to another. I had earned the money to begin flying as a sixteen-year-old and showed some talent for it, earning my private pilot's license before I was a senior in high school. I was streetwise from five years in boarding schools and had good health. I had been late getting my growth and maturing, but by this time I was decent looking and had bulked up to 185 pounds to fill out a six-foot, one-inch frame. I had good core values and quality friends in my peer group and among some of the older people who knew me well. I liked and appreciated girls and women a lot. On the down side, I lacked self-confidence. I did not realize that I had excellent eyesight and hand-eye coordination and considerable potential for physical agility, strength, and endurance. My degree of physical courage was an enigma to me at this point—something that I, like a moth attracted to a candle's flame, needed to know more about. Like many young men, I needed to prove something to myself.

The rest of my sophomore year passed uneventfully and fairly successfully. I did all right in all of my subjects and passed the arcane math that I was repeating in addition to my regular course load. At Yale Aviation's organizational meeting in September, I had been elected vice president. One of the oldest collegiate flying clubs with some prestigious alumni in the aviation community, Yale Aviation had about sixty members and owned two airplanes, a J-3 Cub and a Cessna 140. My duties mostly entailed acting as safety officer, and I spent a good bit of time at Jack Usher's fixed base operation at Tweed Airport talking to the mechanics who kept up our planes. I didn't know enough to contribute a lot, but this was a good learning experience with the working side of aviation. We didn't have any accidents, even though the planes got a lot of use and none of us had very many hours. I continued to fly regularly and checked out in a number of light airplanes, including some four-placers like the Piper Clipper and Pacer and the Stinson Voyager.

That spring I was initiated into Fence Club, one of ten or so fraternities or clubs, pleasant places for eating, drinking, and socializing that some 20 percent of the upperclassmen belonged to. Fence members included the late William Buckley, who had graduated the previous year, and my classmates Bill Donaldson, Dan Lufkin, Dick Thoman, and Archie Douglas, then a junior, were fellow Marine PLCs. We were five out of twenty-two at Yale who joined that year.

After school got out at the end of May, I headed home to work in a surveying crew in the woods to prepare myself physically for Parris Island, where I was to report in July. The job involved a lot of walking and cutting brush with a machete—hot work in the high heat and humidity of lower Alabama. The crew, by tradition, considered it unmanly to carry canteens in the field, so we had to make do with gorging on ice water from our truck's water barrel at the lunch break and later in the afternoon at the close of work. Some days were so bad that I surreptitiously lapped muddy water out of tepid streams and creeks. Hard as it was, this work turned out to be ideal conditioning for what lay ahead at the recruit depot in South Carolina.

EARLY ON A SUNDAY morning, soon after the Fourth of July, I got in my '41 Studebaker Commander four-door sedan and headed east on the narrow, winding, two-lane highways. I made it to the outskirts of Savannah and spent the night in a pleasant roadside inn. On Monday morning I rose early, nervously ate breakfast, and started on the sixty-mile drive up the coast.

Parris Island lies just southeast of the historic seaport Beaufort, South Carolina, a pretty place with numerous imposing antebellum mansions of Northern and Continental flavor and construction. Approaching Parris Island by the causeway and bridge that provided the only entrance, I saw a lowland mass barely rising out of the water, shimmering in the humid heat of midmorning. The island is about 8,000 acres, 4,400 useable with the rest swamp and marshland. The semitropical vegetation consists mostly of cypress, sand pine, live and water oaks festooned with Spanish moss, cabbage palms, and palmetto. Its animal population, besides attractive species like deer, squirrels, otters, and coons, includes all four poisonous snakes native to North America, plus various ants, mosquitoes, sand fleas, and gnats. The waters of Port Royal Harbor and the Beaufort and Broad rivers, which support a healthy population of sharks and alligators, surround it. It has over fifty inches of rainfall annually with numerous thundering cloudbursts; in midsummer it has 100° plus temperatures and very high humidity. All in all, the sultry ambiance of the island fit right in with the kind of maritime terrain associated with most of the Marine Corps' traditional battlegrounds. It did not take much of a leap of the imagination for new arrivals like me to equate it with the French penal colony Devil's Island, which many of us had seen in the movies.

The summer of 1951 was the only time any PLC training was done at Parris Island due to the lack of facilities at Quantico. I have always considered myself fortunate for having had a traditional introduction to the Marine Corps. Our training, based on the premise that a Marine officer has got to do all that his men do, initially paralleled that of regular recruits, with all they got and more. Theirs lasted a little longer and included two weeks mess duty, which consisted of serving chow, swabbing mess hall decks, peeling potatoes, and hosing out garbage cans. Our status as a select group of college men in prime health who had consciously elected to be there guaranteed that we could be force-fed the training under a time constraint that made every hour of every day count. Motivation and guts got us through—we wanted to be Marine officers very badly, and if physically fit with the right mental attitude, you made it. The entire platoon completed the course—nobody quit, got kicked out, became sick enough to lose any training time, or got hurt. We wore no rank insignia as PLCs but were legally corporals for pay purposes during the first year and sergeants during the senior course. At TBS we wore the gold bars of second lieutenants, but while on duty, we did everything that grunt privates did, lived their life in the barracks and in the field, and in fact were often bossed around by enlisted men. The point of all this was that before we ever gave an enlisted man any orders, we would have effectively been what he was for eight months of intensive training and were therefore intimately familiar with how enlisted men thought and their problems.

When I reached the island, I stopped at a kiosk manned by two spit-and-polish enlisted Marines armed with .45 automatics who had gate guard duty. I showed my orders to one of them who matter-of-factly told me where to park my car, then to proceed to the receiving barracks, a white, wooden, two-story building dating from World War II. When I got there, I surrendered my orders to a sergeant manning a desk in the front of a large open room and joined the hushed group of young men who were bunched up by their suitcases trying to look unconcerned. I didn't know anyone but didn't have long to worry because as soon as the forty-eighth PLC showed up, we were told to grab our bags and fall out in front of the building. We formed up raggedly and were greeted by a handsome young buck sergeant, very open-faced in a sincere, all-American way. He introduced himself as Sergeant Wilson, then announced that as one of our junior drill instructors (DIs), he would personally take care of us and see that we made it through the difficult weeks ahead with a minimum of pain and suffering. I don't know exactly what his game was, but it sounded a little too good to be true.

When we got to the company area, our platoon leader, First Lieutenant R. F. Ellis, a reserve called up for Korea, introduced us to our senior DI,

Staff Sergeant. R. L. Lorenzo, and junior DIs Staff Sergeant J. Hephner and Sergeant W. L. Buckley Jr. We were told that there had been a change and that Sergeant Buckley had replaced Sergeant Wilson, who was moving to another platoon in our company. We wondered silently if we were in for it, having lost our protector, but it was probably the best thing that could have happened to us. Lorenzo and Hephner had swapped Wilson to Platoon Fourteen for their contemporary and buddy Sergeant Buckley. From things they later said in passing and from boys we knew in his platoon, it became evident that NCOs and PLCs alike regarded Wilson as a devious, two-faced prick. This served as an important lesson to me: when people tell you how honest and ethical they are and how sympathetic they are to your own very intelligent viewpoints, tastes, and so forth, you had better keep your hand on your wallet and standby for a ram.

We were members of Platoon Sixteen, one of four making up Company M, Third Battalion. The officers commanding the companies and platoons and on the battalion staff filled important administrative functions necessary to run a place like Parris Island openly and smoothly, but they were remote, godlike figures to us. Our three drill instructors at the platoon level were the delivery mechanism for the Marine Corps' message, and they could not have been better picked—professional soldiers, they knew what they wanted to do and how to do it. All three had heavy combat experience in World War II in the Pacific and were just back from the killing fields of Inchon and Chosin. Staff Sergeant Lorenzo, the senior DI, was the executive of the trio who knew all the angles. Staff Sergeant Hephner, a Raider on Guadalcanal and a hard-bitten Marine with a dry sense of humor and a real way with words, sported a tattoo of a bald eagle soaring over a sunset that covered his entire chest. Sergeant William Lawrence Buckley was a West Virginia coal miner, tough, fair, taciturn, competent, and wise. We didn't know anything about their personal affairs, but I'm pretty sure the Marine Corps was home for all three. They were totally dedicated to teaching us the basics of our new job and how to do it right. I can remember no case when they talked about their own combat experiences or glorified war in any way—practical advice like how to beat up soldiers or steal equipment from the army was another story. Parris Island was uncomfortable physically but mostly a head game. They delivered hard-ass doses of stress and work mixed with a good bit of humor.

Our company area consisted of small, metal Nissen huts shaped like miniature Quonset huts. Our platoon occupied four of the 12-man squad bays, another was used for storing our civilian baggage and for stand-up meetings, and the DIs had one with their little office in the front half and their living quarters in the rear behind a partition. The huts were grouped in a quadrangle around the company's combination bath and shithouse, which served two hundred or so men.

I still recollect the first few days of adjusting to all this vividly. The program was designed to take people of disparate backgrounds, which in our case meant colleges from Harvard to Slippery Rock, and all manner of economic and social circumstances and to subordinate the resulting mishmash of values to an acceptance of the Corps' ideals. That first afternoon we were marched, still in civilian clothes, to the lyceum (base auditorium). The commanding general (CG) of the recruit depot, Major General Robert H. Pepper, a burly, tough-looking old man (actually he was fifty-five at the time) with big ears and a big nose, sat on the stage with his staff. Pepper's chief of staff, Colonel John R. Lanigan, ran the affair. Lanigan introduced himself, the staff, and General Pepper and had the head chaplain, a navy captain, bless us and our endeavor.

Pepper then delivered a welcome to the effect that when he and his crew got through with us, we would be Marines and proud of it. He mentioned the Corps' traditional values on which its illustrious reputation was built. He told us that a very careful evaluation would be made as to our leadership characteristics, that future platoon leaders were screened with a view toward eliminating those found to lack the desired qualities, and that this screening process was a very important factor in the training program. He summed up with words to the effect that, most importantly, we would never give up, never quit. If we had a positive attitude and motivation, we would respond successfully to the challenge of our training—the opportunity to be a Marine. It was good advice.

Early the next day we started processing in. Each activity was handled efficiently and impersonally. We were like a herd of prime livestock. First, we were run through the barbershop where civilian barbers gave us a close cut, what is called a "high and tight" today. We went to the supply building where we were accurately measured for our uniforms and shoes and issued with socks, underwear ("skivvies"), towels, and caps. We each got two pairs of "boondockers," high-topped leather shoes with the rough side out, and one pair of cordovan-colored dress shoes. The boondockers were probably the best, most comfortable shoes I have ever had, and in the course of the next six weeks, we wore one pair out completely and got about half way through the second pair. In the field, Marines wore yellow canvas leggings over the boondockers and lower trouser legs, an old fashioned but practical arrangement. Combat boots weren't used until the next year, and by the end of the Korean War, the leggings were all gone. The dress shoes were endlessly shined with Kiwi shoe polish and a little Aqua Velva aftershave lotion, which over time produced a spit-shine gloss finish. I still have the pair I started with in my closet. When we got our clothes, they all fit perfectly and looked good. We wore olive green cotton herringbone utilities, or dungarees as they were called, with soft cotton utility caps to work in. Our dress uniforms were starched wash khaki shirts and trousers, field scarves, and fore and aft caps, "pisscutters" in the vernacular.

We got an intensive mental and physical work over, including a battery of physiological and mental tests with an IQ test called a GCT exam. One of the tests asked us to draw a picture of a man or woman on one side of a blank piece of paper and number it "1," then turn the paper over, number it "2," and draw the opposite sex. I made petty generic Ken and Barbie drawings. Everybody was scared they had missed some secret. I remember one boy took some minor criticism for drawing horns, a tail, and stripes on his male figure and was grilled to ascertain if he had serious hostility to the program. I did pretty well on the GCT test, scoring in the top 10 percent. Dick Thoman, later my son's godfather, made the highest score ever recorded on the GCT exam at Parris Island up to that time. Thoman and I, like about 70 percent of our group, were later briefly interviewed by one of the "talking docs." I remember he asked what I thought about sex and if I had any sexual problems. I responded to the effect that I thought sex was here to stay and that the only problem I had was the extraordinary difficulty in getting girls in my peer group to go to bed with me.

The physical was interesting. Inoculations were given in each arm simultaneously to save time, and on more than one occasion I saw large, tough men faint to the floor under the assault of needle-bearing corpsmen. For the general physical, the whole company was herded into a large room, then told to strip naked and stand in ranks with feet on yellow footprints painted on the deck. Various teams, consisting of a doctor assisted by two corpsmen trooped the lines; the "rear admiral" and his group peering and poking up rectums between spread cheeks; others doing hernia checks by pulling and prodding scrotums; short-arm inspections; ear, eye, nose and throat checks; and so forth. While all this was going on, we were expected to remain at attention with eyes straight ahead. At one point I heard some raised voices coming from in front of an ugly, caveman-looking guy in the rank ahead of me and about four men down to port. By slightly turning my neck and swiveling my eyes, I caught a glimpse of what all the excitement was about. The red-faced subject sported a cabbage-headed crank about the size of a rolling pin, which hung down his right leg almost to the knee. The excited medics who had made the discovery were whistling and signaling all the other teams and administrative personnel to come get a firsthand look, while the rest of us tried to keep straight faces. Things soon quieted down, and the physical finished. From there we were sent through the dental section for a quick check, which completed our mental and physical evaluations.

By the end of the week, we all had our uniforms, 782 gear, and Garand M1 rifles. We were settled in the squad bays, which had three double-deck bunks down each side and a screen door for ventilation on each end. For furniture to sit on, we each had a wooden footlocker, kept locked, for our gear and valuables. We also had a sea bag, a laundry bag, and a wall locker. Though Spartan, this accommodation represented what we had later in the senior course and at TBS as lieutenants. Nobody minded as we were seldom there during the hot part of the day, and at night we were so tired that the rack felt wonderful, and deep sleep was easy to come by, only occasionally disturbed by the collective groans, farts, and babbling of the other eleven inmates. The lack of privacy and enforced togetherness made for a bonding of sorts, but the situation was too harried and stressful for us to make any meaningful friendships, although we supported each other. There were no fights or outward signs of disagreement, and the platoon members helped each other if anybody got behind in anything.

The DIs taught us how to make up a rack so a quarter would bounce on the perfectly tight blanket; how to field-strip and clean our rifles to the point where we could easily do it blindfolded; how to practice military courtesy such as saluting and proper forms of deportment and address; and finally and at great lengths, how to perform close-order drill and the manual of arms. They delivered helpful hints and advice freely. Someone committing the gaffe of calling his weapon a gun was singled out to march around the platoon holding his M1 aloft in one hand and his dick in the other, announcing repeatedly, "This is my rifle; this is my gun. This is for fighting; this is for fun." Once when we were drilling on the "grinder," an asphalt parade ground with daytime surface temperatures of 120°, I was behind a guy who got mixed up and stepped off on the wrong foot at the command of execution. The DI halted the proceedings, walked over to the clumsy one, and planted his boondocker down on an instep with considerable force, while helpfully suggesting, "Next time step off on the one that hurts." At times like this, nobody knew whether to be amused or to feel sorry for the targets of the DIs attentions, but a mistake was seldom made twice.

The DIs mostly worked one at a time, splitting the long duty day into roughly three parts so that they didn't lose their voices or get too hot and tired. Lorenzo, a senior man, took the easier stuff to some extent, but he was still effective, although not as admired as Hephner and Buckley. The language used by the DIs and other enlisted academic and weapons instructors was colorfully profane with heavy emphasis on the F word. Crude, dirty talk can be offensive, but these professionals delivered their ear-burning profanities and blasphemies with such style and grace as to be artistic and often pleasantly amusing. One day Staff Sergeant Hephner assembled us in the hut that served as our indoor stand-up meeting hall and announced that he was tasked with "verbally publishing" an order from General Pepper to all recruits, officer candidates (OCs), and PLCs. The general's order proclaimed that henceforth there would be absolutely no bad language used on people under training. A preacher's son's letter to his father complaining of the terrible verbiage to which he was being subjected had inspired this new policy. The father made an impassioned complaint to his congressman, who in turn passed it on to the commandant of the Marine Corps, General Shepherd, who then took appropriate action. Hephner read the order in precise tones. When he finished, he looked around with a solemn, straight face and indignantly asked, "What the fuck do they want me to say, sexual intercourse?" Work resumed, and as far as I could tell, nobody paid the slightest attention to the dutifully published order, which if carried out would have rendered most of the staff nearly inarticulate.

Our six-week course was divided evenly between physical activities, academics, and weapons training. Midway through, we moved to the rifle range for two weeks, where we became intimately familiar with the M1 rifle and fired the Browning automatic rifle (BAR), M1 carbine, and Colt .45 automatic pistol. The final two weeks were spent working out of the company area polishing our newly learned skills for graduation.

We woke to reveille at 0500 every morning with thirty minutes to shave, wash, use the heads, and fall out for physical drill, either basic calisthenics or some times "under arms," where we used the M1 rifle in a variety of exercises. None of this was overly difficult or unpleasant, and it made a good way to wake up and start the day. After physical drill, we had a few minutes to make our racks up, then police the squad bays, company area, and heads before falling out in formation to be marched to breakfast. Everything had to be spotless and shipshape. After a few object lessons, where the inspecting DI tore all the racks up or kicked a fire bucket filled with sand all over the deck of the squad bay, we got our technique squared away so that we could almost always satisfy their sense of order and cleanliness. Besides calisthenics we got several hours of exercise every day in close-order drill and marches of various lengths, but none over five miles. Marching was usually done at "route march" pace, four miles an hour occasionally punctuated with "double time" with rifles carried at high port. We also ran an obstacle course several times a week in the afternoons. This involved rope climbing and other military-oriented exertions. None of us had any trouble, and it was all pretty tame stuff compared to what was coming in Senior PLC at Quantico.

Our biggest problem was with heat and thirst. The prevailing notion was to limit recruits' liquid intake severely between meals, notwithstanding the extreme heat and humidity, to teach water discipline. The DIs accented our thirst when an opportunity presented itself by halting the formation in front of the various construction projects while they took languid sips of ice water from the workmen's water barrels, often pouring an extra dipper full on the ground to make their point. This was unpleasant, but no worse than I had experienced working in the woods in Alabama. When we had been there three weeks, we heard rumors that one boy had died from heat exhaustion and another's brains had been cooked to the point that he would be a permanent vegetable. A week later, our company was assembled on short notice in one of the mess halls for one of the straight-to-the-point meetings the Marine Corps uses to be sure they have publicly and loudly stated their official position. To our amazement, a young navy doctor in wash khakis stood up on a table and told us that a study on water discipline just concluded in the desert had found that it was not possible to teach the body to do without water, that trying was potentially dangerous and certainly unhealthy, and that accordingly instructions had been issued that we were to be given all the water we wanted to drink. He added that this was serious stuff and that we were to report any DI who interfered with our new rights to plentiful water. Two thoughts instantly crossed my mind and probably everyone else's—first, that this business about the desert tests was "big lie" bullshit to save face for the command about changing the water policy due to the recent problems, and second, that anybody fool enough to put a DI on report over the new policy would probably suffer a fate a hell of a lot worse than heat stroke. Possibly as a result of this, we heard of no more heat-related physical problems; nor did we notice that we were much less thirsty than before.

My only physical problems were sunburn on my face and ears and a carbuncle on my left forearm probably due to the sweaty grime we wallowed in all day. It swelled up and hurt like hell, so I fell out for sick call after chow one night and was marched to the hospital in a small detail from the company. When my turn came, a young doctor and his team of corpsmen examined my arm briefly and made their diagnosis and treatment plan.

Floyd, left, with Dick Thoman at USMC Platoon Leaders' course training at Parris Island, South Carolina.

One big corpsman grabbed my arm and held it while another sprayed the inflamed area with a freezing solution. The doctor stabbed a scalpel into my arm and pulled it through the head of the infected area, then pulled it out and repeated the process from another angle, making an X almost an inch across. The core of the infection popped out, and I began to feel better. These guys didn't have any bedside manner, but they knew what they were doing. I lost no duty time and was healed up in a few days. I still have the X.

Other physical activities consisted of some field work ("snoopin' and poopin'" or "boondockin'") in small-unit tactics, mostly of the rifle-squad variety, bayonet training, hand-to-hand combat, and dirty fighting. We would march from the company area several miles to a wooded maneuver area near the airstrip, Page Field. Once there, the training usually started with a lecture by one of the enlisted academics on subjects like maneuver and tactics, camouflage and concealment, or map reading and compasses. Though very basic and elementary, these talks added substance to our classroom lectures.

Bayonet training was introduced with lectures on theory, after which we split into two-man teams for practical application, done with the scabbard over the bayonet to prevent accidents. We were schooled in the five killing blows used on offense and defensive tactics like the high block, low block, and parry. We spent several periods at this practice and were careful not to hurt each other. The rifle, its butt, and attached bayonet are formidable weapons that can be used with deadly effect, but the order "fix bayonets" must be the worst that grunts ever hear because it means the shit has hit the fan.

We also had some basic training in unarmed hand-to-hand combat, consisting of tactics, holds, and throws, as well as a truly interesting exposure to dirty fighting. We learned the best way to kick a guy's nuts with vigor, gouge eyes, fracture an Adam's apple, and administer killing blows bare-handed, such as by hitting an opponent hard with an upward blow of the heel of the hand to the base of his nose. This maneuver breaks the nose and puts the pieces into his brain, turning his lights off for good.

The academic part of the training took place mostly in temporary classrooms, which were large tents with wooden floors with the sides rolled up for ventilation. We learned about the Corps' history and traditions, organization and branches, and legal system. In 1951 the Uniform Code of Military Justice had recently been put in place in all the military services, replacing the "Rocks and Shoals" legal code of the Naval Service, and this was deemed important enough to merit a good deal of training time. I understood from it that having entered military service, I no longer had any rights as an individual, and my ass belonged to Uncle Sam and the Marine Corps, reason enough to respect orders and discipline absolutely. Much of the classroom work was devoted to infantry weaponry. The NCO instructors knew their stuff and taught effectively in styles ranging from polished to rustic. One redneck opened his lecture with, "Awright you goddamn Ivory Leaguers, today I'm gonna teach ya'll the normanclature [sic] of the machine gun," an exact quote committed to memory while biting my lip to keep from laughing, which would have been a major heresy as the professor was dead serious.

For the third and fourth weeks of the program, we moved to the rifle range, where the company was billeted in many rows of four-man pyramidal tents stretched over wooden frames with wood-plank floors. We each had our own canvas cot. The tent sides were rolled up, and at night cool breezes made it a very pleasant place to sleep. The only trouble was that we had to get up a half hour early, at 0430, so we were chronically sleepy.

At the range, we had one coach for each four shooters. We spent the first couple of days "snapping in," or dry firing in the three basic positions, off-hand (standing), kneeling, and prone. The coaches imparted to us proper sling adjustment, posture, sight adjustment, breathing, trigger squeeze, and other fine points before we ever fired a shot. The range was a carefully run place. Aimed fire under combat conditions is a big part of Marine infantry training. Each section of the massive range had space for fifty shooters side by side. We fired the M1 for record from two, three, and five hundred yards. We spent half the time shooting and half working in the target butts, concrete trenches behind an earthen berm. After each round of firing, we pulled the target down in its frame by pulley, scored it, and signaled the data to the coaches and shooters. Red flags, "Maggie's Drawers," denoted a miss; a tin marker on a pole held up against the target showed the shot's placement and score. Working in the butts was not bad—it was shady, nobody harassed us, and while it was perfectly safe, the sound of hundreds of bullets snapping just overhead was stimulating. We fired fifty rounds from the various ranges and shooting positions to qualify for record. Each round scored 0 for a miss to 5 for a bull's-eye, making 250 a perfect score. Minimum Marksman score was 190 (I shot 195); Sharpshooter, 210; and Expert, 220.

By this time, we had become proficient in basic close-order drill and the manual of arms, and the DIs started to teach us some fancy, show-off variations only done by drill teams. They seemed to enjoy teaching us this stuff, which was elective on their part and outside the canned program. This drilling was mostly administered in short doses on the paved company street fronting our tent area, but on several occasions, when time permitted, we had longer, company-sized drill periods on a big grassy field at the far end of the rifle range. On the far side of this field, near the water, were the senior officers' quarters. I vividly remember standing at attention in the ranks facing these neat, comfortable-looking houses, where like a mirage, groups of young, pretty women in bright summer dresses sat under shade trees and umbrellas on the back patios. They appeared to be sipping ice-cold lemonade from tall glasses and eating cucumber sandwiches. The contrast between the sun and sweat, which characterized our Spartan existence, and the vision of civilized, comfortable pulchritude to our front was stark and served to underscore the differences between military and civilian life.

As PLCs we got liberty every weekend from 1100 on Saturday after weekly inspection until 1700 on Sunday. When liberty began on Saturdays, I always met Mal Gambill and Dick Thoman at my car for the drive to Savannah, our regular weekend port of call. We usually took Archie Douglas and Dick Patton, both in the class ahead of us at Yale, and Joe Provow, a good guy from Tiptonville, Tennessee, who was Mal's buddy in his platoon. On the way into Savannah, we always dropped off our week's laundry at a 24-hour place that specialized in military clothing, a great convenience as it saved us from wasting precious time doing hand-powered washing at the company wash racks. We used the old original DeSoto Hotel as our base and enjoyed it very much. It had a fine bar and dining room and a big veranda with rocking chairs across the front, which faced a shady, pretty little square park where there were always some good-humored black shoeshine boys clamoring for our business. It seemed the height of luxury to sit on a park bench in front of the hotel and have one of these little guys put a professional spit shine on our dress shoes after doing it ourselves so many times. We were required to wear our uniforms on liberty, so there was never any question about who we were.

Besides enjoying the relative luxuries of the DeSoto, we covered the Savannah social scene from top to bottom, often starting an evening with drinks at the Yacht Club, moving on to check out places at Savannah Beach and winding up at a honky-tonk in Thunderbolt, a tough little hamlet about halfway between the beach and the city. One Saturday night at the Yacht Club, I met the young navy doctor who had fixed my arm and bought him a drink. I also met a girl named Mimi Holton whose brother had been at Episcopal High School with me. She was sexy and attractive in a big-chested way and fun to talk to, but too proper to cut out on her date. This was par for the course with college girls, and we had better success with the women in Thunderbolt, although in retrospect I guess we were lucky to get out with our lives and health intact. These weekends were always all too brief, but they served to charge our batteries for the next week's privations.

Before we knew it, our time at Parris Island was almost up. One day we were told to put on our dress uniforms and marched to a photography studio where the DIs and we had individual portrait photos made. Just before popping the shutter, the helpful photographer told each subject to say "bullshit," and as usual, the Marine Corps way, while different, produced the desired result as the pictures were uniformly good. A commercial company had been engaged to make a publication like a school yearbook covering the PLC and OC training at Parris Island that summer, and each of us got one of these books as a valued souvenir.

Toward the end of the course at an evening formation, Staff Sergeant Lorenzo gave us an "at ease" command and asked if any of us had any questions regarding future career fields in the Corps. I asked him what he thought my chances were of going to flight training. He said that he believed this avenue to be open to me, and I would be given an opportunity to apply after being commissioned. As far as I remember, I was the only one in the platoon to express any interest in aviation, although several probably wound up flying for whatever reason.

We had a final formal inspection and big parade, with the CG and his staff on hand to watch us pass in review. Afterwards we said goodbye to the DIs and thanked them for their work. I liked and respected them and felt in their debt for what they had taught me and the way they had done it. Despite its being hot, tired, and uncomfortable, I felt that short time at Parris Island was an extremely positive learning experience—satisfying and fun in many ways, with a lot of good humor throughout. We were in actuality still extremely limited in knowledge and experience, but we had earned the title of Marine as far as the Corps was concerned and would be treated as such from that point forward.

AFTER A BRIEF VISIT home to Alabama, I went back to New Haven to start my junior year. By now my discipline and study habits had improved, and I never had any more trouble in making decent to good grades. We also began to specialize as juniors in smaller, more focused courses taught by some very senior, or at least highly respected, academics. My chosen field was international relations, a political science major mostly favored by people looking to go into the Foreign Service (State Department) or the CIA. I hoped I might get into service flying and wind up as an airline pilot, but beyond that my career aspirations were not well delineated.

In October, I met Rosa Tucker, a freshman at Finch College in midtown Manhattan. I picked her up from school for a blind date one Sunday afternoon and took her to hear Conrad Janis and his jazz band at Central Plaza in the Village. It didn't take long for us to realize that some kind of bonding was taking place. At the same time, my love for handsome women kept popping up, and for a while, I maintained a sort of *The Captain's Paradise* triangle with a beautiful, free-spirited girl from Birmingham at Connecticut College and a pretty, buxom, blond socialite from Cleveland at Vassar. Docking at three ports of call over one weekend made for careful planning, good security, and stamina, but I managed to play this game successfully for a little while, until Rosa, with counseling from her mother, cut the others out.

The school year passed pleasantly enough. When June rolled around,

Mal Gambill came to Chapman where he stayed at our home and worked with me for the lumber company's Forestry Department. In the early part of July, we loaded up my Studebaker and drove to Mal's home in North Wilkesboro, North Carolina. After a short and pleasant visit, we drove on up to Washington to meet Dick Thoman and Joe Provow at the Willard Hotel so that we could report at Quantico as a group and get assigned to the same platoon.

The Marine base at Quantico, Virginia, came into being with the leasing of 5,300 acres from the Quantico Company on April 17, 1917. The Corps was undergoing a very rapid expansion due to U.S. involvement in World War I and was critically short of facilities for garrisoning and training new troops. The site was ideal since it was close to Washington (one of the selection criteria) and on both a mainline railroad and the navigable water of the Potomac River, suitable for deep draft ships. "Mainside," the location of the various headquarters, staff schools, hospital, base exchange, air station, and other facilities lies just east of Dumfries on Route 1 on the west bank of the river, an hour's drive from Washington and halfway between Alexandria and Fredericksburg.

In 1942, the "Guadalcanal Area," a 51,000-acre tract west of Route 1, was added to make more room for field maneuvers with the World War II buildup. Comprising abandoned farmland interspersed with woods, the area had seen heavy traffic from both Confederate and Union troops in the 1860s. In 1950 two new facilities in the area were opened to satisfy the need to train more officers, in effect tripling the capacity of the original on-site Basic School located at Camp Barrett near Mainside. The new places, Camp Goettge and Camp Upshur, mirror images of each other, were miles away from civilization and Mainside's spit and polish. Buried deep in the boonies, they were totally lacking in charm or beauty and set on flat areas bulldozed out of the sandy clay soil. There were no trees and little grass around the Quonset huts used for quarters and the rectangular metal buildings that housed the mess hall, classrooms, support functions, and local administration. All in all, the camps were utilitarian, Spartan settings devoted to military lessons in preparation for probable combat. Sites for practicing any sort of field work—route marches and bivouacs, infantry tactics and artillery, tank and close air support demonstrations—were all within a reasonable march of the camps. We almost never rode anywhere and hoofed it to the training areas in heat, cold, rain, shine, and occasionally snow or sleet.

We reported in and were directed to Camp Goettge, the site of 1952's Senior PLC course. Our scheme to go through as a group worked, and the four of us ended up billeted in a Quonset that held the entire platoon with twelve double-deck racks perpendicular to each side wall and a wide aisle down the middle. Even with four times the population of our little Parris Island squad bays, this hut seemed to have more light and air and was a happier place to live. The adjacent heads lacked privacy but were modern, tiled, easily cleaned places with conventional toilets and even drinking fountains putting out cold water.

We met our DI, Sergeant Jesus Rodriguez, a compact, tough, and darkly handsome young Hispanic from the Southwest who saw to our administrative needs and positioned us for training as called for in the schedule. A former teenage Golden Gloves fighter, he was pleasant and helpful in the execution of his job. He was just back from a heavy dose of infantry combat in Korea and one of those rare individuals, even in the Marines, who genuinely loved the combat experience. He was extremely frustrated with his present safe situation helping train future officers at Quantico. His request to go back to combat in Korea had been denied, and he worried that the war might end before he got a second tour. Discipline, order, and cleanliness were tight, and everybody did everything he was supposed to with absolutely no shirking, but we had risen above the harassment endured in the Parris Island "boot" phase. Rodriguez was there to act as a guide and to show us practical things, and he treated us courteously as fellow Marines.

We were much more self-assured during this training phase. We had entered a middle ground between being raw boots and combat-ready members of the Fleet Marine Force. The work was long and hard but done in a generally positive atmosphere. People got to enjoy each other's conversation and company, and there was a lot more gossip, humor, bitching, and interplay normal to all-male groups, marking the beginning of camaraderie. Other than weekend liberty, we had little time of our own, but there was an open-air slop chute under some pine trees where we could drink a few beers a couple of nights a week.

The training during this six-week course and later at The Basic School wasn't a head game, but what it lacked in mental stress it made up for in extreme physical activity and conditioning. We had a short PT session in front of the hut every morning before breakfast, and on days when we were not in the field, we had to run the obstacle course at 1100, just before lunch. It was much tougher and longer than the one at Parris Island. We were expected to crawl on our bellies under barbed wire strung between metal stakes, cross hand over hand over a slimy mud pit swinging from a slippery metal pipe, pull ourselves over a shoulder high wall, and scale a 20-foot vertical wall via a cargo net hung on one side and then rappel hand over hand down a rope on the other side. This was a timed affair, and we started off running it in skivvy shirts and our dungaree trousers. Every week various items of uniform and equipment were added so that by the end we were running the course in our field clothing plus steel helmet, rifle, bayonet, war belt, canteen, and a full field pack. This was the hardest thing physically that I have ever had to do, but I found I could do it as well as most and better than a lot of the prominent jocks, especially the heavyweight linemen. I got a lasting dose of self-confidence out of this experience, as well as some muscular development and stamina, which served me well in the ensuing years.

We marched to chow immediately after running the course in the heat of the day, filthy and drenched with sweat. The mess hall always had a long, slow line and was crowded, dark, and steamy hot. The chow generally bordered on terrible, and sometimes I just took simple stuff like bread, peanut butter, and jelly that the cooks could not mess up. Most days I was close to throwing up at this point and ate little, just drinking as much cold stuff as possible—water, bug juice (a noxious, sweet, imitation-fruit-flavored drink purchased by the government in large quantities, sort of a poor man's Kool-Aid), tea, milk—whatever was available. I dropped twenty pounds in six weeks, weighing 165 when I finished and in the best shape of my life.

We had continuing classroom instruction in the traditions, organization, and major campaigns of the Corps, plus a lot on infantry weapons, and spent a good amount of time in the field with conditioning marches

Floyd and Rosa Tucker, his future wife, and Barbara and Dick Thoman at Yale.

and demonstrations of supporting arms and tactical problems, mostly at the company level. We spent the middle third of the course at Mainside, where our company occupied the third deck of a multistory, permanent brick barracks. We fired the rifle range for record again with our M1s and went through firing exercises with all the other weapons endemic to an infantry company. We worked with the BAR and machine guns a lot and were exposed to the sinister-looking Browning .30 caliber water-cooled machine gun, which dated back to World War I. The time in the barracks and on the range was more relaxed and fun than our weapons exposure at the recruit depot, and we all enjoyed it. There were even civilian Good Humor men peddling "pogey bait" (ice cream bars, candy, and cold drinks) from the tricycles they drove around the range, and a lot of happy bullshitting accompanied the work. We looked forward to liberty and went to Washington most weekends, but we didn't feel the pressure to let it all hang out like we had in Savannah.

The last weekend before the course broke up, I drove my Studebaker to Lexington, Virginia, to see Rosa. She and her family came back every summer to visit their relatives at the family homestead, Col Alto, a big old mansion set in extensive, landscaped grounds on the outskirts of town. Glad to see me, though somewhat shocked at my haggard appearance, Rosa and her family offered me exceptional hospitality in the form of good company, food, and drink, and we had fun in the short time we had. With so many relatives in attendance, the physical contact Rosa and I enjoyed was limited to some furtive groping in the shrubbery around the perimeter of the grounds, a frustrating circumstance. The time passed all too quickly, and after a big Sunday lunch, I motored back to Quantico.

At formation Monday morning, Sergeant Rodriguez told us that he had finally figured out how to outwit the Corps and get back to combat in Korea. He was a career Marine, and his four-year enlistment was up. Rather than "shipping over" and staying at Quantico, he said that he was going to be discharged and then proceed to the West Coast on his own, where he would reenlist. Ex-Marines with good records got to pick their next duty assignment as an enticement to come back in, and Rodriguez had a plan to beat the system. He said that he would be fighting in Korea in a month or six weeks. During the day we talked about his plan and decided to sweeten it with everybody putting $5 or $10 in an envelope, which we presented to him as a token of our esteem and appreciation. He left on his new adventure the next day with several hundred dollars with which to have a good time before he shipped out to go into harm's way again.

We got a replacement chaser to herd us around for the last few days, and then suddenly we were marching in a final parade with the knowledge that we had made it, with everybody passing out in good shape. If we kept our grades up, didn't get hurt, and graduated, we were going to be lieutenants in another eight or nine months, a fact that gave us a lot of pride and confidence. Mal had to get back for early football practice, so he took the Studebaker back to school, dropping me off at Washington National Airport just off Route 1 south of the city. After resting and enjoying myself for a couple of weeks in Chapman, I packed my stuff and boarded the *Crescent Limited* for New York, then caught the New Haven train up to school to start my senior year.

By now our class of 1953 (motto, "Yale's Greatest Class") had settled down with about 850 survivors out of the initial complement of 1,100. Everybody knew the ropes, and the unstable and those with unsolvable problems were long gone. Most of us had future plans that depended on finishing strong. A big percentage was headed for graduate school—"B" schools like Harvard law or medicine, with a military commitment tacked on one end or the other. Many, possibly half or more, would probably be married within a year or two. We were all at least reasonably intelligent or would not have survived the competition to be there in the first place. By this time, we knew how to think and write well enough to get through the tests and exams in good shape. My own experience reflected a sort of *Pilgrim's Progress*, from the pits of the "Dean's Team" freshman year to Dean's List my last year. As seniors in good standing, we didn't even have to go to class, but I wasn't that smart and therefore rarely used this privilege. The courses were meaty, pertinent, and interesting, taught by top-of-the-line professors who were highly respected in their fields and good teachers. Two of the best courses were David Rowe's in Far Eastern politics and Josef Albers's in design. Both were of lasting benefit to me.

My social life, apart from my family and classmates, was focusing on Rosa, and we got together in New Haven or New York most weekends. By this time we were thinking about getting married, and I had about quit dating other college girls in view of our close relationship. During time at home in Alabama over the Christmas holidays, I saw Joan McCullough from Birmingham one last time. She was the first girl I cared much about, but we were both quite immature as high school seniors and college freshmen. We had passed close like ships in the night soon to drift apart. It was very good to see her once again after several years, but the meeting was bittersweet for me since I knew I was going to marry Rosa. We met again thirty years later when we were both involved in fund-raising work for the University of Alabama, Birmingham, and have enjoyed being good friends since then.

In Lexington over the New Year's holiday, Rosa and I formally announced our engagement. As an unfortunate consequence, I had to sell my faithful '41 Studebaker Commander, a car of classic proportions and good looks that had served me well, to pay to have Rosa's ring designed and set at Cartier. My mother gave me the diamond from her original engagement ring, and my father gave me a new Chevrolet sedan when I graduated so everything worked out for the best.

I had kept up my flying at Yale and often took classmates up with me. I considered enrolling in the commercial pilot ground school that the club sponsored with night classes during the fall term, but I figured I would soon get this training in the military where it would be part of my job. Looking back, I wish I had taken the course, but at the time it seemed a waste of precious time and money. Rosa's father, Harry, owned a four-place Stinson 108 Station Wagon, which he let me fly whenever I visited Lexington. I also flew one that belonged to Usher's Flying Service as well as their Piper Clipper and Pacer, cheaper but snappy little four seaters. One fine spring day, I took Rosa and a picnic lunch and flew the Cub to the short strip on Fishers Island in Long Island Sound southeast of New London. After a nice day in the sun, we got our stuff together and got ready to leave. I was more than a little nervous hand-propping the little plane (it had no electrical system, starter, or radio) with Rosa handling the brakes and throttle from the back seat, but the engine started on the first flip, and I got in with my hand intact. We flew back to New Haven at a thousand feet heading into the late afternoon sun against a strong headwind. The 18-wheelers to our right heading for New York on Route 1 were passing us at the end of this good day. By the time school was out, I had close to 250 hours flying time and was a good basic stick-and-rudder pilot.

Soon after this, I received word to come by the Marine Corps office at the NROTC section where I was sworn in as a second lieutenant with date of rank of June 5, 1953. My mother came to my graduation, and I felt a profound sense of relief to have completed college and its associated rites of passage. I felt like I had done pretty well with the hand I had been dealt and that I might be headed for bigger, better, and certainly more exciting things.

5

Marriage and More Marines

In June 1953, Rosa and I were married. Though both young by today's standards (I was twenty-two; she was twenty), we felt confident that it was the right thing to do, a trust borne out by events. Held on the last Saturday of the month in Lexington, a much smaller place in those days and very civilized, the church wedding and reception at the Tucker's house in town went off smoothly, and suddenly we found ourselves over the threshold into adult life with no going back to the carefree romance and freedom we had previously enjoyed. We spent a week or so in a cottage on the beach at Destin, Florida, and used our honeymoon to adjust to our new circumstances.

I wasn't due to report to Basic School at Quantico until early September, so I worked in the forestry office of the lumber company in Chapman for two months completing a project I had started during previous summer work. This involved making a systematic survey, record, and index of township plat maps covering the company's mineral ownership as it related to all its past and present land holdings. At the time, the property amounted to well over 200,000 acres, and I had to read all of the thousands of title deeds tracing the land into the company's ownership or occasionally out of it. In the majority of cases, the status of the subsurface mineral ownership was straightforward and relatively easy to record and map, but the project was so vast that I had to clarify many cloudy titles with various attorneys. I finished this project close to the time I was due to leave and felt some personal satisfaction for having done a unique, accurate, and valuable piece of work. Nobody gave me any compliments at the time, but when I left the company thirty-eight years later, my workbook was still being used frequently as a handy reference for land matters that had nothing to do with mineral rights.

Rosa and I drove up to Fredericksburg, Virginia, arriving in time for Labor Day weekend during a record heat wave. We had earlier put down a deposit on a nice furnished apartment that occupied the entire gabled third floor of a well-to-do widow's large home in a nice part of town. Our friends Dick Thoman and his wife, Barbara, rented the cottage next door, which also belonged to our landlady, so we had a little social unit to start with. After we had unpacked, explored the town, and sweated a lot, it was suddenly Tuesday morning and time to report to The Basic School. Dick and I donned

Rosa Tucker and Floyd at their wedding reception in her family house in Lexington, Kentucky.

Floyd and Rosa on their honeymoon in Destin, Florida.

our starched khakis, sporting lieutenant's bars for the first time, and headed a little over twenty miles up Route 1. Our class, the Twenty-Fifth Special Basic Class, was held at Camp Upshur, the mirror image of Camp Goettge in Quantico's Guadalcanal Area, where we had been the previous summer. I was assigned to a platoon housed in a large Quonset with double-deck racks, wall lockers, and foot lockers for furniture, where I stored my equipment and changed clothes during the day, though I returned home to Rosa every night unless we had a field problem. Though there was no cooling other than screen doors and a few windows, it was well lighted and a little more spacious than our previous housing. The huts were only a couple of years old and were heated with hot water pipes buried in the concrete floor. Each company area had a modern head and a small slop chute, open briefly after work every day, which sold snacks, cold drinks, beer, and smokes.

That first day in the hut, we had a few minutes between organizational activities, and I picked up my free copy of the *Marine Corps Gazette*, the Marine Corps Association's magazine, which we were exposed to in a bid to get us to join. I started reading an exciting account of the Corps' first night raid in Korea, which had taken place about a year earlier during the trench warfare along the 38th parallel. The object of the raid, which was executed in an exemplary manner, was to jerk several prisoners out of a gook position and bring them back alive for intelligence interrogation. The raiders, armed with sawed off shotguns, tommy guns, and concussion grenades, were led by then Staff Sergeant Harvey Wright, who received the Silver Star for his bravery and initiative in the action. When I finished reading the article, I happened to glance across the aisle running down the middle of the hut at a little fellow sitting on his rack shining his shoes. The name tag on the end of the rack said, "Wright, Harvey." I went over to introduce myself and to find out if he was the man in the *Gazette* story. He was. Harvey had been a 17-year-old rifleman when he was wounded on Iwo Jima in 1945, so he would have been twenty-four or -five in 1953. He definitely looked older than most of us, something like a young Humphrey Bogart with a lightly lined face and sandy hair. He smoked a lot of Camels. After the war he attended the Art Students League in New York on the GI Bill but missed the military life. He went back to the Corps when Korea started and dedicated himself to the proposition of becoming commandant. He seemed to be well on his way, progressing from a young, decorated gunnery sergeant to second lieutenant rank obtained with a meritorious, or battlefield, commission, something that rarely happened in the Corps. Harvey knew how to act and looked like a Harvard Business School grad in his Brooks Brothers gray flannel suit, tasteful tie, and button-down, collared shirt. He drove a new red Buick convertible, was single, and undoubtedly a ladies' man. I looked up to him, and we became good friends. Rosa and I used to have him over for drinks and home-cooked dinners. He was quiet, understated, urbane, polished, and sure of himself. Like Rodriguez, Harvey was one of the few cut out to be a professional killer, something he enjoyed and was good at. When we finished the course, he was going to the French in Indochina as an exchange officer to fight with the Legion. I have not heard any more of him, except for references in articles to his Korean raid, and have always thought that he must have come to an early death, either with the Corps or possibly as a spook with the CIA.

I didn't know anybody when I arrived but soon got acquainted with the people who would be my main partners in the 21-week course. In addition to me, my alphabetically composed four-man fire team consisted of Brian

Maher, a quiet, solid Irish-Catholic from the Northeast who had been at Parris Island when I was there; Dave McKay, a tall, intellectual Southern Californian basketball star from Ojai, who had sort of a beach boy take on life; and Bill O'Hara, an All Pacific Coast tackle who had played out his football eligibility at Lewis & Clark. Brian was a handsome, athletic-looking six footer, easy to work with, dependable, and always pleasant. Dave, a six-foot-four, blond version of Dick Tracy, blended serious intelligence with a sardonic sense of humor and always packed classic literature in college-style paperbacks when he was in the field. A couple of times in fights with the school troops, he got so engrossed in his reading that he tied a white handkerchief to the end of his rifle barrel and propped it up vertically out of his fighting hole, leaving the defense to me, Brian, and Bill. Bill was a mild-mannered, gentle giant with a good sense of humor and a gap-toothed smile—a very nice guy but supremely ugly from batterings his face had taken over the years. He looked a lot like the Swedish Angel, a big-time professional-wrestling villain of the 1940s. Bill told us that during his fifth year in college, which he needed to graduate after his football days, he supported himself as a pro wrestler in the Pacific Northwest. His manager billed him as the "Uncrowned Champion of Ireland," even though road trips playing college ball were as far as he had ever traveled away from his home in Oregon. He said that since he was ugly, he always had to be the bad guy, which he didn't mind, except for the little old ladies sitting in the front-row and aisle seats who would stick hat pins in his ass whenever he got thrown out of the ring and as he entered and exited the arena.

A Marine rifle platoon was organized around three squads, each having three fire teams and a squad leader; each fire team had three riflemen armed with M1s and one BAR man. The riflemen's job was to protect and support the BAR man so as to lay down as much concentrated full-automatic fire as possible. At Basic School we didn't have DIs or chasers; rather, we took turns a day at a time being squad leaders, platoon sergeants, platoon leaders, and company officers so that by the time our five months were up, we had tasted infantry small-unit organization from various perspectives. Since there were a lot of us and relatively few specialist jobs, we spent the great majority of our time as common grunts, a good idea as they were the people we would most likely lead, and we needed to know as much as possible about what they were up against.

Our company commander was Major June, a mustang ex–master sergeant who had been through the big war and Korea and was probably marking time until retirement. He was a mature-looking, dark-haired man in his late thirties, very deliberate and fair minded, competent but no genius either. His executive officer was First Lieutenant Willis, commissioned from the enlisted ranks through Officer Candidate School and not much older than most of us. Willis had a flattop and a pockmarked, scowling, German-looking face with a Clark Gable mustache. Medium-sized, but thick-necked with the build of a weight lifter, he carried himself with an erect posture, walked with a strut, and wore tailored and immaculate uniforms, dress, and dungarees. He also affected a matched pair of Weimaraners, who accompanied him straining on leashes, and always carried an "idiot-stick." Swagger-sticks, carried at times by the British to denote officer status, were briefly authorized for optional use in the Corps. Willis was the only person I ever knew who owned one, much less carried it. While he had a strong comic-opera persona, he wasn't really a bad guy. At least he never gave us a hard time.

Basic School wasn't much fun. It entailed mostly very long days spent in a mixed regime of classroom work and field demonstrations, problems, and exercises. We worked in all weather, which went from extreme heat in the beginning, to a lot of dark, dreary, rainy days in the late fall, to full-blown winter—cold, often subfreezing with sleet, freezing drizzle, ice pellets, and snow. To make things worse, our field clothing consisted of nothing heavier than an issue field jacket, long johns, leather combat boots, leather gloves for cold weather, and a poncho for the rain; we had a couple of blankets and a waterproof groundsheet for bedding. On a lot of days and nights, this rig was barely enough to sustain life, and we endured long stretches of physical discomfort. I have never known whether our dress and equipment were the result of poor planning, the parsimonious ways of the Corps, or just one more way to make our initiation more stressful and meaningful. I do know that the school troops we frequently fought against were superbly equipped with the latest and best cold weather and rain gear that had come out of the Korean experience. We dirty, freezing second lieutenants looked like bastards at a family reunion in contrast to the neatly and comfortably turned out enlisted school troopers, their officers, and our instructors. Most of us bought thermo boots on our own, which we wore on extra cold days without criticism, but the rest of our clothing, at least on the outside, had to be the poor stuff issued to us.

The five-month course was a logical, in-depth, and expanded version of our previous PLC experiences. Though long and sometimes boring, the academic part never seemed all that difficult, and I made good grades without much extra study. During one of the first organizational lectures at the beginning of the course, a fairly senior field grade officer, a lieutenant colonel, gave us stern instructions about political influence, something the Corps felt strongly about. The colonel had a darkly serious demeanor and laid out his text in plain language, telling us in so many words that the Corps knew that many of us were well connected in civilian society and had the means to communicate with the movers and shakers in Washington who ran the government and controlled the military purse strings. While the Corps was glad to have such bluebloods, it would brook absolutely no out-of-channels action to shape assignments or careers. He went on to say in rather poisonous tones that the Corps would know if any of us resorted to political influence and would affix a large "PI" stamp on our officer's records jacket. The guilty would ultimately get their comeuppance, and if any of us wanted to see if this was for real, we should just try it.

During the week, I didn't get home until six in the evening, and I had to leave shortly after five in the morning, but Rosa and I enjoyed ourselves on the weekends. Sometimes we drove up to Washington for dinner and a movie on Friday or Saturday night; other times, we made the shorter drive to Mainside Quantico for drinks and dinner at Waller Hall. Though an "O" club, it was tastefully furnished with good service and food and had the appearance of a very good country club. Occasionally, we had friends spend the weekend with us during the pretty fall weather, and our apartment was nicely set up for entertaining.

Shortly after we got to Quantico, Dick Thoman told me that Barbara was pregnant, and I gave him a sanctimonious little speech to the effect that having babies was not smart for Marine second lieutenants' wives, given the uncertain and tenuous nature of our situation. He took my criticism constructively in his usual intelligent, good-natured way, and it soon became a moot point when Barbara miscarried. Very soon after this, Rosa began experiencing stomach problems and nausea, which she attributed to some bug she had picked up. After she tried to wear this out without success, I finally got her to visit a doctor, who made an easy diagnosis of pregnancy. This event seemed different once it was happening to us, and the Thomans were very nice and supportive. It was one of many times when I discovered graphically that I was not as smart and worldly wise as I had led myself to believe.

In October, we were given the opportunity to volunteer for flight training at Pensacola starting immediately after our February graduation from Basic School. I jumped at the chance to embark on a career I had been considering seriously. By my reckoning, I found airplanes more interesting than anything else I had ever thought about. In addition, I considered military pilots an elite group up toward the top of the aviators' pyramid; as I saw it, naval aviators occupied the top tier of military drivers, and Marine pilots were near the apex of the whole flyer population. Airlines also seemed a holy sort of business to me, combining the highest quality of professional flying techniques, the best and most rapidly advancing technology and equipment, and a glamorous job with adequate pay, as well as travel, adventure, and all the trappings of a fascinating career for a young guy like myself. I planned to spend two or three years flying all-weather, or night, fighters to gain maximum exposure to jets and instrument flying, then to leave the service and get a seat on Delta or Eastern, which I figured would welcome my experience. I wanted this as much as or more than anything before or since in my life. A few days later, I went to Mainside with a few other hopefuls from the company to take the mental exam used to screen prospective pilots. The test was relatively straight-forward and easy so long as the taker read each question's verbiage carefully and followed directions exactly. My flying background counted for nothing, although the questions used aeronautical terms and pictures of instruments and the like, possibly to add some phony or misleading realism to the questions. I passed without difficulty and was surprised to learn that some of the others had failed and were eliminated.

Those of us who passed were ordered to report to the navy hospital at Mainside for a flight physical, which turned out to be the most comprehensive I had in the service. I did fine until the last test, an audiometer exam checking hearing across the frequency spectrum. I sat across from a corpsman with a little wall between us so that I could not see his hands and pressed a button every time I heard a tone in the earphones I was wearing. When we finished, the corpsman said, "Sorry, lieutenant, you flunk." For a second I was too stunned to say anything, then I asked him what the hell he was talking about as I had absolutely no inkling of a problem with my hearing. He told me that I couldn't hear very high-pitched sounds like dog whistles, that the test criteria specified that one's hearing had to be perfect across the board to pass, and that he could not do anything about it. I told him that I needed to talk to someone in authority, and he sent me to the hospital's commanding officer (CO), an elderly navy captain who was pleasant enough, if a little out of touch with practical reality. I explained to him that I had been flying without difficulty for almost six years, had a license and over two hundred hours flying time, and had never had trouble hearing voice or radio range tones, marker beacons, or anything like them on airplane radios. While sympathetic, he told me that I was used to high frequency and very high frequency radios in civilian planes, but military planes mostly used ultrahigh frequency radios, which I would not be able to hear. So that was that.

Still unconvinced (properly so as it turned out), I went to see Major June when I got back to Camp Upshur and asked if he could help. He said that he would do what he could and set me up to go before a board composed of senior field grade aviators who would interview the remaining candidates, the final hurdle to getting into flight training. In due time, I presented myself to these worthies, who listened to my story. When I got through, the president of the board, a lieutenant colonel, told me that they appreciated my attitude but could fill their quota without bending the rules. This was the biggest disappointment in my life, and I even considered asking my father to talk to our congressman and senator about intervening on my behalf, but considering the warning about PI, I rejected this approach and decided to regroup.

We were furnished with a long list of military occupational specialties (MOSs) open to lieutenants finishing TBS. They ranged all the way from staples like infantry, artillery, and tanks to motor transport, supply, and even some exotic, but practically unobtainable, slots, like legation (embassy) duty in guard detachments and detachment duty on battleships, carriers, cruisers, and the like. On a nice morning floating down the Potomac in warm sunlight on an LST in preparation for a landing in amphibious tractors that afternoon, a bunch of us discussed which options we should put down on our preference sheets. We had absolutely no idea what, if any, weight our preferences would be given, so we decided that it would be best just to put what we wanted in one, two, three order and let the chips fall where they might. I chose air controller as first choice, combat air intelligence officer as second, and infantry as third (reasoning that if I wound up as an infantry platoon leader, a likely enough possibility, I wanted it to be something I had asked for, at least in a backhanded way). Soon after the new year began, our orders came out. One of a group of about twelve from our class, I was assigned to Air Control School at Marine Corps Air Station (MCAS) Cherry Point, North Carolina.

Rosa's mother Lillian spent a few days with us in October. Mrs. Tucker, a solidly built lady with a good mind, good values, and a good personality, concealed her considerable intellect and talents with a facade of pleasantries and a strong Southern grande dame persona. It took me a long time to learn her and fully appreciate just how fine and smart she was, but we wound up good friends and, I believe, mutual admirers. She had a couple of rude shocks during her visit in the apartment with us. When she first arrived, Rosa told her about the pregnancy and got an unexpected reaction: horrified, Mrs. Tucker was apparently jolted out of her senses. She must have still considered us children, maybe just on an extended date, as she gravely told Rosa, "Pose, your father and I will stick behind you through thick and thin." Rosa then had to work her through the realities of our situation and point out that the baby was not due until May, eleven months after our wedding. A day or so later, Mrs. Tucker confronted Rosa, telling her that she was thoroughly distraught by what a bad turn our lives had taken, what with the pregnancy and the more or less continual nipping she had observed. More than a little mystified and put out by her mother's lack of understanding and distress, Rosa asked her testily just what she meant by this last. Mrs. Tucker drew herself up and, looking down her nose, said icily that she had in fact observed both of us taking solid hits of wine straight out of the bottle on a frequent basis ever since she had arrived and that our irresponsible sex and debauchery were too much for her to handle. Rosa took her mother to the refrigerator, took out the two wine bottles where we each kept our stash of drinking water, and had her sample each one. Then she sat her down and went though the reality of the impending birth, finally getting her mother's calm and focused attention. Mrs. Tucker, who had a steel-trap mind under all the Old Southern charm and hot air, finally got things sorted out to her satisfaction. She cooked us a fine dinner that night, preceded by a couple of strong old-fashioneds she took to celebrate our good morals and healthy lifestyle. She was always solidly behind us after that.

The physical side of Basic School was active, with a lot of field work and route marches, and we often carried additional equipment, like machine guns, mortars, and ammunition cans, to our exercise sites. We had some exposure to the obstacle course, but without the severity experienced earlier as PLCs. The first time we ran it, Lieutenant Willis went with the company to the site and explained the course rules. The first obstacle was an iron pipe about eight feet high and twenty feet long spanning a sort of hog wallow pit brimming with cold, slimy, muddy water. Willis, natty as always in his winter dress green battle jacket, pisscutter, trousers, and fine cordovan shoes, handed his gloves, idiot stick, and the reins to his straining brace of Weimaraners to the closest lieutenant. He coolly and professionally sized up the geometry of his impending jump, then launched his heavy, muscular frame in a mighty vault toward the pipe. His hands made graceful contact as planned, but then, as if in slow motion, slipped off, dropping him flat on his ass into the depths of the pit—a spectacle too humorous and unexpected to register as believable for a second, but total silence prevailed as the two hundred assembled lieutenants bit their lips and studied the cloud formations overhead. We then all ran the course making sure that none of us fell off the pipe.

After any number of shorter day and night field problems and skirmishes, most involving rural terrain and some in house-to-house combat in a mock town, we set off on a two-day war in the middle of December. Winter had set in for real, and the temperature started to drop rapidly late in the first afternoon as a cold front pushed through under dark-gray scudding clouds. I was a machine gunner and packed an air-cooled .30 caliber Browning, plus ammunition cans, a full field pack, and my M1. My partner carried the gun's tripod and more ammunition in addition to his rifle and gear. Johnson, a salty young guy with a flattop, rosy cheeks, and bright eyes, was short of stature but tough. He had been a corporal serving in the school troops at Quantico before going to OCS and getting his commission, and he was wise to their ways. When we got to the ridge line where our company was to make its defensive position for the night, he and I worked up a sweat digging a good dugout for our gun emplacement with our entrenching tools. We roofed it with pine boughs and camouflaged it as well as we could. We cut a parapet in the front wall of the hole and set the gun up on it to fire through a slot under the roof. The temperature fell rapidly at dusk, and we settled in for the night. I ate a sandwich I had sneaked in from home, picked at a K ration, and began to wonder how we were going to make it through the serious cold of the night (we later found out the temperature went down to 16°). Johnson produced a pint bottle of good cognac brandy, which he offered to share. He said nothing would happen until after midnight. We took one-hour watches, one alert while the other tried to sleep, and kept working on the brandy to fight the cold. After midnight, we started to hear some firing from our front and some bugle blowing, and we saw a flare or two—evidently part of a deception to get our attention while some of the school troopers infiltrated our position in the black dark. About 0200, we were both awake when somebody stuck a rifle barrel in the entrance to our hole and told us to put our hands up and come with him. Johnson and I were both in a foul mood by this time, and the brandy had lowered our inhibitions. Johnson told the trooper that if he wanted us, he could come in and get us, and I made a sincere offer to help beat the shit out of him. The rifle barrel instantly withdrew and that was the end of the prisoner business. Johnson's experience and knowledge of the trooper psychology paid off and doubtless saved us some distress and indignity as mock POWs.

A bit later, the school troops made a big frontal assault on the company's position but were stopped at the wire we had strung a little downslope from our fighting holes and dugouts. With Johnson's help, I kept the machine gun going during the firefights, and things eventually quieted down, leaving us nothing to fight but the cold until dawn finally broke.

In the morning, we had a small, cold breakfast from the rations we carried and loaded up for a march of about five miles. After assaulting a position on another ridge line and running the school troopers off, thereby ending the operation, we gathered up in a large group and shivered through a detailed critique by the instructors and referees, all the while eyeing and smelling a field kitchen that had been brought out from Mainside and set up at the side of the field. Our mouths watering and our stomachs pulsing in anticipation of hot chow and coffee, we eventually lined up with our mess kits at the ready. The cooks had four large stainless steel pots of ravioli, one for each platoon, on top of a nearly red-hot stove on wheels. After everybody else had been fed, it was finally our turn. Two filthy messmen grabbed the last steaming pot by its handles to get it off the stove and, being careless or clumsy or just stupid, managed to turn it loose, emptying all the hot food onto the frozen ground. After this fitting finish to our little trial, we loaded up with empty stomachs in 6 × 6 trucks and rode back to Upshur. Once we had cleaned our weapons and put everything up, it was Friday afternoon, and we were through until Monday. I had a long, hot shower and took off for home. Rosa had gone to a lot of trouble to buy a fresh fish, which she was baking to surprise me. This was not what I had in mind at all. I may have hurt her feelings when I went to the market we used and bought the two biggest, best steaks they had, but we had a happy evening with plenty of good drinking and eating before snuggling up together in a wonderful, warm bed.

Soon after this, we returned to Alabama for two weeks at Christmas time. While I was home, I took the train to Mobile one day to see Dr. Henry Martin, a noted physician who had been the head ear, nose, and throat doctor at West Point during the war. I wanted an independent appraisal of my hearing that I could trust and understand. After a thorough exam and audiometer test, he told me that I did have some high frequency loss consistent with the flight physical finding, which should be of no practical import provided it didn't get any worse. Besides spending a good bit of time around gunfire, explosives, and airplane engines, I had worked in the planing mill at the lumber company one summer, where I stood next to a large planing machine for eight hours a day with no hearing protection. Nowadays these machines are enclosed with elaborate baffling to muffle the tremendous amount of high-pitched noise they make. In those days, the use of hearing protection was virtually unknown in industry as well as the military, and most people who stayed around planing machines, guns, or airplanes wound up with some degree of hearing loss. A year later in Korea, I got to know a couple of flight surgeons who told me that half the pilots in the Marine Corps were probably deafer than I was and that once you got into flying, hearing loss was expected and not viewed as a defect. Soon after I got out of the service, the hearing standard for flight training was amended so that those who could hear normally in the conversational range were accepted, but this came too late to do me any good.

The last six weeks of the course mostly refined what had gone before. We soldiered on from morning dark to black night with early midwinter sunsets. I remember one morning standing shivering at attention in our daily 0630 formation on the pitch-black drill field when I heard Major June, then about ten feet behind his two hundred lieutenants, ask plaintively, "Hey, Willis, where's my company?" The weather was mostly horrible, but that didn't slow down the field work. We actually derived a perverse satisfaction in manning up through the bad days, and I remember often feeling good as we marched along in the cold rain, all of us in the same boat but able to hold our heads up and keep a sense of humor regardless of what was dished out to us.

On a clear, warm Saturday morning in the middle of February, we went to Camp Upshur one last time. The class of about one thousand making up the Twenty-Fifth Special Basic Class turned out in winter dress green uniforms, cartridge belts, and M1s to form up for a big parade. The band from Mainside played some good music as we passed in review in front of a stand loaded with big brass, and then we were finished. Rosa and I cleaned out the furnished apartment, stuffed our car with our worldly goods, and set out for North Carolina and my next assignment.

On a bright and warm Monday afternoon, we arrived at MCAS Cherry Point in good spirits, optimistic that we had come to a good place. This new country had a nice feel to it, and the land was flat with pine trees everywhere, which made me feel at home. I checked Rosa into the guest house on the base and reported with my orders to the headquarters of the control group. The personnel people told me that I would be assigned to one of the three air control squadrons in the group, which were located at Cherry Point and Edenton, North Carolina, and Miami, Florida, all part of the Second Marine Air Wing, which supported the Fleet Marine Force, Atlantic. Since I was one of the first men to report in, I was given my choice. I acted on my premonition that we were going to like Cherry Point and asked to stay, so I was assigned to Marine Air Control Squadron (MACS) 6, located on the north side of the base on the Neuse River. They also told me that I would be attending controllers' school at the group for a month before becoming a functioning member of the squadron, where I would receive on-the-job training under the supervision of squadron personnel.

A Marine air wing is the aerial equivalent of a division. Its principal mission is to support the ground force in expeditionary operations. The wing has various kinds of aircraft in different air groups, each group comprising several squadrons. The aircraft range from transports and tankers to strike aircraft (mostly fighter bombers), day fighters, night or all-weather fighters, photographic reconnaissance and electronic countermeasure (ECM) planes, observation aircraft (then both fixed wing and helicopter), and helicopters of various types. The wing's specialty was supplying close air support in close proximity to the ground force on the battlefield. To do this effectively and safely requires the full faith and confidence of all concerned and a lot of cross training to achieve the desired results.

Each air wing had a control group that operated a tactical air control center (TACC), at which the overall commander had his command post and a plot of all air activity in the wing's area of responsibility. The group also operated several MACSs, each of which was responsible for a sector using powerful long-range search and height-finding radars to provide the data for the TACC's master plot and to control the wing's aircraft plus other friendlies. The air control squadron's tactical mission was to detect and identify all aircraft in its sector and to control the wing's fighters in making intercepts of any hostiles (bandits) resulting in their destruction. In addition, the group had specialized control units using exotic short-range radars stationed near the front lines to provide precise guidance for precision bombing at night and in bad weather. Finally, the forward air controllers, all aviators, who called in air strikes visually from observation points on the ground overlooking the battlefield were part of the group. The control group's commander, his senior staff officers, and the subordinate unit commanders were all aviators, as were a good percentage of the controllers in the MACS squadrons.

I signed up for a quarters assignment in Hancock Village, an attractive new officers' housing area consisting of one-story, ranch-style duplexes with pine trees, nice lawns, winding streets, and sidewalks. It cost a little more than the other off-base government housing administered by the wing, and a lot of the tenants were captains and majors. We spent two uncomfortable weeks in a bare-bones, well-used trailer located in the base's temporary housing area, an ugly, mildly unpleasant and spooky place, and Rosa never felt safe while I was at work. We were very glad to leave it and move into our nice, new quarters.

Air Control School was conducted in a classroom at Group Headquarters located in the central part of the base near the Wing Headquarters and offices. The twelve of us just in from Basic School spent eight hours a day for a month absorbing the rudiments of our new line of work. We had specialist instructors in subjects like meteorology, communications and radar theory and equipment, aircraft armament, navigation theory and equipment, airways, and airport rules and procedures. We learned the history and theory of the use of radar in aircraft control with particular emphasis on ground-controlled interception (GCI) techniques and the RAF's role in pioneering them. We learned the controllers' and pilots' specialized vocabulary invented by the Brits, as well as a lot of useful items that we committed to memory, such as a shorthand for writing down weather reports, tricks to figure compass heading reciprocals instantly, and specific weather patterns that might signal hazardous flight conditions. We made field trips to various units on the base, such as aerology, where the weathermen reinforced our classroom lectures, telling us about the things they watched the most, like the temperature–dew point relationship, or "spread," that signaled fog, as well as pressure gradients, air mass characteristics, thunderstorm and frontal weather, freezing levels and icing conditions, and the like. We toured selected tactical and transport squadron areas and got to sample the aircraft cockpits and flight decks.

The most interesting part of the course covered intercept and fighter tactics. Our teacher was Captain John "Blackie" McManus, an ace with six victories in Corsairs flying off the *Bunker Hill* in the Pacific. Then thirty-four and reputedly the oldest captain in the Marine Corps in terms of service, he was a handsome, outgoing guy and a great combat pilot, though an unhappy camper in the peacetime service. Blackie tried to impart to us the basic fighter tactics and attack patterns, discussing which ones worked well for the pilots and which did not. He emphasized points like trying for position between the sun and the hostile, the advantages of speed and altitude for energy management, the futility of tail chases, and other useful nuggets of information about the fighter pilot's trade. Our job as fighter directors would be to place our pilots in the most advantageous possible position relative to the bogey to initiate a successful killing attack once they acquired a visual or, in the case of night fighters, picked the target up on their airborne radar. Blackie supplemented the technical information imparted by previous instructors by going into the good and bad characteristics of our fighters and those of the Communists.

After a month in our little school, we received a certificate of completion and joined our squadrons. MACS-6 was both a functioning unit in the tactical scheme of the wing's business and an on-the-job training establishment to qualify officer and enlisted personnel in air control and send them through the pipeline to Korea as needed. The CO, Major Les Penn, a handsome fighter jock with a good-looking blond wife, always wore a khaki summer flying suit, flight deck shoes, and a pisscutter in the squadron area. He looked like the actor Robert Conrad who played Pappy Boyington in the *Baa Baa Black Sheep* TV series. He flew a lot and didn't come around the squadron much. I gathered that he left most of the administration to his flunkies, which suited me fine since I wanted to focus my energies on learning the technical aspects of my job as rapidly and thoroughly as possible and to deemphasize the drill and "pomp and ceremony" rituals that had previously taken a lot of time. Marine aviation had tough people who got the job done, but it was a kinder, gentler version of the grunts' Corps. From the time I got there, I was comfortable and well treated and felt like a junior member of a good club.

The tactical part of the squadron consisted of radar, communications, the combat information center (CIC) or radar room, and attendant controllers and enlisted operating and support personnel. It was run by Major Ernest "Lightning" Mitch, who had earned his nickname because of the slow-motion way he eased around. A serious, no-bullshit, soft-spoken, medium-sized man from Missouri, he was about thirty-four and a well-respected aviator and fighter pilot. He delegated almost all the work to First Lieutenant Dick Clough, his assistant operations officer and a PLC. A squared-away, urbane young man with a lot of charm, Dick was very good at his job. The NCO in charge was Master Sergeant Laing assisted by Staff Sergeant Jim Sentenn. Laing was a tall, sparse, leathery-faced guy, tough but fair. Sentenn was a tall, handsome, smooth-faced, rosy-cheeked young man who had been a radar operator in night fighters before joining the squadron. He was very sharp and competent, fun to talk to, and eager to pass his knowledge along to anybody who wanted to learn.

I was one of a half dozen new trainee controllers who joined the squadron at the same time. I was hot to trot to become professionally qualified in a facet of the aviation business, having decided that if I couldn't fly then I would be the best controller possible. Clough, Laing, and Sentenn noted my attitude, and I very quickly developed a strong rapport with all three. Besides standing watches on the scopes and at the other stations in the radar room, I devoted a lot of time, a good bit of it in addition to my assigned schedule, to learning the business. We were studying the procedural part, as well as how to talk, plan, and execute with the aircraft under our control in running intercepts, how to make airport surveillance radar (ASR) approaches, and how to feed planes to the ground-controlled approach (GCA) final controller, in addition to learning about all the nuances of a radar-approach-control facility. As trainee controllers, we had to log a considerable number of intercepts and ASR approaches, then be approved for our designated MOS, 6709 (senior air controller), by Major Mitch on the recommendation of Dick Clough, who kept up with our progress through the watch supervisors and senior NCOs.

My training and progress in becoming qualified as a controller went very well. I was intensely interested in anything to do with aviation, and becoming a professional insider in such an important part of it had its own satisfactions, though I still felt something like a eunuch in a harem being so close to the cockpit yet still so far removed. I ran as many intercepts as I could arrange under supervision and to some extent on my own. It really wasn't difficult to "get up a game" since the wing had a training group that served to qualify new pilots from Pensacola and Corpus Christi and to requalify older ones who had been out of the cockpit, and they also needed the practice to finish their own syllabi. In addition, there were a lot of tactical fighter squadrons with pilots eager to jump on unsuspecting targets. Everybody leaving or entering Cherry Point's airspace had to talk to us anyway as we were the facility's approach control, so we always had an entree to get some "trade." In addition to the actual intercepts and surveillance approaches, I did a lot of work on the old synthetic trainers that we had in a dark room alongside the CIC running intercepts. Laing or Sentenn acted as the "pilot" under my control while they worked the trainer's panel, giving direction and speed to the blips on the scope, a fairly accurate facsimile of the real thing.

While we were not required to fly and got no extra pay for doing so, we were told that it would be good experience if we found the time. Some of the other new guys stayed firmly on the ground; a few tried it once and didn't go back; I flew as much as I could. My favorite hop was to fly right seat (copilot) in Beech SNB-5s used as target aircraft on "RO bogey" missions run by the training group. My pilots were Major Mitch, Captain Lewis, and First LieutenantTony Lochran, and I got to do eight or more of these flights lasting a little over two hours each. They were flying these hops to maintain proficiency and to log the minimum four hours of flight time a month, then required for flight pay. The military flew the SNB with one pilot as minimum crew, so officially I was just along for the ride, usually with several enlisted men dozing in the back while they also logged flight time for pay purposes. My pilots, all squadron mates, were aware of my interest in flying and wanted to encourage me. They did the takeoffs and landings and all the ground handling, while I worked the ARC-1 VHF communications radio. Once we were airborne, they usually turned the controls over to me and lay back in their seats to sleep until it was time to come back in. I would check in with our squadron, code name Langdale, for a vector and an altitude assignment, which always took us east of Morehead City out over the Atlantic. We flew up and down the coast on 30-mile legs acting as the bogey, or target aircraft, for Lockheed PV-2T Harpoons used to train airborne intercept (AI) radar operators before their assignment to night fighters. For me this was highly educational as well as a lot of fun—I was getting to drive a military airplane that seemed the equivalent of a small airliner.

I hung around operations in the training group and picked up several rides in the Lockheed PV-2T Harpoons used to attack the SNBs. In the fleet, they had eight nose-mounted .50 caliber machine guns for their maritime reconnaissance role. For training, the guns had been replaced with an AI radar as used in the night fighters. The fuselage behind the flight deck had plenty of room for three radar positions, each manned by a student operator who gave directions to the pilots when their turn came. An instructor worked with each student one by one. I watched each intercept with one of the idle students standing up at his side and observing the blips on their scopes. This was educational but not much fun. All the windows were painted over to darken the interior, and it was very warm in the back from all the electronic gear. The normal airplane smells of hydraulic fluid, leather, and sweat were overlaid by the pervasive odor of stale vomit from previous unfortunates, and I was always glad to get out of the hot, stinking black hole after the last intercept and sit on the floor of the flight deck behind the pilots in sunshine and fresh air on the ride back to the base. The PV was a heavy brute of an airplane that took some technique to operate properly, but my pilots, usually second lieutenants not long out of flight school, seemed to cope very well, and I didn't know enough about what was involved to be scared.

I was also able to get a couple of rides in the radar operator's position in the Douglas F3D Skyknight, or "Whale," my first experience with jet flying. The Skyknight was a big, straight-winged airplane powered by twin jet engines, each with 3,400 pounds of thrust. It was armed with four 20 mm cannons and carried a powerful Hughes AI radar—very expensive and sophisticated for its day. Its configuration was unusual in that the radar operator (RO) sat to the pilot's right in what would normally be the copilot's seat, with the AI scopes and radar-operating controls in front of him. The plane did not have ejection seats, but there was enough room between and behind the two seats for a tunnel that, like a laundry chute, led to the bottom of the fuselage. In an emergency one just undid the straps and radio and oxygen connections, jumped into the hole to hit a trap door at the bottom, fell out, and then pulled the rip cord manually. The F3D was a reliable plane, and I never heard of anyone bailing out. My hops were good experience, although the purpose of the flights was pilot proficiency, mostly doing GCA approaches at New River. It did let me experience maneuvers in a fighter decked out in hard hat, oxygen mask, life jacket, and parachute and helped me to appreciate the military aviator's trade with some knowledge of what flight crews experienced. It felt good to get out of the equipment and breathe fresh air after one of these hops, and I always had the feeling I had just gotten out of an aerial cement mixer.

In early April, I was one of a party from the squadron and group who made a field trip to the southeast headquarters of the North American Air Defense Command located at Dobbins Air Force Base at Marietta, Georgia. The air force was responsible for defending the continental United States against aerial attack from Soviet long-range bombers, and our radar capability and fighter aircraft were plugged into their overall net. Their facility, effectively a sector command post for threat evaluation and response, looked at all air activity showing up on radar, much as the FAA's centers do now. It was large in typical first-class air force style, something like a glorified version of the bare-bones TACCs operated by the Corps. I enjoyed the trip, especially the flights on our transport, which was the general's private R4D (military DC-3), outfitted for about a dozen passengers and very comfortable for a military plane. Soon after we took off from Cherry Point in the early morning, I walked up to the flight deck to watch the crew at

work, thinking that I would see some real experts at the controls. This il-
lusion was shattered when I opened the door and stood in the narrow aisle
between radio racks on the right side and a crew baggage area on the left.
The enlisted crew chief was sitting on a fold-down jump seat in the aisle
between and immediately behind the two pilots, who both had their seats
pushed as far back as they would go with their feet resting comfortably
on the bottom of their respective instrument panels. The big bird droned
down the airway on autopilot, while all three crew members devoted their
rapt attention to the full-color skin magazines each had open in his lap. In
those days, *Playboy* and its host of imitators had yet to be born, but some
very rare, racy, and desirable male reading materials existed. On the floor
behind the pedestal sat a stack about a foot high, undoubtedly the general's
private stock. I spent a pleasant twenty minutes occupied with the view out
the windshield, the instrumentation and mechanisms on the flight deck,
and as much as I could see of the beautiful naked women on display. Not
a word was said, and I finally retreated to my seat in the cabin to reflect on
the stress and strain involved in flying big airplanes.

One day in early May 1954, Dick Clough told me that Major Mitch
wanted to see me and took me to his office. I knew both of them well by
this time, so I went into the meeting with some curiosity but no trepida-
tion. Major Mitch told me that he had approved my designation to a 6709
MOS and that I was the first of our group to become a fully qualified GCI
controller. He also told me that he needed someone to take over as assistant
operations officer when Dick got out in a couple of months and that they
both wanted me for the job. If I took it and gave it my best, I would be
assured of staying in the squadron with him for the rest of my tour in the
Marine Corps. It didn't take me any time to accept his offer with enthusiasm. I liked what I was doing, Rosa was almost ready to have our baby, and
we enjoyed our life at Cherry Point, where we had plenty of friends and
nice quarters. Additionally, the operations section was the nerve center of a
MACS outfit and controlled everything from the standpoint of the tactical
work, so I would be in a powerful slot for a junior officer. I went back to
work with a sense of renewed enthusiasm and started spending all the time
I could hanging around operations during office hours, observing how they

did things and handled problems.

Rosa went to the base hospital operated by the navy for her prenatal care and checkups, and as her pregnancy advanced, she became increasingly nervous. She saw a different doctor every time, which did not inspire her confidence. While the medical care was probably perfectly adequate in a technical sense, it was the equivalent of later socialized or managed health care schemes, and she became adamant in her desire to have the baby at home. I put her on a Piedmont DC-3 at New Bern for the trip across the mountains to Lexington one day near the end of April.

I made arrangements to take two weeks leave on a moment's notice so that I could spend as much time as possible with Rosa and our baby when the time came. As in a lot of life's situations, events failed to follow our well-laid plan. The attending physician, a general practitioner who used the small hospital in Georgetown for his obstetrics work, had been selected by virtue of having successfully delivered Rosa's sister's first child. After Rosa had been home with her parents for several weeks, the doctor said her time was very near and to send for me at once, though he doubted that I would get there for the delivery. I took her early-morning call, notified the squadron, and jumped on a handy Piedmont flight, making it to the hospital that afternoon. Rosa was sitting up in an uncomfortable little bed in a small room and feeling fine, with no signs of the baby's arrival being anywhere close at hand. I spent the next two nights sleeping on the floor by her bed and tried to talk to the doctor several times in the course of his rounds without much success. Surly and uncommunicative, he made no effort to raise our spirits. After a couple of days, we decided that everybody concerned would be more comfortable at home, and the doctor agreed, giving us the impression that he was glad to get rid of us. Rosa was too uncomfortable to go out anywhere, but we walked and drove on some rough country roads every day in hopes of speeding things up. She finally went into labor for real a couple of days before my leave was up and delivered our son, Norman, on May 23, three days after my own birthday. He gave his mother some difficulty with the birthing, arriving badly bruised and marked up around the head from the quack's forceps, but otherwise very healthy. We were happy when it was over, and I went back to the squadron in a good mood.

I got back into watch standing, working for Mitch and Clough, and gained experience and knowledge in a hurry. As in any business, you have to experience some of the weird things that happen to learn the parts they don't teach in school. One stormy night, I was working the last watch of the day, holding down one of the scopes in the radar room, when we all noticed some unusual activity due east of Cherry Point, some seventy-five miles out over the Atlantic. We were plotting what appeared to be some six aircraft targets in a "racetrack" holding pattern moving at what would have been a low cruise, or loiter, speed for tactical aircraft. Neither the group nor the North American Air Defense Command had any idea who the bogies were; we just knew that they were definitely not any of our side's assets. After a few minutes we got orders to launch the duty all-weather fighter, an F3D at readiness, and run an intercept to determine their identity. The weather consisted of low ceilings in rain squalls, and thunderstorm cells were also plentiful on the radar. The watch commander had me call to brief the alert pilot on what we had in mind for him and to get him airborne as quickly as possible. I had visions of the gung ho, heroic, night-fighter pilot and his RO grabbing their gear and running out to mount their jet in the rain to light off the engines and be headed out to sea in a very few minutes. I was probed for additional information about the plots and told to "stand-by one." After a few minutes the duty pilot on the other end came back with some story to the effect that they had a mechanical problem on the jet and could not respond; perhaps the air force had one somewhere that could run the mission. We reported this to higher headquarters, scrubbed the mission, and watched the targets fade away after a few more minutes. I learned two things from this. First, you could not always believe seemingly hard physical evidence, even if you and others nearby agreed it was real (the radar targets and their consistent behavior). Second, all-weather, or night, fighters had self-imposed, unwritten limitations and might, or might not, be available when needed.

Rosa came back with Norman in June, and we started learning about parenting. He was a strong, healthy baby with a good disposition, which made this adjustment easy for us. Some of the wives in Rosa's circle were a little cool because she had gone home to have her baby, which violated the code the regulars lived by, but neither of us worried about it. I kept working hard on the technical and operational aspects of my job, but neglected to have a public relations program aimed at pushing my personal visibility and reputation beyond Major Mitch and the people I worked with. My credo has always been that actions speak louder than words, and I never developed any facility for brownnosing to advance myself. I avoided the headquarters people and only ever spoke to Major Penn at happy hours and parties for the squadron officers and their wives. My style probably had a hand in setting me up for what came to pass in the latter part of July.

Major Mitch took off on an extended leave telling Dick and me to keep an eye on things. It was the last time I ever saw him, although he had a strong influence on my future. A week or so after he left, I was told to report to the adjutant's office along with several others from my group who had just received their controller's MOS designation. We were each handed a thick set of mimeographed orders that had us leaving the squadron in a week to proceed as rapidly as possible to join the First Marine Air Wing in Korea "for duty not involving flying." The adjutant said the orders were in response to a priority draft calling for eight controllers, which the wing was meeting by stripping our squadron and those at Edenton and Miami. Only qualified people with a year's service remaining met the criteria for this posting, an irony of sorts since the slow learners and lazy ones, most unmarried, didn't have to go.

Even though this unexpected development busted up the comfortable sinecure I had planned for the rest of my service, I felt a shot of adrenaline and excitement from the news and resolved to make the best of the experience. When I went home that afternoon, I put on a shit-eating grin and told Rosa that I had some bad news for her. Her reaction was unexpected and volcanic—she came totally unglued. She grabbed up some pots and pans and started throwing them at me while shouting through angry tears and calling me every variety of son of a bitch her vocabulary could formulate. It probably made her madder than anything that has ever happened in our years together. She sensed that I was a little proud to be going, which only fanned the flames of her rage. I finally got her to calm down long enough to tell her that I had not volunteered and was just as surprised as she was.

I reiterated that the needs of the Marine Corps came first, that orders were orders, and recited the old saw, "If the Marine Corps had wanted you to have a wife, they would have issued you one." She finally cried her anger out, and we managed to have a couple of drinks and a good dinner.

I spent the next week processing out, which consisted of getting a battery of overseas shots, turning in my weapon and other gear, and completing the paperwork to be detached from the squadron. On my last Saturday, I drove onto the base in civilian clothes to go to the post exchange and noticed a large group of reserve Corsairs in the landing pattern for the northwest runway. A road paralleled the landing area to my right, so I pulled off and parked to watch the "U-Birds," which were somewhat of a romantic rarity by 1954. After a few minutes, a pickup truck with a flashing amber light drove up, and a grinning MP corporal got out and asked for my ID card. When he saw that I was an officer, he was extremely pleased. Since I was in a prohibited area (no signs were posted to that effect), he would have to run me in to the provost marshal, and I was to follow him. We drove a short distance to the security detail's headquarters where the corporal presented me directly to the man, a grunt lieutenant colonel with a mean face and a flattop. After listening to the corporal's recital of my infraction of the rules, the colonel told me with some pleasure that he would have to take my base driver's license away for two weeks and asked me if I had anything to say. I told him that this was perfectly fine with me since I was already detached from my squadron and was leaving with my wife and baby on Monday for Korea. He told the corporal to get out, brightened up, and told me to forget the crap about the driver's license. He wished me luck and gave me a firm handshake. I left in a much better mood and flipped the sulking corporal a one-finger salute as I passed him in the outer office.

Just before we left, Major Bruce, who occupied the other side of our duplex with his family, did a nice thing for us. A dog lover, he had bought a champion-quality miniature Dachshund bitch when he was stationed in Germany. He bred her just before coming back to Cherry Point, and she produced a litter of beautiful tiny pups, which we admired very much. They were the same age as Norman, and the major let us have one of the girls, who already bore the name Friedl. She was intelligent, very pretty, active, and aggressively protective of Norman. She always slept in the bed with us.

On the last Monday in July, the mover packed up our sparse furniture for storage. Rosa and I loaded up our Chevrolet sedan with Norman and Friedl and started out on the two-lane highway heading west to Lexington, where they were to stay with the Tuckers. I spent the rest of the week with them and got to fly Harry Tucker's Stinson a couple of times. On Sunday, Rosa drove me to the airport, and we held each other for a long time before I turned around and walked out to board a TWA Lockheed Constellation for the flight to Los Angeles.

6

An Oriental Adventure

When I landed in Los Angeles, a cousin on my father's side, young Dr. Frank Winter and his wife, Irma, met me at the airport and took me to their nice home in Santa Monica, where we had drinks in the yard in the last of the warm, soft sunshine that filtered through the mist over the nearby beach. This was my first visit to California, before the smog and traffic gridlock around Los Angeles, and I found it attractive—with lots of nice homes, flowers, and eucalyptus, citrus, avocado, and palm trees—if somewhat artificial and glitzy, just a little too pretty. After they had showed me around the next morning, we drove down the coast to Laguna Beach, enjoyed swimming in the strong surf of the Pacific, then after lunch headed inland to El Toro, the Marine Corps Air Station, where I presented my orders and reported in.

El Toro, Marine Aviation's West Coast equivalent of Cherry Point, lay on 4,700 acres about an hour's drive south of Los Angeles. It seemed smaller and rougher than Cherry Point. I was assigned to a four-man room in the transient bachelor officers' quarters (BOQ), a plain, wooden, two-story barracks left over from the big war. It was nothing but a place to sleep, and our racks were the same double-deck narrow metal cots that we had at Parris Island and Quantico. It was easy to get splinters in your feet if you walked barefoot to the communal head down the hall.

My roommates were John Dunphy, John Van Dusen, and a major we seldom saw. Dunphy, a former member of the Harvard hockey team and an outgoing, funny ladies' man, was a compact, tough Irishman from Boston who had been at Parris Island and Quantico with me and was a fellow air controller at MACS-6. Van Dusen, a recent graduate of NAVCAD and AD training, was a second lieutenant headed to join VMC-1 at K-3, which flew AD-4Ns in an ECM role. He was a tall, handsome, serious guy who knew a lot about airplanes, and I believe he had flown some before coming into the military. Our fourth roommate, the major, was a handsome blond man in his early thirties with an exhausted, frazzled look. He had three rows of ribbons from previous World War II and Korean fighter tours and was headed back to join VMJ-1, a photo squadron flying unarmed Banshees out of K-3. He seemed to be making the most of a hectic social schedule pursuing wine and women at all hours like a squirrel hoarding nuts for the winter.

We had a lot of orange juice, sandwiches, and beer at an officers' snack bar just down the street and usually ate dinner at the officers' club, a small and simple building across the road. We spent the first couple of days attending lectures to prepare us for overseas duty given in some large pyramidal tents set on wood floors with the sides rolled up. They discussed oriental customs and culture and laid out some dos and don'ts to ease our transition and preserve good relations with the Koreans and Japanese. One lecture on the evils of "bean bagging," or going to bed with foreign nationals, stated blandly that the Corps did not countenance such reprehensible behavior and would not tolerate fornication or adultery. This later proved to be one of those sanctimonious policies that, like Staff Sergeant Hephner's order at Parris Island to swear off profanity, had little punch to it.

After our lectures, we took care of the remaining paperwork concerning pay allotments (I had two-thirds of mine sent home to Rosa), next-of-kin listings, and other miscellaneous details. Then we were free to do what we wanted to for the next couple of weeks, as is typical of the military's hurry-up-and-wait style of doing things. We checked in every morning and got the next two weekends off before being alerted to stand by for immediate movement. We spent a good bit of time in a nice bar half a block up the hill from the ocean in Laguna Beach. There were a lot of attractive girls around, and I found myself not a little uncomfortable and frustrated as I was twenty-three years old, married, a long way from my wife, and in a look-but-don't-touch situation. My friend Mal Gambill was in an engineer outfit at Camp Pendleton and shared a bachelor pad in the hills behind Laguna Beach with some other lieutenants. I spent a lonely Friday night there on a couch in the living room while the other guys and their dates retired to the bedrooms. I resolved not to put myself in that situation again.

USMC 2nd Lt. Floyd McGowin, in South Korea.

Mal and I drove up the coast in his car to Los Angeles both Saturdays and spent the night with my cousin Charles Abercrombie, who lived alone on the edge of Santa Monica. A couple of years older than I, he seemed dedicated to having a good time. Though trained as a concert pianist, he gave it up in favor of less demanding work, such as being a part-time private detective and postal worker. Entertaining company and a fun drinking buddy, Charles liked pretty women and took us to the big burlesque theater in downtown LA on both trips. The featured stripper was Tempest Storm, then at the top of her profession. With red hair, green eyes, long legs, and large, exquisitely shaped breasts that she knew how to present, she was one of the sexiest women I have ever seen.

The Monday after our last visit to LA, our little group got word that we were leaving for Korea that afternoon on a Marine R5D (DC-4). We boarded the plane excited and glad to be on our way finally, but this feeling didn't last long. The first leg took us up the coast to Moffett Field, the naval air station outside Palo Alto just inland from San Francisco. Soon after we landed, our group was told to get off the plane, collect our baggage, and go to the transient BOQ as we were being bumped in favor of higher-priority travelers.

We spent four or five days there, checking in every morning to be told to come back the next day. We used the delay to good advantage, seeing the sights in San Francisco, where we always made the scene at the Top of the Mark for late afternoon drinks before heading back to Moffett. This famous bar on top of the Mark Hopkins Hotel, with its spectacular view and tasteful surroundings, had a lot of atmosphere and figured in many novels and memoirs of World War II. We were latecomers and on our way to a dormant combat zone, but going up there had a special meaning for us, representing as it did a romanticized phase of military service.

On our final morning at Moffett, we got the word on checking in that we would be leaving that afternoon on a chartered bus for Travis Air Force Base between San Francisco and Sacramento, the principal Military Air Transport Service (MATS) base on the West Coast and the jumping off place for most trans-Pacific flights. To celebrate finally getting on our way, we had a fine lunch at the officers' mess on the air station and were impressed with the difference in style between the navy and its Marine Corps ward. The mess was as attractive as a good civilian club with white linen table clothes, fine china, and full silver place settings. Highly trained Filipino messmen in starched white coats served first-class food. Like the air force, the navy saw to its people's creature comforts in tasteful surroundings—a stark contrast to the lot of the raggedy-ass Marines, who with few exceptions got by on a sort of "less is more" philosophy and seemed to do all the better for it.

After a pleasant bus ride that afternoon, we pulled into Travis, a large base with a lot of transport activity plus a few B-36s droning over head with their peculiar sound from the rear-facing (pusher) big engines. The next morning, we had an early breakfast, then boarded a big C-97 and settled in for the long trip to Tokyo with brief stops at Hawaii and Wake Island for fuel, servicing, and crew changes. The well-soundproofed and roomy C-97 had comfortable airline seats for eighty passengers. Though the military version had only six windows on each side, I sat by one, which helped satisfy my intense interest in the proceedings. We were soon airborne and launched on our 2,082 nm (about 2,400 statute miles) journey. The flight was sunny and smooth with fair-weather cumulus clouds over the empty ocean, and the time passed agreeably. We were free to move around and visit the spacious cockpit to watch the large flight crew (two pilots, navigator, flight engineer, and radioman) at work. After about ten hours, we landed at Honolulu and taxied into a terminal on the air force side of the international airport. We had about an hour and a half to stretch, walk around, and eat a light meal of sandwiches, fresh fruit, and juice before reboarding the freshly serviced and cleaned-up airplane.

We departed Honolulu flying almost due west into the setting sun for the long run to Wake Island—a legendary U.S. forward base for aircraft and submarines and the scene of much combat with the Japanese during World War II—which lay 2,183 nm ahead on the other side of the International Date Line. Everybody was getting tired and grungy, and most slept fitfully for a few hours in the darkened cabin as the big plane droned smoothly through the night. After about ten and a half hours, we began to let down in the still, clear dawn to begin our approach to the island's 9,800-foot east-west runway. As we turned final, I noted the wreck of a large ship nosed up on the beach next to the runway, a ghost of the recent big war. It was the *Suwa Maru*, a 10,000-ton Japanese freighter torpedoed by an American submarine in 1943 while bringing supplies to the island.

We deplaned for about an hour while our C-97 was being cleaned, serviced, and restocked and ate breakfast in a dining room adjacent to the terminal. We were soon airborne with a fresh crew and climbing out to the northwest for the final 1,709 nm leg to Tokyo. We flew through the day in good weather over the empty ocean and saw nothing except a few clouds and Marcus Island, a Japanese possession located directly on our track about 800 miles out of Wake. After about seven and a half hours, we began letting down for our run into Tokyo's Haneda Airport, located south of the city on the west side of the bay. After thirty hours on the airplane, multiple cups of coffee, and a lot of cigarettes, we were ready to find a hot shower and a bed. Upon landing, our little group of Korea-bound Marines repaired to a transient BOQ near the flight line to clean up, rest, and wait for a flight out the next day. A couple of the guys took off for downtown Tokyo to sightsee, but I was too tired. The next day we caught a flight down to Itami, the airport serving Osaka, about 200 miles west-southwest of Tokyo. We had a few drinks and a simple meal at the ratty little Marine-operated officers' club and got a good night's rest on cots in a communal bunkroom, more than a little excited as the next morning would see us on a flight to Korea where new jobs and a new culture awaited us.

After a predawn break-
fast the next day, September
1, 1954, we reported to the
nearby flight line to board
a four-engine Douglas
R5D-3 (DC-4) for the 310
nm flight to Korea. After
an hour-and-forty-minute
flight west across the Sea of
Japan, we landed at Pusan's
K-9 airport so that a team
of neutral Third World military officers could inspect
our plane's personnel and
cargo manifest, part of the
previous year's truce agreement protocol designed to
preserve the existing power
balance between the two
sides. We stayed on the

Lieutenant McGowin and friend in Korea.

plane during the short stop and soon took off for the last little 50-mile run
north up the coast to Pohang's K-3 airport, home of the First Marine Air
Wing. The 6,000-foot east-west strip was located on the southwest side of
the large bay, which made Pohang a good harbor for seagoing ships. The Japs
built it during their long occupation and used it as a fighter base, complete
with underground hangars in the sides of the hills along the southeast side
of the runway where Zeros were stored. The runway was on flat land by
the water, but hills and small mountains were very close at hand. The land
had a bleak, worn look with few trees of any size since most were cut for
firewood at a young age. The Communists had pushed south past Pohang
four years earlier to be stopped along the Pusan perimeter. The combination
of fierce fighting and the burning of houses and buildings to deny their
use to the other side contributed to the wasted look. The Koreans eked out
a bare subsistence from farming, raising rice and other crops, and a lot of

fishing. Human waste, or "night soil," was the fertilizer of choice, and the country had a pervasive stench that had to be experienced to be believed, though, as with most things, we eventually got used to it.

The main base at the strip was on both sides of the runway and constituted a small city—in addition to housing more than 10,000 Marines, it employed a lot of Koreans as labor. While not pretty or luxurious in any way, the quarters and infrastructure buildings kept out the worst of the dirt, heat, and cold, and the main roadways on the base were paved. Our living conditions were good, with ten or twelve lieutenants and captains sharing a Butler hut. We each had a semiprivate cubicle, with a cot plus lamps, a homemade desk, chair, chest of drawers, wall locker, and a locker box. Very competent, pleasant, and well-paid Korean houseboys kept everything neat and clean and took care of the laundry. All in all, it made for fairly nice living conditions. The only drawback was the lack of privacy. I had to listen to the incessant, loud, boring, and banal conversation of two of the stupidest officers (both first lieutenants from the Northeast) I was ever around. It got very cold at night during the Korean winter, and I slept with five blankets plus a trench coat on top of my rack. Homemade space heaters that ran on contaminated jet fuel kept things fairly comfortable during the day, but were prone to blowing up, presenting both an element of danger and a lot of soot and fumes.

A good size club near our living quarters housed a nice, large bar, a lounge with a big stone fireplace, and a well-furnished, pleasant dining room. Behind the bar stood a life-size photograph of a drop-dead-gorgeous blond with beautiful, statuesque tits prominently and lovingly displayed, along with some pubic hair, a daily reminder of what we were all missing. Beer cost a dime, and mixed drinks, a quarter. I drank on a regular basis before dinner but never to excess. Our food was generally good since a lot of field grade officers—majors and colonels—ate with us though at separate tables. A team of black sergeants—gunnies and master sergeants originally enlisted for "mess duty only"—did a good job running the mess. We had white tablecloths and real napkins, and young uniformed Korean women, some very pretty, waited on us. Many of the officers were avid hunters, and as the indigenous Koreans had not been allowed to own firearms for over fifty years under Jap and U.S. occupation, the countryside was teeming with game, including ducks, geese, pheasants, doves, and beautiful miniature deer. Our mess sergeants prepared wonderful all-you-could-eat feasts from the game on Saturday nights and at Thanksgiving and Christmas.

Upon our arrival at Pohang, we reported to the group personnel office to pick up our assignments. When my turn came to talk to the warrant officer running things, he said with a bored look, "Well, Lieutenant, you are going to the tactical air control center here at K-3." I felt a rush of outrage and disappointment, much like I'd experienced when cut out of flight training. I had neither the right MOS (6708) nor the desire to work in the TACC. I thought about all the hard work and effort I had put into learning the air controller's trade and how this stupid son of a bitch was wasting it. There were two Marine control squadrons in Korea, MACS-3 near K-3 and another one on the Yellow Sea near the west coast airbase K-8. We had been told at Cherry Point that both had a critical need for rated controllers, which had occasioned our rushed up draft. I put on the best face I could and begged him to reconsider my assignment, saying that I was really interested in the control business and that staying involved in it meant a lot to me. He frowned, then told me that there was absolutely nothing that he could do and that I should make the best out of filling "the needs of the Corps." He also added that he had a job to do and that I should be careful not to waste any more of his time. I hadn't yet heard the expression "life ain't fair," but I was catching on fast.

The assignment to the TACC turned out to be a bland, mostly boring experience—neither uncomfortable nor really unpleasant but also not the kind of lesson to impart much more than humility. To gain entrance to the control center proper—a large underground bunker made of reinforced concrete in the side of a hill about a quarter mile from our quarters, club, and mess—you went through a security check in the person of an armed guard, ducked through a sandbagged door, and then walked down a flight of steps into an anteroom with a bulletin board listing watch schedules and other pertinent notices. By tradition, we mustered in the anteroom and entered the control center proper through a steel blast door to relieve the watch a few minutes early. The watches, manned by a crew comprising a captain or senior first lieutenant, a couple more lieutenants, and about ten enlisted men, lasted a very long six hours. Tardiness was not an option.

The center had a dark, spooky feel and smelled of electronics, cigarette smoke, and coffee. It was fairly large and resembled a small theater with two tiers of balcony positions along the front wall. The upper one, reserved for the general commanding the wing and his battle staff, was only occupied in cases of genuine emergency "red alerts." The next tier down was for the officers in the duty crew and the senior NCO, a staff sergeant or higher. Enlisted men manned a pit in front of us filled with communications consoles and teletypes. In front of the back wall stood a large back-lighted Plexiglas plotting board with a map of Korea and reference information, such as air fields, prohibited areas, ranges, the DMZ, and the like, delineated in orange grease pencil. Several enlisted plotters wearing headsets stood on a platform behind the board adding and deleting traffic plots, as well as raid and combat air patrol information. They resembled a troop of literate but dyslexic monkeys in that they had to write backwards, usually rapidly, to make their data legible to us. In the event of action, the commander could view the tactical plot as it unfolded on the board and make his decisions as to how to deploy his aerial assets.

In addition to the plot, we had current information as to the status of everything that flew on a real-time basis as well as what was planned. The First Marine Air Wing worked under the Fifth Air Force and got its orders and plan of the day late the night before in a lengthy "FRAG" order, which poured out of one of our teletypes onto the floor on reams of yellow paper. These orders emanated from the Joint Operations Center (JOC), the highest theater headquarters located at K-55 air base at Osan to our northwest, south of the capital at Seoul. Our job was to collate orders and data from the JOC, the wing, and its groups and squadrons and to have up-to-the-minute knowledge of all this, plus the weather, the status of the radar at the MACS locations, and a lot of other data and intelligence information. We worked nine or ten watches a week, which started at midnight and changed every six hours on a continuous, week-in, week-out basis. Usually nothing much happened outside of observing the wing's routine operations, but there were occasional moments of high drama, excitement, and sometimes a little apprehension as to what might happen next.

John Van Dusen came over to our club for drinks and dinner a couple of weeks after we checked in. He got lucky and was assigned to VMC-1 as a pilot flying their AD-4NA Skyraiders in the ECM role. As an additional dividend, the squadron was to be pulled back later in the fall to MCAS Kaneohe Bay in Hawaii—a tropical paradise blessed with a comfortable climate, beautiful flowers, and women in abundance and probably the most desirable duty station in the Corps—so his tour in Korea would last less than three months. After an early meal, he took us down to his squadron's flight line and showed us their airplanes, which were parked close together in a neat line with their wings folded to save ramp space. They made an impressive picture in the last of the day's soft sunlight, very strong, purposeful looking, and warlike in front of the old Jap hangars carved in the hillside behind the ramp.

John climbed up on the left wing walk of one of the planes and slid back its bubble canopy. I stood on the right wing walk with the canopy rail of the big plane coming up to the top of my chest and watched and listened as he patiently explained the myriad controls and instruments. My attention was a little spotty for I was hit with a profound sense of envy and loss at having missed out on the opportunity to be a pilot with a front-row seat in the military aviation business. The cockpit seemed very complicated at the time, and John's explanations were too numerous and detailed for me to absorb with total understanding. It seemed a very complex machine and reinforced my belief that a military pilot had to be something special to master his trade. All too soon, this communion with the great airplane was over. I never saw John again, but I like to believe he was dedicated enough to have made flying his life work.

One day I was listening to the talk on one of the fighter squadron's discrete frequencies (VMF-115 and -311 operated Grumman Panther jets in the fighter-attack role) between a major and his charge, a young second lieutenant on a "FAM" (familiarization) flight. These consisted of a syllabus of eight or so flights designed to orient a new pilot to the area with its ranges, prohibited areas, "no-fly" lines, the DMZ, and the spectrum of navigation and communication facilities. It also served as instruction on the wiles of the gooks and their electronic booby traps. Everything seemed to be proceeding smoothly as the major led his junior wingman around the area at 25,000 feet. Talk between tactical military airplanes is kept to a bare minimum for various reasons, so there wasn't much to listen to. It was a pretty day outside our dark hole, and I didn't anticipate any problems, although in aviation big-time trouble can, and usually does, develop in an instant when least expected. All of a sudden, I heard the major tell his wingman to "close it up," followed by a string of strident warnings to "pull-out, pull-out." The lieutenant's jet had rolled off the flight lead's wing to go inverted into a vertical dive. The major peeled off and followed him down, offering increasingly desperate pleas and suggestions—all to no avail. In less than two minutes, the jet and its mute occupant were buried at the bottom of a deep smoking hole in the inhospitable Korean countryside. The shaken major reported the crash and returned to base alone. I did not know either of the parties, but I was around a lot of the young fighter pilots and sensed that a few of them were scared to death. We never knew whether this young man was the victim of oxygen starvation (hypoxia) or had been apprehensive enough to hyperventilate and gulp so much 100 percent oxygen that he created the same effect, slowly losing consciousness. Both circumstances happened occasionally as a by-product of nervousness—misuse of the oxygen equipment and/or its connections or breathing too quickly.

One night in the early fall, I experienced my first "red alert," which was interesting but not dangerous. Working the graveyard watch, we heard around 2100 that unidentified aircraft were flying over Seoul in a gaggle of about ten. Sirens went off all over South Korea. Nobody knew what the crazy gooks might be up to. It was felt that the intruders might be a diversion created to mask some more sinister purpose. They were PO-2s, primitive biplanes that had been used five or six times during the 1950–1953 war for various nuisance-type activities, mostly at night. With a maximum speed of 88 mph, they were almost totally safe from attack by our side's jet night fighters, and the air force had in fact lost two Lockheed F-94s in stall-spin accidents flying against them. On this particular night, the "bed-check Charlies" milled around over the ruined capital city for about forty minutes while their observers chucked leaflets overboard. The F-94s were scrambled but had no luck as usual. The gooks finally tired of the sport, thumbed their noses at the jets, and went back home to the North. A little while later, the alert was canceled, leaving us more than a little amused at their audacious style and the Blue Suiters' impotence.

I had the same watch one night about a month later. The Korean winter was starting, and the weather was unsettled with low clouds and rain squalls breaking out all over South Korea. Suddenly, another red alert was set by the JOC, and we all concentrated on what was developing. The threat this time was a flight of several IL-28 jet bombers, probably originating from the Antung airfield complex north of the Yalu, the home of most of the MiG-15 fighters deployed against our forces. The Red jets went down the peninsula just inland from the west coast. When they got to the bottom of the country, they turned east along the south coast and its outlying islands before turning north and heading back home. At my level, we didn't know what to make of this, although I would suspect that they were testing our defenses with ECM equipment and recording the location and frequencies of all our radar facilities. As I recall, they stayed at a relatively low altitude and never got much above 10,000 feet. They were speeding south at about 500 knots totally unopposed, as the weather was too bad for our "all-weather" fighters to launch. We did not know it at the time, but these aircraft were almost certainly crewed by Russians, who in fact accounted for a majority of the air assets used by the Communists in Korea. In little more than an hour, the "raid" was over. The bombers were last seen heading north across the Yalu, again leaving us marveling at their nerve and tactics.

The Reds were not the only ones who employed snooper and spy planes. On more than a few occasions in the TACC, we followed the progress of our RB-45 bombers with a heavy escort of F-86s north along the west coast past the 38th parallel. They were supposed to stay just outside North Korean coastal waters while gathering intelligence with ECM recording gear and oblique cameras. The other side didn't like this a bit and usually responded by scrambling a gaggle of MiG-15s and heading them toward the imperialist intruders. To my knowledge, nobody ever got hurt, but shots were traded back and forth during most of these confrontations.

Except for pulling long watches conscientiously in the TACC, following orders, and getting along with everybody, all very easy to do, junior officers like me had no other official duties and a lot of free time. I tried to stay busy to make the days pass. The group had a small but very good library, which I visited several times a week. The latest publications, magazines, and books of a wide variety were flown in from the States on a continuous basis, so there was almost always interesting stuff to look at. I read *Aviation Week*, *Life*, *Time*, and various newspapers to keep up with current events, and I always had several books checked out. I kept a log of my reading and averaged about two and a half books a week while I was at the TACC. The group also showed movies, and I was a regular customer. Most were obscure B pictures that we would never have heard of or looked at in the States. Many of them were made by the same Jewish gentleman in Hollywood, who probably sold most of his output to the government. They were often so bad as to be funny, generating outrageous comments from the culture-hungry audience, and we enjoyed them immensely.

I had my first R&R in Japan in the latter part of October. R&R stood for "Rest and Recreation," and we got eight days off (not counted as leave) for every seven weeks. Some realists also called this break I&I ("Intoxication and Intercourse"). Besides our not having to pay income tax (Korea was still technically a combat zone), R&R was our only reward for working seven-day weeks, often day and night, during our year of overseas service, which didn't receive any campaign ribbons, glory, or even much public awareness or appreciation. We and our families knew we were doing something of real value, and that was all that really mattered.

One Monday morning, I got on one of the R5Ds with some other lieutenants. We ran up to Seoul to deliver some people and mail, then headed east to Itami, where the air force had brought about wondrous changes. In the place of the dinky little Marine "O" club stood a large, modern, concrete structure that housed a fine bar and large dining room—every bit the equivalent of a first-class, stateside commercial eating and drinking establishment and far superior to most Marine facilities at home. It looked to be built to last at least fifty years. We checked into the air force's transient BOQ, where we were amazed to find that we each got a small, neat private room. Those fellows knew how to live, and the culture difference compared to what we were accustomed to was striking.

I spent this first R&R in Japan mostly luxuriating in the club with its fresh milk, good steaks, and nice bar. We operated as a group and made a couple of runs into Osaka that entailed traversing the thousand-yard dash between the main gate and train station. Even then Japanese trains were very efficient, fast, and dependable, and it didn't take long to get into the great seaport city. The street was lined with bars, tailors, and tattoo shops and a lot of cheap-looking women. On one such trip, we repaired to an attractive rooftop bar on top of one of the big hotels and got into numerous quart bottles of Jap and Aussie beer (Asahi and Emu) while we planned our next move. We went to a wonderful music hall–type theater that was an oriental takeoff on the Folies in Paris. The women in the cast were strikingly beautiful, dressed in gorgeous costumes that accented their charms without encumbering the view. The show had elaborate props with the girls coming down from the ceiling in little birdcages spotlighted to show all they had. After the show we went to a good restaurant where we took off our shoes and sat on cushions around a low table. Kimono-clad young women with hair coiffed and faces made up in the traditional style served us warm sake and a good meal of thinly sliced steak, rice, and various unknown condiments and side dishes. The food was good and the atmosphere interesting and pleasant, but we were too young and provincial to appreciate it for what it was. Most of the time we tended to eat American-style chow at the military clubs or Japanese hotels and restaurants that catered to Westerners.

My impression of Japan after spending almost two months in Korea differed notably from my initial reaction to it. Everything at first had seemed gray, grimy, and rundown. The few Japanese automobiles in evidence had been tiny, crude-looking cars that crawled along the crowded streets among equally rinky-dink trucks. The pervasive musty smell and hazy atmosphere, while not grossly unpleasant, had seemed mildly depressing. Overall, we had seen Japan as backward and different, lacking in sophistication and certainly not up to our standards. Two months later, Japan appeared much more comfortable and attractive and presented a stark contrast to the squalor, destruction, and pitiful living conditions we saw in Korea. There was order and much beauty sprinkled around the landscape. Many of the women were very attractive and looked more and more Western to our starved eyes. I found that I liked Japan a lot and looked forward to coming back. All too soon, the week had passed, and it was time for a dawn takeoff in the trusty R-5D across the straits to K-9 at Pusan and on to K-3.

November passed in slow motion with one day exactly like another, except for the weather, which was very changeable and worsening rapidly. It was getting extremely cold with bitter winds coming down from the north, and frequent storms and squalls often spat out sleet and sometimes snow. I had a homemade calendar in the notebook I used to record things and, like a convict doing jail time, crossed off each day. One day in the first week of December, several of us reported to the headquarters office where we were told that we were now first lieutenants—an automatic time-in-grade-based promotion that everyone received unless he screwed up in some spectacular way. We were glad to replace our gold bars with silver ones, which made us feel more salty and at ease in the culture.

Christmas was coming on, and I got a lot of mail from Rosa in Kentucky and my family in Alabama. Rosa sent me some cheerful presents and pictures of our son, Norman, and while I was very glad to get them, they served to make the separation even more painful. I missed my wife and child and thought about them a lot. Communications and travel were much different then, and except for some kind of ham radio deal called "MARS," which I never tried, phone calls were not practical. My mother talked about taking Rosa to Japan on a far-ranging cruise where I could meet them on leave, but this never materialized, probably because of my mother's deteriorating physical condition.

I had the duty starting at midnight on Christmas. I remember walking through the cold, still night to the command bunker, wearing a loaded sidearm and looking up at a sky lit with brilliant stars and a staff pilot's moon, full and providing lots of light. I thought about the shepherds and the magi on their way to the Christ Child's manger and of my family tucked in on the other side of the world. It was a painful loneliness, but I took some satisfaction in being a part of protecting their way of life and doing my duty. For the next six hours, we saw Christmas come in down in our hole over the usual numerous cigarettes and cups of coffee. Not much broke the monotony except for the plotters starting a track called in by MACS-3, or Wild Fire, which purported to be Santa Claus and his troop of flying reindeer.

I got off watch at 0600 and emerged from the bunker into a bright, cold Christmas morning. I went back to my space in the hut and opened the little presents I had laid out on my rack the night before, feeling glad and sad at the same time. I had the rest of the day off and spent it reading in the library in the morning, then in the afternoon seeing an entertaining B flick about Marine officer and football great Elroy "Crazylegs" Hirsh, who played himself in the picture. As one reviewer put it, "This movie demonstrates why he decided to stick to football." That night we had a blowout at the club with a lot of booze and a feast featuring wonderful pheasant and venison, as well as the traditional turkey and dressing.

The next day, I got on the big bird for my second R&R in Japan, armed with a lot of good advice about people and places and what to do from Bob Gregory, a tall, handsome fellow with good taste who knew his way around. This time I caught a ride to Tokyo, where I checked into a good new downtown hotel, Japanese owned and operated but Western in style. I spent a couple of days wandering around, getting a feel for the city. I saw the palace and its gardens and had late-afternoon drinks in the bar at the Imperial Hotel, the Frank Lloyd Wright architectural masterpiece where Douglas MacArthur had his original headquarters after the war. In subtle ways, Tokyo's cosmopolitan and sophisticated nature reminded me of New York.

After a hard run on the town, we used to go to the Tokyo Onson to sweat out the previous night's excesses. This well-run and -equipped bathhouse occupied the whole fifth floor of a big downtown office building and catered to Western businessmen, diplomats, and officers. You entered an attractive lobby, paid your yen equivalent of three or four dollars, and paired up with one of the attractive girls demurely standing around in white panties and a bra. Together we would go into one of the many identical little rooms. After shutting the door, the girl would punch a large alarm clock and motion for you to take all your clothes off while holding out a bath towel and looking away. This pretense at modesty only lasted a minute or so, after which you were put through alternate hot and cold baths, including total and intimate scrubbing, manicure, and pedicure, and ten minutes or so in a sweat box where you sat naked on a stool with just your head sticking out of the top. The best part came after this when the young lady put you on the massage table and worked you over with vigor, first front and then back. The massage always peaked with the girl jumping up on your back to apply the pressure by walking around and rubbing with her bare feet. In spite of the operation's let-it-all-hang-out style, it was a strictly ethical place, even though the Japanese were not burdened with any Puritan hang-ups about sex. One time, in the ecstasy of one of the rubdowns, I decided to see if that reputation was for real by asking my girl what it would cost to take the exercise into the next dimension. Without a pause or even change of expression, she answered, "million dolla." plainly shutting off any further conversation in that direction, and a minute or so later, the alarm clock went off signaling the end of the hour session. I have always missed that place and its high-class, wonderful service, which always made you feel fresh and well and very alive.

I caught a Marine twin-engine R4Q "Flying Boxcar," which left Haneda just at dark for Itami with an intermediate stop at Nagoya. It was my first ride on one of these transports, a modern postwar design by Fairchild Aircraft. We sat on bucket seats along the side walls of the big cargo compartment, and I noticed that the bulkheads across from and behind me were covered with flack curtains, which seemed odd. When I asked why, the crew chief dryly explained that the armor was installed to keep people like me from being killed if a blade let go on one of the power-recovery turbines that were a part of the particular Wright R-3350 engine's exhaust system used on the plane.

It was dark when we landed at Nagoya. I relaxed when the main wheels gently kissed the runway, marking a good landing. Just as the nose gear lowered to roll on, a huge tail of bright flames shot out the starboard side trailing twelve or fifteen feet back from the engine, which I observed through the port holes on either side of the flack curtain. I am almost never frightened in airplanes, but for a couple of seconds, I thought maybe we were about to meet a fiery end due to some catastrophic engine failure. The fire went out as quickly as it had started, and the helpful crew chief explained that it was just the engine grumbling about being revved up into reverse and not to worry.

I spent another couple of days hanging around the air force installation at Itami, eating steak and eggs for breakfast, going into Osaka, and slaking a newly acquired taste for Stingers in the club bar after dinner. Then, all of a sudden it was back on one of the VMR-152 R5Ds for a predawn takeoff to the Land of the Morning Calm.

When I reported in, I had a message to call Major Broker, the operations officer at Wild Fire (MACS-3), the control squadron located adjacent to K-3 on the tip of a point of land sticking out into the Sea of Japan eight miles east of the air base. I knew who they were and what they did, and in fact I talked to them by land line and radio frequently, but I had never been there or met anyone from the squadron in person. Major Broker matter-of-factly told me that his chief henchman, George Baker, the assistant operations officer and head controller, was leaving in about two weeks for flight training at Pensacola. He was looking for somebody to come in as a direct replacement for George, and I had been nominated as one who could do the job. Time was of the essence, and if I agreed to come, he and George would do everything they could to get me fully qualified in their operations so as to fit in smoothly. It took me probably five seconds to tell him that I would be happy to come and was prepared to give him everything I had. He told me to get my stuff together and catch the squadron mail-run truck that afternoon; orders transferring me to the squadron from the TACC had already been approved by the group. To this day, it remains a mystery to me why I was put in the command post when I first got to Korea, then when they needed somebody good to join the control squadron and essentially run its day-to-day tactical reason for being, the command structure plucked me out of my sinecure and turned the radar work, an important and responsible job, over to me with no explanation. Being young, I guess I thought I was just getting my due at the time, but I am sure there was some bigger story behind it. Maybe Major Ernie "Lightning" Mitch, my boss at Cherry Point, and Dick Clough wrote a powerful fitness report on me and passed some strong verbal endorsement up the line. All I know is that, at the time, I appreciated the opportunity to get back to doing an interesting, challenging job that involved considerable responsibility and personal integrity, one that also did wonders for my personal development and probably helped me do well in leadership in later life.

When I got out to the point and reported in, I met Major Broker and George, a first lieutenant. A heavyset, serious, and competent man of about thirty-five, Major Broker had been one of the original air controllers during the big war in the Pacific and knew the business thoroughly. He had become a commercial pilot in Montana after the war and was called back up for Korea. Having organized the squadron's operations, radar and radio equipments, and personnel efficiently and effectively, he worked from the background and functioned more as a coach than a player. George, a hardworking, pleasant ex–enlisted man commissioned through OC, couldn't wait to start flying, but he had to get me checked out and qualified before he could leave. He worked with me openly and enthusiastically, sharing information about what to expect and watch for from the officers and men, as well as the equipment and its support infrastructure.

There were three crews composed of six or seven officer controllers and fifteen or so enlisted men. A senior first lieutenant led each crew with a buck sergeant in charge of the enlisted men. George had one crew, and the others were run by Kevin Lyons and Ed Chapman, both good officers. The other controllers were roughly half ground officers and half aviators, and to me they seemed very capable with few exceptions. The two senior NCOs in operations turned out to be Master Sergeant Laing and Staff Sergeant Sentenn, who had taught me the business at Cherry Point—both fine men and very capable, save occasional episodes with too much booze. Our clerk, Corporal Jacques from Panama City, Florida, handled all the paperwork and reports very efficiently and capably and managed the military clap-trap and inspections perfectly. Jacques was also an extremely talented professional gambler, a master at cards and dice, who routinely cleaned out a big part of the squadron's enlisted payroll every payday. His success was constant and rewarding to the extent that he had something of a problem disposing of all the money. I remember once he wired the Oldsmobile dealer in Panama City the funds for a brand-new 98 convertible for his girlfriend's birthday present. Occasional speculation that his luck stemmed from marked cards, loaded dice, and the like were unfounded. His winnings continued, especially from the staff NCOs like Laing and Sentenn, who like Mafia capos were not to be trifled with. The only bad luck I ever knew him to have was coming down with a drip after an R&R in Japan, a problem diagnosed as "nonspecific urethritis," with a course of penicillin shots administered as a precaution.

The CO was Lieutenant Colonel Ahee, a small dark man with very black hair, penetrating eyes, and a heavy shadow of beard. He was Lebanese, quick, very intelligent, irreverent, and outspoken, with a reputation as a mean hard-ass. I respected and admired him and got along with him beautifully. Those who didn't like him tended to be lazy or incompetent. He had flown TBMs in the war, fighters, and, more recently, transports. He had a sharp wit and could be very funny on occasion over drinks in our little club.

Major Jack Perrin, our executive officer responsible for the squadron's routine operation, had been a controller on Okinawa during the World War II battle and went through flight training after the war. A nice, mild-mannered man, tall and thin, he kept a lower profile than the colonel. They spent their time flying and keeping up with group and wing protocol. They insisted that we have a first-class operation in both perception and fact and that we give consistently good service to the wing's aircraft and their pilots. Like Major Broker, they stayed out of the actual control business but were very well aware of what we were doing. They were quick to question and criticize, and occasionally compliment, when they felt there was reason.

Late in the afternoon after I arrived at Wild Fire, George took me into the combat information center (CIC) to look at the radar, radio, and communications equipment and to meet some of his crew who had the watch. We entered through an anteroom that housed a coffee mess and some electronics equipment and went through a blackout curtain into the radar room proper. As I went in, the unique smell of the powerful electronics operating in the air-conditioned, darkened little theater hit my nose, and I had a very strong and good feeling of coming home again. This wasn't going to be flying, but it was a closely associated and meaningful part of the business; it was also my opportunity to get back into the loop and achieve some personal satisfaction from being responsibly involved.

I shook hands with the watch commander, several controllers, and the NCO in charge of the enlisted crew members. Sergeant Manuel Fernandez, darkly handsome and personable, was from New Orleans and spoke with the Brooklyn-type brogue of an Irish Channel native. In his early twenties, he was a little older and more experienced than most of his men, and he got good work out of them using an easygoing, helpful style; he knew his stuff, and he never let me down. The enlisted crew were mostly PFCs and corporals, and while they were clean and had proper haircuts and shaves, they presented a classical raggedy-ass appearance. In those days, the Corps saved its spit and polish for parades and liberty and, in keeping with its parsimonious ways, let the troops do their work in utilities (dungarees), which were often faded and threadbare to the extreme. Rank chevrons were crudely stenciled on jacket sleeves and, in more than a few cases, were covered over with a rectangle of black ink, indicating that the wearer had been busted (demoted) in rank. The utility covers (caps) had no stays or stiffness and often gave the wearer a rakish, salty appearance. Officers and staff NCOs always wore proper uniforms, maybe sweaty and dirty in the field, but as neat and clean as conditions permitted. The junior enlisted men at work resembled the college kids of the 1960s, when it was fashionable to see who could wear the rattiest, most torn getup.

In the radar room, illuminated only by the master plotting board, its flanking status boards, and the greenish glow from the various radar scopes, the crew was going about its work. There was a raised dais in the front of the room where the watch commander and two others sat at a communications console that overlooked the floor area. There were two planned position indicator (PPI) scopes on each side of the room with hard-to-read, height-finding scopes alongside. At the far end of the room was a raised Plexiglas plotting board with range and bearing azimuths radiating from our location in the center. The map ran from west of Taegu, east to the coast where we were, near Pohang, and on across the Sea of Japan almost to the Japanese Home Islands. It went up north into Communist territory beyond the 38th parallel and below Pusan to the south. The geography depicted on the translucent plotting board had a radius of about 250 miles, the effective limit of our radar. Two plotters skilled in writing backwards with grease pencils on the back of the board stood wearing headsets, constantly plotting and erasing tracks passed to them by another enlisted man at one of the PPI scopes closest to the board. On each side of the main plotting board were status boards with details of current weather, radio frequencies, local missions, and so forth. The concept, layout, equipment, operating procedures, and even vernacular for Wild Fire were all straight out of the RAF's Battle of Britain experience.

Wild Fire was the focal point of MACS-3, also known as a GCI squadron in trade talk. Without radar like ours to protect its turf against intruders, the First Marine Air Wing we belonged to would have been in the same position as a boxer in the prize ring wearing a blind fold. The Brits had been the first to prove and exploit the concept in the summer of 1940 during the epic battle, and the RAF's brand-new GCI radar tipped the scales in their favor, causing the Luftwaffe to stand down in October of that year. Many factors contributed to Churchill's statement that "never in the field of human conflict was so much owed by so many to so few," but GCI radar was among the most important. Besides the tactical mission of providing detection, identification, and intercept of unknown or hostile "trade," we had another important duty, namely to serve as what is now called a radar approach control (RAPCON), which provided radar positioning and control services for transient and local aircraft. These included military aircraft from all Allied forces as well as a few civilian airliners, notably Northwest Orient's, whose service to Seoul made landfall where the airway from Japan passed over our station. The other RAPCON function was to handle traffic in and out of our airstrip (K-3) located some eight miles west of us. At that time our fighters and attack aircraft had only an automatic direction finder (ADF) receiver for navigation, which was subject to various problems, at times rendering it unusable. In any event, an ADF "jet penetration" using our local low-frequency nondirectional radio beacon—called "Uncle Tare"—was not a precision approach, and because of the steep terrain near the air base, it had high minimums. It wasn't trusted in bad weather at K-3 for another reason. A couple of years before, the Communists had figured out that they could achieve a victory by covertly lugging their own high-powered counterfeit UT beacon to a nearby mountaintop to wait for a combination of low weather and sick radar to fire it up. When they did, it entrapped two flights of F9F Panther fighter bombers returning from a mission. Seven of the eight jets hit the mountain, killing the pilots. The gooks were good at tricks, especially electronic ones, and in this case their success probably exceeded their wildest expectations.

GCA, or ground controlled approach, a precision radar procedure directed from a radar shack at the strip, was used for the final approach and landing of the tactical aircraft. The GCA radar was very short range, covering only the area leading to the runway, and required that our facility vector every aircraft to its approach gate from its initial approach, necessitating communication and coordination between the GCI and GCA controllers on each approach. When everything worked, this very good system could land aircraft safely in appalling, zero-zero weather conditions. It required little skill on the part of the pilot, assuming he could fly instruments well and didn't get vertigo. All he had to do was respond to directions for altitude, headings, and speed, then drop flaps and gear when told to, and he would end up on the center line of the runway near the threshold. The only trouble was that the GCA radar seemed to sense when the weather really got low and bad in rain or snow and would decide to go down for mechanical reasons. When this happened, the GCI controller had to earn his money by guiding the aircraft from initial contact far away from the base all the way to the runway in what is now called an airport surveillance radar, or ASR, approach. Assuming that the controller was proficient (not all were, but when things got tight we took the weaker ones off the scopes) and the pilot kept his cool, we did some good work, at times recovering aircraft in situations where it was either land or bailout because there wasn't enough fuel to go anywhere else.

On one such occasion in 1955, I handled a U.S. Air Force Republic F-84 whose pilot had missed his refueling tanker rendezvous en route from Okinawa to one of the air bases near Seoul located about 250 miles to our northwest. He checked in with me when he was some 150 miles south of our station at high altitude over the sea. After running through the mandatory authentication procedures using a voice challenge and response from the code of the day issued to all duty controllers and pilots, and a "parrot check" that positively identified the aircraft by displaying an electronic tag along side his aircraft's skin painted "blip" (raw radar data) on the scope, we were ready to do business. It was nearing dark on a gloomy, freezing late winter day. The ceiling was a variable 200 foot with about two miles visibility in snow. As usual, the GCA precision approach radar had decided to pack it in for the day, so it would be up to me and the best ASR approach I could pull off to get the fighter onto the strip at K-3 on the first pass. The pilot was a cool individual who matter-of-factly gave me the elements of his fuel emergency. In essence, if he stayed at his cruise altitude of angels 40 (40,000 feet) as long as possible, then closed his throttle to come down at the standard jet rate of descent (4,000 feet per minute), he would probably make it, assuming nobody made any mistakes. If this didn't work, it meant an ejection followed by a landing, most likely in the sea. Even though the pilots wore "poopy suits" (uncomfortable rubber anti-immersion waterproof garments put on over flight suits), the water temperature at that time of year was such that thirty minutes was as long as a pilot in the water had before he died from hypothermia, assuming he was in good shape when he landed.

The F-84 pilot and I worked well together. As he got closer and closer to land and the strip, I kept blowing up the picture on my scope, reducing the range and area depicted to enable constantly more precise guidance to the runway, so that by the time he was on final approach, I had a fairly large-scale, clear plot of the fighter's position relative to the center line of the runway. Since our long-range search radar was not designed for this kind of use, there was a permissible error of several hundred feet in depicted position, but a good controller with practice could usually make his own luck and put a competent pilot in position to glimpse the runway and threshold environment, take over visually, and land if he had any kind of ceiling at all. The first part of the procedure was fairly relaxed with the necessary course and altitude directions being issued by the controller as needed and "rogered" by the pilot. The object was to get the aircraft to a predetermined final approach fix on the extended center line of the runway about five miles out at an altitude of 2,000 feet above ground level and slowed to initial approach speed. At that point, the controller would tell the pilot to drop his gear and flaps and not to acknowledge further transmissions until calling the runway in sight; recommended altitudes would be furnished each mile on final. The mark of a good controller, apart from knowing what he was doing and keeping his cool under pressure, was to deliver a patter of cogent directions in a monologue, in effect lending a calming and reassuring psychological backup to the pilot. We all had our personal styles of doing this and were recognized by many of the individual pilots flying out of K-3. Some of us, known mostly by our voices, mannerisms, and controller numbers, had a reputation for dependable service. On this occasion, the pilot told me that he had the runway and went off the air. K-3 tower told us he had landed safely, which we all thought ended the incident; however, about forty-five minutes later, the pilot rang up on the land line to thank me personally, saying that I had saved his bacon and that the reason he had abruptly gone off the radio was that the jet had flamed out on rollout and had to be towed off the runway. Pilots normally didn't talk to us like this, usually taking our work for granted, so this made me feel good. I told him he had done an outstanding job and wished him further success in getting outside a few jars of Scotch at the MAG-33 "O" Club where he was headed.

MACS-3 WAS A HAPPY unit with a good feel to it. The setting was picturesque and pretty, perched on a long, narrow headland. Our squadron had the area to itself and was a self-contained little community. Wired in with water on three sides, we felt fairly secure. The buildings were Butler and Quonset huts, and we had the usual parade field, motor park, and mobile radar and communications vans dispersed around the site. There were sandbagged slit trenches adjacent to all the facilities. Everything was neat and clean with walks laid out and bordered with whitewashed stones. There were no trees and not much grass. Our area looked something like the set of M.A.S.H., but with buildings instead of tents.

I was assigned a cubicle in one of the Butler huts used for officers' quarters. Seven of us, all controllers, lived in two rooms in one end of the building and shared a head. Colonel Ahee and Major Perrin's quarters were behind a wall at the other end of the hut. We had a nice little club just down the hill from our quarters that overlooked the harbor, as well as a communal mess hall, with one kitchen and separate dining areas for the enlisted men, staff NCOs, and officers. Everybody ate the same chow. The food was adequate but not as well prepared as we had enjoyed at the group mess. The broccoli served once or twice a day often contained large green caterpillars, which could be picked out or eaten depending on one's taste. This led to a lot of speculation as to probable skullduggery in the military procurement system.

We had a little dispensary manned by two navy corpsmen, both first-class petty officers (equivalent to a technical sergeant), who had a daily sick call and tended to inspections of the mess and sanitary facilities. They also had oversight responsibility for a whorehouse operated for the sole benefit of the squadron's enlisted men in the little village near our camp. The girls were strictly forbidden to service any Korean men on pains of having their establishment shut down. They came to the dispensary as a group every Wednesday afternoon just after lunch for a box check and penicillin boosters administered by the corpsmen. At the time, none of us thought much about this as it seemed just a practical Marine Corps way of keeping the troops happy and healthy. It is impossible to imagine something like this in today's political climate.

I was happy in my new slot and threw myself at the work as hard as I could. Instead of reading a lot to make the time pass, I saturated myself with work in operations and as a watch commander and had no trouble catching on to the routine. The operations were similar in many respects to Cherry Point but with more varied and interesting "trade." We did a considerable amount of work with air force fighters, mostly F-86 Sabres, and occasionally controlled various navy airplanes, Republic of Korean (ROK) air force P-51 Mustangs, and airliners operated by Northwest and China Air Transport, a CIA-controlled outfit. The winter weather often got bad in a hurry, which put a premium on our ability to supply dependable and often much-needed service to the lightly equipped tactical aircraft. I also had to pull a 24-hour tour as officer of the day (OD) about once every three weeks, hold periodic rifle inspections of the troops in our section of the squadron, and teach an occasional class on various weapons to some of the enlisted men. All this made the time go by agreeably, and I felt challenged by my various jobs and responsibilities. Everything seemed to run smoothly, and there were no major problems in the squadron, a sure sign of good leadership and administration.

George left for flight training at Pensacola on schedule and made me a present of a nice army windbreaker. I scheduled myself for a heavy load of watches in the radar room every week and was always sure to pull as many as, or more than, any of the other officers, correctly figuring that leading from the front would keep me in good regard with those under me. I also spent all my available daytime hours working in the Operations Office, often eight hours or more, and was commonly on duty for seventy-five or eighty hours during a typical seven-day workweek. Saturdays and Sundays were regular workdays. Every Saturday night we grilled New York strip steaks at our little club and had a party attended by all squadron officers not on duty. We paid for the steaks, which had been flown in from Japan, and I always looked forward to the event.

These happy hours were excellent mixers and gave the colonel and the other field grade officers an opportunity to let their hair down and mix with their juniors on an informal basis, which promoted mutual understanding and trust. In retrospect, I am sure that the Marine Corps had its share of senior officers who were less than desirable, but all the ones that I served with or knew were well deserving of my respect, and I guess I was naive enough to think they were all that way. At my first Saturday night happy hour at our club, I witnessed an interesting verbal interchange between Colonel Ahee and my Yalie friend Don Nelson, a second lieutenant and junior controller in my crew. Seemingly undaunted by the fact that besides holding inferior rank, he was much younger, smaller, uglier, and less experienced and proven than the colonel, Nelson was coming on strong, advancing some inane position in a heated argument they both seemed to enjoy. Colonel Ahee's patience finally ran out, and he cut Nelson off, saying, "Erg, you shut up and listen to me," advice Don had enough sense to abide by. Later, somebody got up enough nerve to ask the colonel what the "Erg" handle meant. Obviously pleased by the question, he explained that an erg was by definition "ten pounds of shit in a five-pound Kraft paper bag." I think they really liked each other, but the name fit Nelson well, and he was known as "the Erg" to the other officers for the rest of his time in the squadron.

McGowin with an aviator.

Major Broker rotated home after his year in Korea a couple of months after I joined. I was told to keep running things as I had been and to be the acting operations officer. I served in this capacity for a couple more months with some success and was conceited enough to believe secretly that I might get to keep the job. This was not to be. It was properly a major's slot, and the group administration was just waiting for the major they, or more likely Colonel Ahee, had chosen to become available. In any event, one day Major Alfred Anton showed up to be my new boss.

We hit it off well from the start. He was Lebanese like Ahee, with dark hair, a swarthy complexion, and a strong build, though he was a bigger man than the colonel. He had flown Corsairs in combat in the Pacific and, I believe, early in the Korean War. I don't think he knew a lot about the technical aspects of our operation except from a pilot's perspective, but he didn't concern himself with the details and let me keep running things about like I had been. He had a good personality and was easy to talk to and a nice guy to work for. Soon after he reported in, I got a call to report to the colonel's office one morning, and I went in with some degree of apprehension, wondering what I might have done to get myself into trouble. I entered in the prescribed formal military manner braced for the worse. Colonel Ahee put me at ease and told me to sit down. In plain language, he told me that he personally appreciated the job I had been doing running Operations and the CIC and that he wanted to thank me for it. I was somewhat taken aback by this as it was highly unusual, at least in my experience, and because of my respect for the tough little colonel, it meant a hell of a lot to me. Soon after this, he finished his tour as CO and was replaced by Lieutenant Colonel MacDanial, a big genial guy with a pleasant, open personality and a fondness for strong drink and hell-raising on R&R, as well as another veteran pilot of the fighting in World War II and Korea.

The controlling was generally routine, but it did have its moments. My crew, officers and enlisted, were excellent and easy to manage. Besides Tony Plattner, Cecil Parker, and Dick Hansen, our other pilot/controller was Don Kelly from Dallas, Texas, fresh out of one of the Panther squadrons at K-3. All of them were superior aviators and took their flying to a serious and professional level, which was commendable and not all that typical of the flyers. We also had Don Nelson, Ed Reardon, and Bob Anastasia working as controllers. All were second lieutenants doing the best they could, but with limited knowledge and experience in the deeper aspects of the controller's art. Sergeant Fernandez ran the enlisted part of the crew, and in the main we got good work out of them with very little trouble.

We had one shit-bird whom I'll call Smith. He was one of "the ten percent who never get the word," the Marine expression covering the small group that always makes 80 percent or more of the trouble in any organization. Nowadays the Corps gets rid of as many of these as possible in boot camp. A further 30 percent or more are identified and given discharges before their first year of service is over through a fairly simple administrative process. In my day, this procedure didn't exist, and every outfit had to carry a few fuck-ups, a bad situation for the unfortunates as well as their units. They were usually foisted off on another unsuspecting unit when the opportunity presented itself, a ploy developed to highly sophisticated levels in corporate America. The really bad ones wound up on the rock pile as brig rats and often went on to get BCDs (bad-conduct discharges), though the percentage was very small.

Smith, a pasty-faced, vacuous-looking young man of average build with a reddish blond crew cut, always presented a scruffy appearance. He had a talent for getting into minor trouble on a continuing basis and had attained his permanent rank of private by the time I knew him. He was in love with one of the girls who worked in the squadron's whorehouse, and they had reportedly married in some sort of gook voodoo rite not recognized by the Corps. One day when I was serving as OD, the sergeant of the guard came to me to report that Smith had just been apprehended sneaking back into the camp from a conjugal visit with his "wife." This was a fairly serious breach of discipline since he was confined to the base at the time as punishment for some minor infraction. I took this under advisement and decided that I had no choice but to enter it in the OD's log book, which would start the ball rolling on a court-martial for Smith. I had just picked up my pen to start making this entry when Master Sergeant Laing presented himself and asked if he could speak with me privately. I had a lot of confidence in him and told him to stand at ease and tell me anything he wanted to. He said that he had heard about Smith's trouble and wished to make a proposal for handling it. As Smith was his man and his responsibility, he asked that I permit him to handle it in his own way. This would, he continued, avert a court-martial conviction and possible brig time for Smith and save the rest of us a hell of a lot of time, trouble, and red tape. I was leery about this and hesitant to give Laing my consent. Appreciating my dilemma, he proposed putting the matter directly and clearly to Smith and letting him decide between having me run him up for a court-martial or taking his punishment directly from his authority figure. I had never come across anything like this before, but I respected Laing's judgment enough to tell him to proceed. He came back later in the day to tell me that the matter was concluded and not to worry about it. I saw Smith the next day, and aside from a few cuts and bruises on his face, he looked all right and seemed cheerful enough. I heard later that he took his whipping from Laing's fists and a belt buckle like a man and was relieved to get out of fairly serious trouble so easily.

I was OD several months later on the day that Smith and a small group of enlisted men were leaving on a 6 × 6 truck to start their long journey back to the States. The girls from the whorehouse were lined up outside the gate to see them off, and I vividly recall Smith's "wife" moaning, crying, and yelling, "Oh, my husband go over sea," between racking sobs. I didn't know whether to laugh or cry.

Operations had responsibility for maintaining the pilots' flight-time records and log books, which were kept in the office. We also had handbooks and test booklets covering the performance and systems of each aircraft type operated by the wing. I found all of these things very interesting and went through all the material systematically. The log books were very informative and gave good insight into who really liked to fly, as represented by the frequency and multitude of types flown by the pilots who were really hot to trot. Don Kelly was obviously such a guy as he was already qualified in most everything we had in Korea, plus some exotic types like the North American FJ (a naval version of the F-86 Sabre). Several of the duller aviators had references to "gear-up" landings in their past, and one lieutenant had gone so far as to cut out the offending entry from his book, fooling nobody in the process.

The prevailing thought at the time was that naval aviators by definition had the training and confidence to tackle a new mount without any more background than reading the book and passing a little oral exam. We gave these, then issued the candidate (who always passed) a signed chit saying in effect that he was "ready" to fly a new type of plane outside of his previous experience. These chits were presented to the Ops people at the outfit who "owned" whichever new plane the aviator planned to have a go in. A qualified pilot or an enlisted crew chief would show him the switches and starting procedure, and off he would go. This rather casual system had its beginnings in the days of simple biplanes and worked surprisingly well most of the time. As the equipment grew more sophisticated, it tended to produce an increasing number of destructive and often fatal consequences until the NATOPS standardized flight manuals and put into place a much more rigorous training and qualification system.

I recall one instance when a captain attached to the wing in a staff job came to grief in the course of his first takeoff in an AD Skyraider. He had previously flown jets and probably believed the myth about their being the exclusive province of the hot sticks. For whatever reason, he did not take the mighty "Spad" seriously. Obviously suffering from overconfidence, he lacked preparation and didn't understand what to do—and, more importantly, what not to do—in it. The AD's engine put out 2,700 hp. That much raw power in a prop airplane produces considerable torque, or "P factor," which, when suddenly applied on takeoff, pulls the plane to the left. In a balked landing with the plane airborne but slowed up, it can produce a "torque roll" where the airplane rolls left around the prop. In the captain's case, he rolled out and stopped in takeoff position lined up at the end of the single runway and waited for the tower to clear him to go. At this point he neglected to lock the tail wheel. In most of the high-powered aircraft of this and earlier vintage, the tail wheel needed to be locked in fore-and-aft position to help the plane run straight on takeoff and landing; the tail wheel was left unlocked to free-swivel for taxi and parking. Failure to lock the tail wheel for these evolutions was an open invitation for an uncontrolled trip to the weeds unless the operator was lucky, had ideal wind conditions, or was very skillful. This pilot's second error, equally grievous, was to set 5° left rudder trim instead of 5° right, which served to accentuate the plane's propensity to turn to the left instead of canceling out the swing. His third error, which compounded the first two, was to cram in the power when the tower cleared him for take off, instead of running it up to thirty inches manifold pressure (approximately half power) before releasing the brakes and then putting in the remaining power gradually and evenly to produce maximum rudder authority for directional control early in the run. I don't remember what the wind was like that day, but I know from experience in the AD that if he had a strong left cross wind, he would have needed to be alert and timely with his control and brake inputs, even if he had done everything correctly up to that point.

The mighty Skyraider went berserk from the accumulated neglect and abuse and made a 30° left turn on its own, dragging its left wingtip before it got even halfway down the runway. The startled tower crew, sitting in their lofty cab atop spindly steel legs, observed the bellowing aircraft bearing down on the base of the structure and thought it was all over until the plane roared by, trailing a rooster tail of sand and dust, narrowly missing them. It then ran through the parking spot normally occupied by the general's R4D and was still on the ground. A black sergeant who worked at the air freight barn located between Base Ops and the tower looked up at this time to see the approaching monster and reportedly ran through a beaver board wall in his haste to escape, leaving a cutout silhouette like you see in cartoons. The Skyraider then ran through a ditch, across the main road, and through another ditch, shedding parts as it went. It finally came to rest in a twisted heap when the four-bladed prop and the big 18-cylinder engine separated from the plane. The captain then undid his harness and stepped out unhurt, certainly sadder and possibly wiser. I don't know what happened to him as a consequence, but his and similar operating problems with this fine airplane were in my mind and helpful when I finally got to fly it years later.

Another Skyraider episode happened in the fall of 1954, while I was still working in the TACC at K-3. It involved a plane that had been decoyed north of the "no-fly" line near the DMZ's eastern end by a gook radio scam and hosed down with their waiting 37 mm antiaircraft artillery. The pilot coaxed the mortally wounded AD back south of the DMZ and pancaked into a rice paddy when the shot-up engine quit. A survey team led by a Marine colonel was dispatched to the crash scene and arrived at the headquarters of the ROK army unit responsible for the area the next day. After suitable introductions, our colonel and his Korean counterpart exchanged gifts and hospitality, then made their way to the wrecked aircraft where they found an unfortunate soldier guarding it asleep. In an effort to salvage some face, the ROK colonel offered our man the opportunity to shoot the kid, which he politely turned down. According to the story, the colonel then blew the Korean boy's brains out with his own pistol without bothering to wake him up.

Soon after I joined the squadron, Colonel Ahee took a small group of us to a reception at K-3 honoring the main commanders in the wing. I still have a strong memory of shaking hands with Lieutenant Colonel Marion Carl, then the CO of VMC-1, a photoreconnaissance squadron flying unarmed F2H-2P Banshees. I had heard a lot about him and probably talked to him on the radio, but I had never met him. A tall, good-looking, taciturn man who exuded a solemn reserve, he had distinguished himself as one of the Corps' leading aces in the Pacific (18.5 victories) and test pilots (he set world altitude and speed records in the Douglas D-558-1 Skystreak in 1953).

One day in early May, all officers were required to attend an open-air meeting in a secluded part of the squadron area. A Criminal Investigation Division (CID) captain from the wing told us that Colonel Carl had just taken VMJ-1 to Tainan Air Base on Taiwan positioned to fly photo missions over mainland China. We were warned that this operation was extremely delicate and was to be conducted in utmost secrecy; anybody who said anything about it would get into most serious trouble. Between May 5 and June 12, VMJ-1 flew seventy-seven sorties against the Reds, who were bulking up forces to attack the Nationalist-held islands of Quemoy and Matsu in preparation for an amphibious assault on Taiwan. Colonel Carl and his wingman were jumped by Chinese MiG-15s on their first mission, over Fukien Province, flying at an assigned altitude of 40,000 feet. In a display of superior airmanship, he led his flight to a safe escape. He scrounged up four armed Banshees to accompany the toothless photobirds on subsequent missions, usually flying one of the fighters himself. He received his fourteenth Air Medal (citation classified) for this operation and was promoted to full colonel in October 1956, jumping over a good many men who were senior to him on the promotion list. This is yet another example of the kind of high-stakes poker both sides played in the Cold War, which could have resulted in an escalation of hostilities and serious casualties, situations that nobody outside those involved knew about at the time.

I enjoyed knowing Don Kelly, who like me had started flying early and was ferrying Stearmans for a crop duster by the time he was seventeen. He was from Dallas and had gotten some college in Texas before becoming a NAVCAD. He was a purist about flying and loved the whole business, especially the fighters. I kept up with his log book in operations and noticed that he seemed the most eager of all our pilots, flying more different types and accumulating more hours each month than anybody else. He had made himself a volunteer maintenance test pilot and as such made sure that the planes were fixed properly and flew well when they came out of the shops before going back on the line. He took me with him a couple of times in a Beech SNB-5, and I could tell immediately that he was a good stick who knew exactly what he was doing. Once airborne, he would give me the controls, and I savored every minute I got to fly the airplane. We had a good time exploring the south coast, flying over an island reputedly populated by a gang of tough Amazon-type Korean women (we didn't see any) and a ROK air force fighter base southwest of Pusan, where we saw a bunch of North American Mustangs neatly parked on the line.

While making his rounds as OD in the dark of the night, Don and one of the sentries saw a bunch of gooks worming under the wire, cutting their way in. He told the boy to keep them under surveillance while he went for help, but almost as soon as he turned his back, the kid started shooting at them, which started a wild and confused melee. During the subsequent chase, he saw one of the gooks run full bore into the side of a Butler building, whereupon a pursuing Marine clubbed him over the head with his M1, breaking the stock, but the Korean took off running again as if nothing had happened. Three of them were finally clubbed into submission and captured when they got tangled up in the barbed wire at the bottom of the hill below my hut, near our "O" Club. Don marched one of them up to our little brig with his .45 stuck in the gook's mouth for safekeeping, and they were locked up. The next day, a big black CID sergeant and the Korean agent Don had known at the MAG-33 "O" Club, ROK Captain Kim, came out and gave the prisoners the third degree, which caused them to identify the other three who had somehow escaped. They were all deserters from the Korean Marine Corps living off the land and stealing whatever they could. We heard that the others were soon picked up and that the Korean Secret Service man had them all executed within twenty-four hours.

Tony Plattner, another of my pilot/controllers, also loved to fly, and he knew the AD very well. He organized a sort of air show with three of the other lieutenants one Saturday. They showed up around noon over the squadron area in four big, noisy Skyraiders and proceeded to have a spirited, two-on-two, low-level dogfight, what today's fighter pilots call a "fur ball." They got very low and were pulling contrails off the wingtips in the humid, early summer air from heavy G loadings in their spirited maneuvering. The short, wild exhibition was a big hit with everybody, officers and enlisted men alike, and was seen by all of the squadron except those on duty. Everybody had so much fun that Tony decided to put it on again the next Saturday and produced an even wilder, lower show that we all enjoyed hugely. The only trouble was that our group commander and his staff picked that time to visit our squadron, and they witnessed the whole thing. Nobody got into any real trouble, but the colonel told our CO that there had better not be any more such escapades, effectively ending the impromptu shows.

Tony did pull one more deal with an AD that could have gotten him into a little trouble and that worried me a lot at the time. I had the watch one morning when he was flying, and when he checked in on the radio with us after takeoff from K-3, he said he was going to make one very low pass over our area and be gone before anybody got his side number. I went outside into the sunshine to watch him roar past, bank almost vertically just over the ocean, and disappear from sight around the headland to our south just as suddenly as he had arrived. I rushed back in to call him on the radio and congratulate him on a superb buzz job, but he didn't answer. We called him repeatedly on all our radios using all the tactical frequencies with no luck. We were getting worried, thinking he might have had an engine failure when he went around the point or flown too low and hit the water, a fairly common accident. We tried to raise him on guard channel (the emergency frequency, which all pilots were supposed to monitor all the time), and when we got no response, I got really worried. I didn't want to get him into trouble, but I kept thinking that he might be injured and in the water in a wrecked plane, or in his life jacket or raft, in which case, time would be of the essence. I called the squadron that owned the plane, and neither they nor K-3 tower or GCA had heard from him, so I initiated a search-and-rescue operation to look for the downed aircraft. Just as we were getting into high gear, Tony announced his initial approach to the field. He was a free spirit and had turned off all his radios to better enjoy the feeling, a sort of inner peace, that real pilots get sometimes when flying a good airplane on a nice day. I felt very relieved that he was okay but more than a little silly and embarrassed about the commotion I had caused, and I was also afraid that he might get into trouble as a result. When I got off watch, I walked around by myself for about an hour feeling very lonesome and put out. The colonel spoke to me later that afternoon and told me that I had done the right thing. Tony also spoke to me when he got back and apologized for putting me in an awkward position, saying that he appreciated my concern. As it turned out, nothing else happened, no harm was done, and nobody got into any trouble.

By the end of June, the frigid winter was long gone, and I was going home after a year in country on September 1, so I was in an optimistic mood when I boarded an R4D-8 to fly to Japan for my last R&R. I could have gone to Hong Kong, a popular place with a lot of the guys, but it sounded like a tourist trap to me, and I had come to like Japan a lot. I planned my week carefully and made it all the way to Tokyo, where I spent the first couple of days, then caught an express to Kyoto. This was before the high-speed, streamlined "bullet trains," but the railroads were fast, efficient, clean, and heavily used by the population as the principal means of getting from place to place. Even though I spoke no Japanese, there were enough signs and helpful people, including neatly dressed school children and railroad personnel, to make this an easy trip. The Japanese were by nature clean and polite, and having lost the war, they were able to make a rapid and total accommodation to the new order of things and go forward with a positive, constructive attitude. They were almost always pleasant and easy to deal with. I sensed that wearing the uniform of a Marine officer gave me an extra measure of respect and acceptance in their society with its warrior tradition. My service had faced their best troops in such hellholes as Guadalcanal, Tarawa, Peleliu, and Iwo Jima. The fighting was some of the bloodiest of the entire war with neither side asking for, or giving, quarter. There were few prisoners but many dead and wounded on both sides. The Marine Corps had kicked their ass and prevailed in each instance, earning their respect, which was still accorded to people like me.

After an interesting and not unpleasant four-hour ride on the crowded train, we pulled into Kyoto's station in the center of the ancient capital. I caught a cab to the Miyako, my hotel on the eastern side of the city. Built in 1890 on a 16-acre hill, it was a Western-style oasis set in beautiful woods and gardens. This part of Japan has the same climate as Alabama, and the trees and shrubs were very similar. All in all, the Miyako and its environs reminded me of Mountain Brook, the beautiful suburb on the southeast side of Birmingham where my mother's family lived.

The hotel had a sort of faded grandeur and was very smart and first rate in an understated way. It had always been the favored hostelry for crowned heads, diplomats, and high rollers on their grand tour of Japan. I had a simple, pleasant room on the third floor overlooking woods and gardens. After washing up, I went down to the restaurant and got an American-style lunch (club sandwich and a quart of Asahi beer) and made my sightseeing plan.

Kyoto, now a city of over one and a half million, was Japan's capital from 794 to 1868. The influence of Zen Buddhism is felt in the great number and variety of temples, gardens, and plantings, which reflect nature at its grandest. That first afternoon I saw the Nijo Castle near the city center and the Kinkaku-ji, or Gold Pavilion, on the northwest side of town. The latter was just reemerging, after having been torched by a mad monk in 1950. The next day I made a walking tour from the Nanzen-ji Temple (built 1293) with its famous sliding door with a tiger painting on it, on to the Eikando Temple (a.k.a. Zenrin-ji Temple, founded 856) and its beautiful garden. I walked the mile-long Philosopher's Pathway along a canal lined with cherry trees and did some reflecting of my own about my life, my little family, and my future possibilities. I wound up my tour by looking at the Ginkaku-ji, or Silver Pavilion, built by a shogun in 1482 as his retirement villa. This worthy died before the structure could be overlaid with its planned silver plate, leaving the beautiful wood exposed. The interaction of the building with the subtleties of the gardens and their sand, rocks, stunted trees and moss, small pools, and luxuriant bordering shrubs and foliage gave the place a great feel. Kyoto did not give the impression of largeness or hustle and bustle like Tokyo and Osaka, and its beauty made it the most pleasing place I saw in the Orient.

The next day, I took the short train ride to Osaka and caught a flight from Itami to Iwakuni in southwest Honshu, where the First Marine Air Wing maintained its main presence in Japan. I checked into the transient BOQ and ran into several lieutenants from K-3 whom I knew. That night over dinner we decided to visit Hiroshima the following day to view the site of the atomic bomb drop that had precipitated Japan's surrender in 1945.

The next morning we caught a local train for the 25-mile trip northeast along the shoreline of the Inland Sea to Hiroshima. It was a bright, fresh, sunny day, with a brisk wind making small white caps on the blue sea to our right, altogether a cheerful setting. We soon pulled into what had been the large city and disembarked for a walking tour to get a feel for the place. Even with the pretty weather, the mood abruptly turned somber. We obtained directions and walked several miles from the station to the ruin of the Industrial Promotion Hall (Chamber of Commerce) at the edge of the Ota River. This had been the target, or ground zero, for the Enola Gay's bomb that exploded over it in an air burst. There wasn't much to see on the flat plain but freshly paved streets, block after block of cleared rubble in between them, and the hulks of a few large buildings sticking up randomly. We could see the city coming back to life in the distance on the hills overlooking the harbor. Even after ten years, what had been the heart of a large, bustling port remained empty. The few Japanese we saw looked away from us, although one group of tough-looking sailors balled up their fists and glared at us as if spoiling for a fight. We kept on through the empty streets until we reached the target now referred to as the "atomic dome." It was preserved as a monument to the event with the steel structure at the top serving as evidence of what the gutted large building looked like before the blast blew away most of its masonry. We stayed for a few minutes and gave alms to some of the burned beggars sitting around, then silently retraced our footsteps back to the station to catch the first train we could back to Iwakuni. While an extreme illustration of "war is hell," this place in reality was no more awful than the firebombed Japanese cities. I am sure in my own mind that the dramatic destruction at Hiroshima and Nagasaki was needed to make the fanatical Japs lay down their arms to create an instant peace. The bombs saved a million lives, 75 percent or more Japanese, by ending the war.

The air station at Iwakuni had been developed as a major base by the Japanese navy and had a facility to support flying boats in addition to its runways. The Marines had taken over operating the base when they moved in from Itami the year before, and the navy had a detachment operating big Martin P5M Marlin flying boats at the seaplane facility. They were the last of a long line of their waterborne flying machines and somewhat of a rarity even in 1955. The town had a highly developed entertainment district outside the main gate, and that night our little group repaired to one of the gin mills catering to officers to improve our mood. The next morning, somewhat hungover and worse for wear, we were roused out of our racks at 0430 to get early chow at the nearby base mess hall before getting on an R5D for a 0600 departure. The mess was large and stark with bright lights over the steam tables and dining area and spooky darkness elsewhere. We were standing around in the building's large front hall waiting for the chow line to start moving at 0500 when the double doors behind us slammed open, announcing the arrival of the wing brig's population and their attendant chasers. I had seen this platoon-sized group once or twice before on previous visits, but the orchestrated ritual of their entrance and subsequent movements was always worth watching closely. With few exceptions, the inmates were hardcore fuck-ups, generally scruffy nonconformists, usually antisocial personalities sprinkled with a few sociopaths in among the thieves and rebels, who generally had a sloppy and undisciplined appearance in their regular units. The brig had seemingly worked a powerful, in-depth, Parris Island–like transformation on them. They all had tight haircuts and freshly scoured and clean-shaven faces. Their worn and ragged utilities, obviously turn-ins from previous users drawing replacements, were clean and starched, with a large, white "P" stenciled on the front and back of each jacket. They held their heads up and looked straight ahead with wide-open, glazed eyes. They were never at ease or still. They marched in using a peculiar lockstep, which they maintained when the group halted, like a bunch of mechanical monkeys dancing in sync. The chasers—squared away, tough, and mean looking, like DIs from hell—were armed with twelve-gauge pump shotguns in addition to .45s and billy clubs. They obviously had the presence and means to enforce total and continuous order, discipline, and obedience. Anyone who resisted the brig's ethics and code of conduct was put in the hole (solitary confinement on bread and water) for attitude adjustment.

After a few minutes, the chow line opened, and we all went in ahead of the prisoners. We watched them go through the serving line and sit down for their ten-minute meal like dumbed-down military academy plebes, their every move still part of minutely controlled, mute group action. I have no way of knowing if the brig's methods effected permanent reform in the lives of their charges, but I do know that brig time had a reputation strong enough to make most want to avoid it. As a result, it usually was reserved for those few who were truly incorrigible, and they probably stayed that way in later life.

Back at the squadron, I settled in for my final seven weeks in-country and fine-tuned plans for my trip home. I had been promised air transportation, which had the advantage of being relatively quick and dependable, since junior officers returning to the States had a higher travel priority than was the case outbound. I could have volunteered to come back on a troop ship in charge of a party of enlisted men, but I was afraid I might get rung up in some disciplinary action during the voyage that would delay my release from active duty. I had been negotiating with the Fairmont, one of San Francisco's grand old hotels, for six months to get a confirmed room for my reunion with Rosa. We planned a sort of second honeymoon seeing the sights and living the good life together, while I was being processed off active duty at the navy base on Treasure Island in San Francisco harbor.

My work was routine and held few surprises. I was starting to feel burned-out from the long, irregular hours, uninspired food, too much coffee, too many cigarettes and APCs (the military-issue pain killer, containing aspirin, caffeine, and something starting with a p), and not enough physical exercise. During the summer, the weather was generally good, and there were few problems handling aircraft, altogether a much safer and more forgiving operating climate for tactical aviation than the brutal winter. We were able to run a lot of practice intercepts during daylight hours and some at night, usually at mid-level and high altitudes in clear conditions. There were some interesting aspects to this, the main one being that without radar, the high-speed jets we worked with were essentially blind. Even though the air was crystal clear, we often had to run a friendly day fighter almost up his opponent's tail pipe before our keen-eyed young pilot visually acquired his target and called "tally ho." This is a vision phenomenon that has to do with the human eye's ability to focus when there are no reference points in one's field of vision.

Early one foggy, humid Sunday morning during the 0400–0800 watch, I was faced with the same phantom target phenomenon that I had seen one night the previous year at Cherry Point. Our radar picked up a half dozen targets orbiting in a racetrack pattern about twenty miles offshore, half way between our base and North Korea. Their maneuvering was similar to tactical aircraft in a hold before making their run-in for a raid. We were not getting any hits with the height-finding radar, but it was never as reliable as the search radar depicted on our PPI scopes. It was also not capable of detecting very low-flying aircraft. I immediately thought of the IL-28 jet bombers operated by our adversaries and our almost total vulnerability should they decide to take us out in round one of a renewed conflict. The TACC assigned the plots a raid number and talked to the alert fighters at the strip, telling them to stand by to launch. They also told us that they had neither knowledge of any friendly naval or air activity in that area nor intelligence that the Reds were up to anything. This last didn't really mean much as we never seemed to know anything they did until after the fact, or at least such knowledge never made it down to my level. Over the land line, I told the chief controller at the TACC about my previous experience with ghost targets during a temperature inversion (where the temperature is higher aloft than at the surface). I added that we might well be tracking UFOs and not bandits, and he decided to wait and watch a while longer before committing any sort of response. After ten minutes or so, the targets faded and then disappeared, and we all breathed a sigh of relief when the TACC scrubbed the "raid." This kind of stuff kept us on our toes—our heads telling us not to worry, that it had to be a false alarm, and our guts saying that we might get snuffed by a well-directed bomb on our radar at any moment.

While pleasant, my work in operations was time-consuming. I delegated just about all of the activities outside of running the radar and controlling airplanes to the other lieutenants, who took care of the drilling and other work with our enlisted personnel. When I was OD, I took the morning formation with its color-raising ritual and reading of the plan of the day, court-martial proceedings, and other matters orally published to the troops. I always enjoyed this as well as inspecting them and their weapons, which

I considered good training for handling my self in later life.

I was truly "short" by this time. Fewer and fewer un-crossed-off days were left on the calendar I had made when I arrived the year before. All of a sudden it was time to face life after the Marine Corps with which I had grown quite comfortable. Several of the captains and majors told me that I ought to voluntarily extend my active duty tour. They said that I would certainly make captain at the earliest opportunity and had a shot at going regular. This held no appeal for me. I knew that the air control field, however essential, had zero potential for a career leading to high rank and command. One needed to be an aviator flying tactical aircraft or a grunt to go very far in the Corps, and I was neither. One morning I got a call that the CO wanted to see me in his office. I formally reported to Colonel MacDanial, who, relaxed and friendly, told me to sit down and asked what I planned to do when my tour was over. I told him that since I could not go to flight training, I was determined to get out and make what I could of myself as a civilian. He told me that he would be glad to write me a "to whom it may concern" letter of recommendation. I was taken aback and humbled by this gesture and told him that such a letter would be much appreciated and useful to me. He wrote a nice letter commending my initiative, resolve, responsibility, and ability to deliver dependable, high-quality results, and he said that it had been his pleasure to have me work for him. I appreciated what he did very much.

One day at the end of August, I packed up most of my belongings in two footlockers for their long voyage home. I inventoried and signed off on all the secret and restricted material under my care and turned in my weapon. I said my good-byes to my enlisted and officer friends and stood for several rounds of drinks at the club that night. The next day, I enjoyed the ride down to K-3 sitting in the back of a 6 × 6 with my bags and several enlisted men to be dropped off at Base Ops to get on the big R5D for the first leg home. We flew to Kimpo outside Seoul and then to the naval air station at Atsugi south of Tokyo. I was traveling with several lieutenants, and we went as a group to the big naval base at Yokosuka to check into a BOQ and wait for our flight call stateside. This had been the headquarters of the Imperial Japanese Fleet before and during the war, and it was an imposing place. I bought a nice Rolex watch for just under $100 at the post exchange the next day before getting on a bus for the ride to the flight line at Base Ops at Haneda.

The airport was still small, worn, and ratty looking around the departure area of the little military operations and terminal building. We handed in our orders and looked around before being called to board our flight, a DC-4 (R5D) operated by Overseas National Airways (a supplemental airline that flew troops for a number of years) as a MATS charter. The airplane was clean and fairly comfortable with two abreast seats on each side of the aisle. We retraced our outbound route, with short stops at Wake Island and Honolulu for fuel, servicing, crew changes, and a little food and drink. It was thirty-seven and a half hours of flying over the trackless ocean, plenty of time for me to think about where I had been and what I might do in the future. I had been assured an entry-level job in my family's company back in Alabama, and I wanted to give this a shot and see where it might lead me. Forestry and logging had seemed interesting to me as a schoolboy doing summer work, and I hoped I might find a future there. Also, still extremely interested in anything to do with airplanes, I was strongly motivated to learn more about flying, maybe using the GI Bill to finance training toward the professional ratings—a seemingly daunting task as I had little money and a family to feed, and getting very far along in flying seemed likely to be an impossible dream. When we landed at Travis Air Force Base, our little group took a bus to San Francisco, where we checked into the Marine Memorial Club to soak in a hot tub and crash in a real bed until the next morning.

I had been working for months with the Fairmont Hotel to get a nice room for my reunion with Rosa, who was to arrive that afternoon on a TWA Constellation from Louisville. They could not take us until the next day and arranged for a broom-closet-sized room at a decidedly second-rate hotel for our first night. I moved my stuff to the little hotel and walked out on the busy street to find the downtown airline terminal to get a bus to the airport. I saw an attractive, well-dressed blond walking toward me and tried to ask her for directions, but she just raised her nose a little higher, kept her eyes front and center, and breezed by me. I thought I looked salty and maybe even handsome in my summer Class A uniform, but I got the message that people like me had little status with certain segments of the civilian population. I thought about the signs warning "sailors and dogs" to keep out of the nicer parts of another navy town, Norfolk, Virginia, and figured some of the people in San Francisco must have felt the same way.

The big, beautiful airliner arrived on time, and I spied Rosa walking down the high steps to the ramp in the soft, mid-afternoon, Mediterranean-like sunshine. We were too choked up to say much initially and just kissed and held onto one another for a couple of minutes. We were very happy that the pain of our separation was over. Getting back together after more than a year was a powerful thing for both of us. We got back to the dingy little hotel as quickly as possible and tumbled into bed to play out the old saw about sex being the thing that you can get the most behind in while catching up on the fastest. We were very happy, and our surroundings didn't make any difference. We moved over to the Fairmont the next day and settled into its grand and comfortable ambiance. I had to go out to Treasure Island for a couple of hours every morning for the next three or four days for physical exams and paper work, a new reserve ID card, and other housekeeping affairs before going on thirty days' terminal leave. I was still in good shape, but weighed 165 pounds, twenty less than my normal 185. We had a good lunch together every day and spent the afternoons in bed and sightseeing. I took Rosa up to the Top of the Mark, where I was looking forward to having some drinks in the romantic and famous old bar overlooking San Francisco in all its glory. When we started to go in, the maitre d' blocked our entry and demanded to know in inhospitable terms how old Rosa was. We told him twenty-two, but that wasn't good enough, and he demanded identification that she did not have. Her wallet and driver's license were at the hotel. I showed him my ID card and a picture of our son, Norman, and pointed out that I had been out of the country for a year protecting the likes of him. Marine officers, I added, did not lie, and I really wanted to show off the place to my wife. He answered that he didn't care who I was as the city had a campaign to punish establishments serving underage drinkers, and he became progressively more unpleasant and rude. I was getting close to decking him when Rosa told me that we were leaving and that she did not want to spend any more time in the place.

A couple of days later, I was glad to leave the land of fruits and nuts. At the Oakland railroad terminal, we boarded the *California Zephyr*, a crack streamlined train with Vista Dome club cars and settled into the comfort of a Pullman compartment. We enjoyed the 50-hour, 2,400-mile trip through the Sierras, the Rockies, and the Midwest Corn Belt on the way to Chicago, the first leg home to Kentucky and Alabama where a new chapter in our lives was waiting.

Part III

The Company

A pilot must have a memory developed to absolute perfection. But there are two higher qualities which he also must have. He must have good and quick judgment and decision, and a cool, calm courage that no peril can shake.

— Mark Twain, speaking about
Mississippi River pilots

Chapman Mill.

7

The Strike

After a weekend with Rosa's parents in Lexington, Kentucky, we loaded Norman, then a big, strong, 16-month-old boy, and Friedl, his miniature dachshund companion and protector, into our Chevrolet sedan and motored down the winding roads to Chapman. As my plan to land a seat on a major airline as a professional pilot just as the jet age was dawning had died with my inability to get military flight training, and as I was attached to my family and our little town of Chapman, I decided to take an entry-level job in the company to see where I could go as a fourth-generation lumberman. We arrived home in the latter days of September 1955 and settled into an apartment on the second floor of the old Will McGowin house, two doors up the street from where I was raised.

My first job was in the Sales Department, where I clerked for Gene Jackson, the sales manager, maintaining a running inventory of stock on hand for him and acting as his go-between and gofer with the mills and Shipping Department. I got to talk to customers a little when he was away and found the job an excellent way to begin learning the business seriously.

Chapman had changed a lot since the last time I had been home—not least because officials of the International Woodworkers of America, CIO, had called a vicious strike against W. T. Smith on July 20, and the plants and logging operations had been down cold since that date. While strong in the forest industries in the Pacific Northwest, before 1945 the unions hadn't had much of a toehold in the South. Immediately following World War II, however, they made a determined effort to organize the region's sawmill companies, generally unsuccessfully. Because the industry was very fragmented, with most of the mills being small and nondescript, they concentrated on the larger, more stable and profitable ones, successfully getting contracts at three or four in Alabama, including W. T. Smith.

The brothers didn't like what the unions represented or having to deal with them, but they were as always at pains to obey the letter of the law. The other organized lumber companies were more practical minded and were successful in getting rid of their locals in short order using whatever means it took. Bill Harrigan at Scotch, always an extremely bright man in my view, had the classiest exercise in this regard, which worked as follows. The union always negotiated the dues-checkoff provision into their contracts (union dues were deducted from the members' paychecks by the company), which Bill perceived as their Achilles' heel from the beginning. A shrewd judge of character, he made an initial, ultimately correct assessment of the union's business agent. He turned the dues collected under the checkoff over to the agent in cash, small bills only, nothing larger than a twenty. Scotch was a large operation, employing hundreds of workers, so the dues amounted to a considerable amount of money. Predictably, the temptation proved too much for the agent, who had probably fiddled with the money from the beginning. After some period had elapsed, he disappeared with a suitcase full of cash, breaking the local at Scotch, which was ultimately decertified.

The union at the company never amounted to anything but a beachhead in Alabama for the International in Portland, Oregon, exhibiting its reach and power and acting as a source of income. The decisions influencing the locals' conduct were made from on high with little input from the workers in Chapman and Greenville, half of whom were black. As segregation was the law in the South at the time, the colored members found themselves in a somewhat delicate position, caught between the International's promised brotherhood of labor but working every day alongside their redneck associates, whose ingrained attitudes precluded much fraternizing. The local union leaders at W. T. Smith tended to be bigmouthed whites who resented their social position. One of the main ones in Chapman was Charlie Cooper, a middle-aged man with his own little place east of Mill Hill, who had done time in the state pen on a bootlegging charge. The company had made the mistake of giving him his job back when he got out, and I had him arrested again a few years later after I caught him red-handed setting the company woods on fire just north of Chapman. That was the sort of union man the company was expected to deal with.

The company had a history of treating its employees well, providing wages and benefits as good as any in the industry in Alabama and better than those in 90 percent of the mills. I believe this would have been true even if the union had never been there. The lumber industry then was very competitive and labor intensive, but not extremely profitable, so wages and benefits were materially lower than is now the case. Fair and decent treatment and job security, along with freedom from race baiting in the work place, were prized job values that had always been in place at W. T. Smith.

During its ten years at the company, the union had not been much of a problem, except for a nine-week strike in the fall of 1949, which began shortly after I matriculated at Yale, so I have no first hand knowledge of it. While shorter and much milder than the 1955 work stoppage, union thugs did bomb the home of one aged black man who decided to break the strike. Although he wasn't hurt, the action presaged later events.

By the time the union contract expired in 1955, W. T. Smith was the only unionized lumber company in Alabama. The brothers had never liked dealing with the unions and tired of this lonesome, suckerlike status, they resolved to end it once and for all. As they were above employing any underhanded or illegal means, they decided on a simple strategy that they knew would ultimately work. Accordingly, when the talks opened to renegotiate the contract, they stated up front that while prepared to bargain over issues involving wages, benefits, and other matters of concern to the hourly employees, the company would not agree to a continuation of the dues-checkoff provision. Progress was made on most of the issues, but the International's officials and agents finally got it that the company would not back down from its position on the dues collection. Knowing that many of the rank and file workers had little or no interest or faith in the union and trusted the McGowins over it, the union officials figured a switch to voluntary dues payments would lead to the end of their last presence in the Alabama lumber industry. Workers arriving at the plants on the morning of July 20, 1955, were met by sound trucks blaring out the news that they were on strike and should report to the union hall immediately. A few of the white workers and all but one of the supervisors came in to work, but production was shutdown for three months.

As CHAPMAN WAS AN incorporated town, the streets were public roads, with striking, nonstriking, and management employees living hard by each other. The union set up picket stations at both entrances to Chapman on Highway 31 and in front of the depot, as well as at picket stations at the entrance to the Greenville mill. They ran picket lines in front of the office and the main elements of the plant, as well as along the roadside in the woods where the logging equipment sat unused. As Chapman alone had several hundred idle union workers, the pickets made more than a token presence. Most of the picketers carried "walking sticks" that were actually stout cudgels, but this turned out to be only for show. The union did commit a great deal of dangerous violence during the course of the strike, featuring arson, bombings, shootings, and assaults, among other mischief and sabotage, but this was all conducted under cover of night, some of the worst incidents committed by professional goons brought in from Mississippi and Oklahoma for this express purpose.

My father, Earl, and Julian and occasionally Nick, the lawyer brother from Mobile, were almost totally engaged in facing the strike, a volatile situation presenting grave physical danger for a lot of people and also very costly in terms of nonproductive expenditures and lost business. Since we weren't manufacturing, our sales and shipping activities didn't amount to much during my first couple of weeks on the job, and I was handed the additional duty of acting as a security officer for the balance of the strike, a job I shared with Elisha Poole, recently an agent with the U.S. Air Force Office of Special Investigations and experienced in criminal investigations. At twenty-seven, Elisha had grown adept at dealing with tough situations and bad people and was not one to back down when the going got tough.

The union's signature weapon was dynamite. The first blast was heard in Chapman on June 21, the day after the strike started, and bombings continued for the next four days. The last two targeted the homes of Foster Owens and Grady Aplin. Owens, an hourly employee, took his family and moved away from Chapman. Grady Aplin, the plant superintendent, stayed the course in his well-built new house, which was only lightly damaged. The dynamiting continued with regularity for about nine months and occurred in several surrounding counties at the homes of some of our new employees after the plants reopened as the union pulled out all the stops to intimidate the scabs. In the first year, there were forty-two blasts, one of which seriously injured several employees and hospitalized eleven. This self-defeating strategy served only to stiffen the resolve of all of us who were working, young and old alike, and put public opinion solidly behind us—at least in the minds of most responsible people who knew anything about what was going on.

We were also fortunate in that all of the public officials and law-enforcement officers involved, as well as our own attorneys and advisors, were talented people dedicated to doing the best job possible. From the public-sector people we wanted only honest, impartial application of the law, and as far as I know, that is exactly what they delivered. It may sound too good to be true, but all of these people displayed conspicuous guts and character, and in this they resembled characters in a movie portraying rural Southern good guys matched against—and eventually besting—some really mean, dangerous, and unscrupulous low-class adversaries.

Werth Thomas was the sheriff. Fifty-eight years old, tall, lean, and handsome, he wore glasses and a nickel-plated Colt Model M1911A1 automatic. He was a kindly, good man who carried himself with dignity and was easily approached by all people of good will. Henry Stanford, the chief deputy (later sheriff), had an imposing physical presence, being tall and very strong. He and Sheriff Thomas were absolutely fearless and honest, and I saw these qualities displayed firsthand on several occasions.

The circuit judge was Werth Thagard, a small, wiry, white-haired man. Handsome with piercing eyes, he had courage, a keen intellect, and great respect for the law. Joe Kettler, from Luverne in Crenshaw County, was a dedicated and competent circuit solicitor. Paul Hartley, the Butler County district attorney, was sort of a brilliant screwball, unconventional but very smart. When heavily engaged in thought he would take out his false teeth and suck his gums, which was disconcerting to those with him. On occasion I saw him come up with detective deductions worthy of Sherlock Holmes after such deliberations.

Willis Darby was the government man in charge of Mobile's National Labor Relations Board office that had jurisdiction over the strike and a reputation for being left-leaning and pro-union, but Mr. Darby conducted his hearings and made his decisions based on his strict, impartial review of the facts, evidence, and law. Our expert advisors were very respectful of him.

Elisha Poole and his father, Calvin, were our local attorneys, and they spent a lot of time on the strike. Mr. Calvin Poole, then sixty-three, was a wise man and extremely adept country lawyer. He looked and was tough, but underneath he was a good man with a highly developed, dry sense of humor. Mr. Calvin had always negotiated with the union as the company's spokesman but requested expert help when the company told him, going into the bargaining, that there would be no continuation of the checkoff. John Curran, a well-respected labor consultant from New Orleans, was retained to work with Mr. Calvin. At about six foot three and close to 300 pounds, he was an imposing man, and we called him "Oodles" after the large *Dick Tracy* character by that name. He was also very knowledgeable and tough, with massive experience dealing with unions, and projected competence and power. John looked people straight in the eye with an unsmiling poker face and tended to turn purple and wheeze when he got worked up, whether for real or on purpose to get his adversary's attention. Helen Humphry, a labor lawyer from Washington, D.C.—attractive in her way, tough and somewhat mannish, and extremely intelligent and effective—became a key member of our team a little later after the violence escalated.

THE LONG AND TORTUROUS strike was an intense experience for me. A picket station was manned twenty-four hours a day just across the street from our apartment, in plain view from our front windows. The pickets were in a position to observe all our comings and goings but never caused us any harm, although Rosa got a couple of anonymous phone calls alleging that "Little Mr. Floyd" was diddling one or more of the young women who worked in the office. Though I wasn't in any more danger than a lot of our people, I did pass several character-building gut checks to my own satisfaction. I also carried a concealed .38 Detective Special snub-nosed revolver for two and a half years, but never had to use it. We had multiple physical injuries on our side, some very serious and permanent, and it was a miracle that nobody was killed. The strikers had zero casualties although several of them, along with their hired goons, were convicted and sentenced to jail time.

Two and a half months into the strike, on the night of October 7, I went to my parents' house on the Edgefield property for dinner, along with my brother Greeley. My uncle Nick was spending the night there along with his client Zack Brooks, a successful oil operator (independent driller) bringing in oil wells in the developing Citronelle Field north of Mobile. Over cocktails before dinner, we mostly talked about how bad the situation had gotten with the union's threats and violence. Mr. Brooks, a tough old man in his sixties who had earned his spurs as a roughneck in the Texas oil fields, was brash, outspoken, and full of ego and self-confidence. I think he sized us up as a group of overeducated candy asses and proceeded to lecture us on how we didn't know what tough really was. He dominated the conversation throughout the meal with tales of the fights he had endured and won in the great state of Texas, and we all shut up and let him run on. After dinner, we went back into the living room for coffee, which was in a large silver pot sitting on a tray on the low coffee table in front of the sofa. As my mother reached for the pot to start pouring, a violent explosion jolted the house, causing the empty little demitasse cups to jump up and clatter down on their fragile saucers. It was immediately evident that no real harm had been done as the large bomb had exploded near the outer reaches of the driveway, well away from the house, evidently just a psychological weapon. The most striking effect was on Mr. Brooks, who said only a few quiet words the rest of the evening.

Three days later on October 10, more than 150 pickets armed with sticks massed near the center of town for about three hours. I don't recall that we ever knew the reason why—perhaps it was just a show of force to demonstrate the union's resolve, or maybe they thought we planned to start up some operations. In any event, they constituted an ugly-looking mob. As a result of this and the many bombings, assaults, arsons, and drive-by shootings, it was decided to supplement Chapman's one man police force (Elbert Newton, who also supervised the town's cleanup and grounds maintenance crew) with officers brought in for the duration of the emergency. John Curran put Elisha Poole and me onto some rent-a-cops in Pritchard, a tough suburb of Mobile, and six of them were sworn in as town cops and Butler County deputies to deal with strike-related matters.

As we had a good-sized log inventory on the yard at Chapman that was close to spoiling, we made plans to sell it. I talked to Hubert Browder at Bradleyton, thirty miles northeast of Chapman, where he had a veneer mill. I sold him the soft hardwood log inventory, about ten truck loads, warning him that he would have to pass a picket station and penetrate a picket line to get to the logs. It would not be a Sunday school picnic. I told him I would meet him and provide what help I could but that I could not guarantee safe passage.

Hubert stood about five foot ten with broad shoulders and no neck or hips; he probably weighed 220 and looked like an all-American guard on a big-time football team. About thirty-five, he was a veteran of heavy infantry fighting in North Africa, with bright eyes, rosy cheeks, and a mouth full of white teeth. He always wore a slouch hat and clean, neat khaki shirts and trousers and drove a sporty Ford coupe with a loaded M1 carbine at hand on the seat by him. Hubert let me know right quick that he could take care of himself and that he would arrive ahead of his trucks on October 24 at about 8 A.M. I met him on the way into town and told him exactly where to go. A little while later, I watched him ease up to the picket line at the entrance of the log yard, where he stopped his car and got out. In addition to his physical presence, Hubert had a nickel-plated .44 Magnum revolver stuck in his belt. He walked right up to the dozen or so slovenly pickets and told them firmly and politely that he was Hubert Browder from Bradleyton, a peaceful man, who had come to get the logs he had bought and that he would tolerate no interference. He added that he would personally shoot any son of a bitch who laid a finger on one of his little niggers. The pickets just kept shuffling along, looking at the ground. Hubert turned around, got back in his car, and led his log trucks through the line onto the yard. He left after a while, telling his drivers to proceed back home individually as they got loaded. All went well until the last load of the day, which several car loads of strikers ambushed on Highway 31 just north of Edgefield. They ran the truck off the road onto the shoulder, where the terrified driver made his escape on foot by running into the woods, not to emerge until he got almost to Greenville. The pissed-off strikers, enraged by Hubert's one-upmanship earlier in the day, were armed with ball bats, axes, and clubs.

They knocked out the truck's headlights, windshield, and windows and put as many dents into it as possible in a minute or two, apparently to show Browder what big men they were.

The company also made deals with Dick Bennett and the Rainey brothers, sawmill owners in Greenville, and with Grover Little from Andalusia to buy our substantial pine log inventory. We made these arrangements as secretly as possible as it was to everyone's advantage to keep the deal quiet. With so many people involved though, we were very fearful that the union might have gotten wind of our plans.

Each of the buyers was to use three log trucks to haul their logs away from Chapman, always in company with other trucks and an escort. The logs were already cut into sawmill lengths, and the loads ran about twelve tons aboard short single-axle pole trailers. In view of Hubert Browder's experience, we planned to make a considerable show of force in an effort to avoid any violence. We met very early, about 4:30 on the morning of November 3, at the Raineys' sawmill on the east side of Greenville. It was still, cold, and clear, with a sky full of bright stars, and I was glad I had on a good sweater and a navy goatskin flying jacket with a fur collar. Somebody had the foresight to build a huge bonfire out of sawmill cutoffs, and the twenty-five or thirty of us formed around it. Each of the nine trucks had a man riding shotgun with the driver, and we had lined up escort cars to be positioned at the front, middle, and rear of the convoy. Mr. Calvin Poole briefed us. He had seen combat in France in World War I as a 24-year-old infantry captain and spoke clearly and unequivocally, his face lit by the roaring fire. Like any good leader, he knew that men always behave best when they know what is expected of them. He explained the simple rules of engagement: we were not to stop for anything on our way into Chapman and the mill, we were not to say anything to pickets or other union people, and we were to maintain the integrity of the convoy at all costs. His parting words were, "Boys, don't shoot anybody unless you have to." I got into the lead car, Bob Aplin's company green Ford sedan, along with Joe Norman, a tough, intelligent guy, strong of body and will, who'd been a 17-year-old seaman on a jeep carrier in the Atlantic fighting U-boats during the war. I carried my Smith & Wesson .38 Combat Masterpiece revolver, which I'd had in Korea as a supplemental sidearm, as well as my little Colt belly gun. We didn't talk much on the way to Chapman. We didn't know what we might get into, and I suspect most of us felt a healthy amount of anxiety. We were all absolutely committed to what we were doing, and nobody wanted to look bad or let the others down. I said a silent prayer as we came down Highway 31 in front of Edgefield in the dawn's early light, primed for what we might see when we topped the hill in front of Julian's house to go down the slight grade before turning off to the right where the pickets had a station at the north entrance to Chapman. I saw immediately that they were in their normal mode, just four or five of them sitting around a camp fire in the road median. We felt good seeing this, and a couple of minutes later, we penetrated the picket line at the log yard with no difficulty; the strikers on duty just turned their backs and kept pacing. This exercise lasted a full workweek, and we got all the logs out without a hitch. We met at the Rainbow Café in downtown Greenville when it opened at five each morning for the rest of the week and enjoyed a warm camaraderie over breakfast.

On November 10, the Greenville plant that Greeley managed reopened. Notices in the local papers and broadcast over the radio stated that all employees were entitled to their old jobs and to all the rights they had enjoyed before the strike, provided that they had been guilty of no misconduct during the strike and had not been permanently replaced in their jobs by new employees. On November 17, the Chapman plant reopened with the same notices. As the area economy was poor, there was no shortage of applicants willing to cross picket lines to get permanent jobs. Many of them didn't work out or quit on their own, and there was a high turnover for a while until things settled down. The workforce demographics had also changed, being now 100 percent white and comprising mostly young men as the blacks were too afraid to cross picket lines run by whites.

We had good intelligence by then as to the union's intentions and learned that they intended to deploy mass pickets on the day the mill reopened, hoping to scare away returning employees and scabs through a show of force. Helen Humphry and John Curran told us that strikers on picket lines most feared cameras, which they said were much more useful and safer than guns. Someone suggested that we contact WSFA. Known as the "poor folks' channel," this was the only Montgomery station powerful enough to be picked up clearly by the rabbit ears most people in the area had. On Friday, November 14, I called the news anchor, Frank McGee (later the award-winning anchor for NBC's Today Show), apprised him of the anticipated situation, and asked if he might like to cover it. Frank thanked me for the information and said he would have a crew on hand. At the beginning of the workday on Monday, a large white van marked prominently with WSFA signs was parked near the entrance to the planing mill, and a couple of cameras were rolling. The several dozen pickets there knew they had best behave, and we got through the startup without incident. I called Frank twice more in the next few weeks, and he responded with a news crew each time, a totally legitimate response for him as a responsible newsman, but one that helped us a great deal.

To inhibit bad behavior on the part of the union, we used another psychological weapon that was fun and interesting, although of questionable effectiveness. Some of our cops highly recommended a team comprising a retired lawman and his partner, a talented tracking dog. They lived in southern Mississippi and did freelance work locating escapees from jails and prisons and hunting missing persons. I contacted Mr. New, and we agreed that he would begin with a trial engagement of a week to ten days. Our people believed that the strikers, especially the black ones, would fear the dog and ascribe magical powers to his ability to track people who had been present at a crime scene. I arranged for them to stay at the Rocky Creek Inn and went to visit when they arrived. I knocked on the door and was invited in. Mr. New, a tall thin man of about seventy with erect posture, snow-white hair, and a large mustache, was sitting in a rocking chair with a very large black-and-tan bloodhound lying by his right side on the floor. Both looked at me alertly, and Mr. New stood up. Already dressed in our uniform of gray cotton shirt and trousers and wearing a western-looking black-string tie and a black Stetson hat, he looked exactly like the caricatures one sees nowadays of old Confederate colonels. After we shook hands and had a short talk covering his job and rules of engagement, he looked down at his mate and said, "Rube, meet a friend." The dog stood up without hesitation and stuck out his right paw to shake hands with me. Standing about twenty-seven inches tall and weighing about 110 pounds, he looked very dignified, intelligent, and controlled with a solemn, wise face on a large head. He and his boss made regular rounds in the plant area in full view of the pickets, and we hoped that they were suitably impressed.

The union stepped up the dynamiting over the month after the Chapman plant reopened, with a dozen or more blasts resulting in considerable damage to employees' residences and outbuildings across the area. Though ostensibly conducted to discourage employees, particularly the hated scabs, from coming in, I suspect these blasts stemmed partly from frustration as the union was pretty much beaten at this point. My father had already written to the International's Southern director to announce that the Chapman and Greenville mills had resumed operation, most of the jobs had been permanently filled, and not wishing "to impose on its employees bargaining representatives they had not selected," the Company would no longer recognize the union's Chapman and Greenville chapters. Still, the union did not concede defeat, and the worst violence was yet to come.

At that time, much of our output was shipped by rail. The company operated a diesel-electric switch engine over an extensive internal rail system. The little engine would pick up empties dropped by the L&N local freight from the side track next to the main line between the town and Williams Crossing and deliver them to the pulpwood and pole yards, the chip-loading facility, and the dock near the planer mill where lumber and timbers were loaded. Often as many as twenty to thirty cars were loaded each day, and the mill could not operate without a switch every day. Recognizing the importance of the rail movements, the union did all it could to impede them, tampering with switches on both the L&N and company tracks and derailing cars on two occasions. Many of the loaded cars were left in dark, remote areas, surrounded by woods, and the air brake hoses on some were cut almost every night, meaning that the brakes locked up, and the car could not be moved until a new hose was installed. The union also stationed pickets at the yard limits on the main line, which the train crews, rabid unionists almost to a man, honored. The pickets would stop the train, and the crew (engineer, fireman, brakeman, and conductor) would get off to socialize with the pickets or lie down in the shade of the trees near the track. The railroad had to send a couple of station wagons loaded with supervisors, detectives, and occasionally executives, along with a large quantity of air brake hoses, to Chapman to meet the local, install new hoses where needed, and do the switching. The railroad men came from Montgomery and Mobile on alternate days and wore their normal attire of business suits and hats while doing this work. I saw them on a daily basis, and we developed a pleasant relationship, often eating lunch together at the hotel. Once I asked how and where they recruited supervisors, thinking that their workforce must be so poisoned by union hatreds as to be off limits as a source. They told me that the best talent they had came from ex-union officers, men with talent, brains, and imagination who had gravitated to the union posts as a way of exercising their attributes and who craved responsibility and an opportunity to make decisions and earn respect. This interesting revelation taught me a lesson in human behavior.

I have a strong recollection of the above events, which were among the scariest of the strike for me. On the several occasions when massed pickets formed to interfere with the switching, we had Sheriff Thomas and Chief Deputy Stanford on hand to keep order and allow us to exercise our lawful rights. The union's action clearly violated the Interstate Commerce Act, thus federal law, but we never could get the FBI to lift a finger to help. I would accompany the law officers, and we would have to walk through the mob to get to the engine on the track. I always just looked through the strikers, keeping a straight face and saying nothing to them. They were riled up, and the situation could become uncontrollable if something happened to touch off a riot. Civil wars, family disagreements, and strikes bring out some of the most intensely hostile feelings most people are capable of, and there were plenty of such feelings in Chapman at that time, often between people who had known each other for years and were in some cases related. I saw Earl Skipper, a friend from my grade at the little Chapman school, lie down across the track in front of the engine one day, determined to stop it. I had always liked Earl, who was rough but intelligent, outspoken, and determined, with tobacco juice usually running down his chin, and everybody held his breath, waiting to see what would happen next. Not intimidated by Earl's bluff, the supervisor at the controls revved the big GM engine and started it moving slowly forward. Earl's nerve broke when the engine was about two feet from him, and he scampered off the track like a squirrel running from a dog. Everybody breathed a sigh of relief as the situation was defused.

We had a good Christmas not withstanding the almost constant reminders of the strike around us. The pickets, huddling around their little fire in front of our apartment, looked forlorn, uncomfortable, cold, and poor. They were mostly pawns in the International's bigger game, holding out hope that the union's empty promises would make it all worthwhile. I felt sorry for their families but not for them.

Six dynamite blasts during the week of Christmas resulted in no injuries and only minor property damage. One of the bombings was at the home of the Reverend J. N. White, president of the Chapman local, and knocked out some of his windows. As far as I know this was the only case of damage to a union member's property, and the perpetrator was never apprehended. He might well have been someone on our side who wanted to mix some "eye for an eye" with the Christmas cheer he was imbibing, or perhaps the preacher or some of his agents sought to gain sympathy for their side at our expense. Nobody paid much attention to the incident as the militant Holiness preacher had few friends by that time among the law-abiding citizens of the community.

The most serious instance of violence in the strike occurred soon after the new year on January 9, when a dynamite blast injured eleven employees. I got to the scene a few minutes after the bomb exploded. The powerful charge had been placed inside a steel drum used by the workers at the planing mill as a make-shift stove. Its fuse had been ignited by the roaring fire the workers lit to warm by for a few minutes before clocking in, as was their custom every day in the winter. The blast "fragged" the 55-gallon oil drum, turning it instantly into thousands of pieces of red-hot, jagged shrapnel, which mowed down the eleven men closest to the fire and scared numerous others out of their wits. All that was left was a smoking hole ringed with debris over a wide field. The wounded had been moved to the paved area in front of the planing mill and were lying on coats and blankets, still in shock, among large puddles of blood. The worst injured were Ephrum Atkins, a middle-aged, grey-haired man, and Marion F. McCormick, a younger man. One side of Atkins's face, including an eye, was blown away. McCormick had been partially eviscerated, his abdominal cavity laid open and impregnated with scraps of his several layers of clothing. The blood had its own odor, and you could also smell the fear and anger in the large crowd of loyal company people who had assembled waiting for medical help and transport for the wounded. My father and his brothers soon arrived with disbelief, worry, and frustration etched on their faces. People and experiences I had known in the Marine Corps helped me in all that went on during the strike, but nothing in my past held a candle to the horror of this situation, which I saw up close and personal. The crime was never officially solved, but I have reason to believe that responsibility lay with a pair of professional goons, Claud Hill and Stuart O'Bannion. Both had violent records and were operating in the vicinity of Chapman at the time of the blast as paid agents of the union. While we never were able to bust them, they were hardened bad guys, probably sociopaths, and certainly the most dangerous men we were up against.

DESPITE ALL OF THE strike happenings, Rosa and I enjoyed being back at home. I was interested in cars and had always wanted to own one like my father's before and during the war. I ordered a '56 Buick Special from Brunson Kierce, the dealer in Greenville, and got it just before Christmas. It was a handsome, powerful car, made to my specifications, shiny black with custom red seat covers. Rosa and I took pride in and enjoyed it, but the family criticized us for the purchase, mostly behind our backs. They considered the car ostentatious and inappropriate for young people like us to own before we had earned a lot of money.

We also desperately wanted a house of our own and thought a lot about how to get one on our limited income. Greeley lived in one of the small frame houses next to the old dairy, which had been remodeled into a basic, but attractive, little place. It was next door to the dairy building, which had been made into a rambling, comfortable residence for Jack Hopkins, who ran the Retail Yard Division. Greeley thought he knew a lot about house building and financing, and Jack really did. They conceived the idea of W. T. Smith's creating a small subdivision in the woods east of Highway

31 for company management and supervisory personnel. Greeley and I were both extremely dedicated to W. T. Smith and thought that having a nice housing area close to the mill for key people would be good for morale and team building. We determined to build the first two houses there on adjacent lots if we could line up financing. When the idea was approved a bit later, a street was paved through the stand of mature pines covering the lots, and a Montgomery architect who did work for the Retail Yard Division customized existing plans. Greeley and I indeed bought the first two lots, side by side, each just under an acre in size.

In February, Grady Aplin, the Chapman plant superintendent, had a bad heart attack, which put him out of action for an indeterminate period. Greeley was immediately assigned to take over his responsibilities, and I became the new manager of the Greenville plant in addition to my responsibilities with security. I was given a well-worn, aged pickup to drive and raised to $85 per week, all of which pleased and excited me. I knew very little about the job I was taking over, and once I went to it, I would be totally on my own. Both Julian and Greeley had cut their management teeth in this position before me, so I knew I was following something of a tradition.

The plant supervisors saw to it that I learned the business properly and didn't make any bad mistakes. They were a good crew and were all nice to me. Roy Dunn and Bobby Branum ran the office, and Frank Parmer, Curtis Sexton, and Roy Callins were the principal supervisors. Ralph Perdue, who had previously lost a hand and forearm in an accident, checked the green lumber in, Irby Owens ran the planing machine, and over the next year, Parmer Chetham taught me how to grade the lumber. Mr. Irby Hinson was a company land and timber buyer who answered to Julian. A feisty little man then seventy-five or older, with eyes that sparkled behind wire-rimmed glasses, he stood about five foot six and weighed about 120 pounds. He offset his small stature with tough talk and a well-developed little man's complex. He always wore a hat and several cardigan sweaters, one on top of the other, and had a dip or a chew going. I had known and liked him since I was a kid, and he joined in with the others as a tutor. I think they all informally took on the task of turning another young McGowin into a competent manager and took pleasure in feeding me the true gen. For my part, I had enough sense to look, learn, and listen before making any changes, something I had been taught at The Basic School at Quantico.

I enjoyed the year or so I spent running the Greenville operation; it was a valuable experience full of self-discovery. My job was to buy the raw material, logs and rough green lumber, competitively and effectively so that we never ran out. I supervised the operation, mainly by informing the foremen of our current objective and letting them achieve it. I was responsible for over a hundred men and was attentive to their well-being, safety, and morale. I interfaced with the big Chapman sales and accounting departments, working with Gene Jackson and Melvin Brown daily to produce their orders on a timely basis and to a high quality standard, and we had no complaints on the products we shipped. The lumber had to be properly kiln dried, manufactured, and graded and packaged. My personality is about quality work, and I was always careful to see that the customer got a little better material than the bare specs called for. Back then half to three-quarters of our production was shipped by rail, and I ordered the cars and arranged for trucking the balance.

I found very quickly that I thrived on command and responsibility, something I had previously experienced in Korea, and I remember thinking that it probably didn't make a lot of difference what I was running; it could just as easily have been a shoe factory as a lumber mill. I enjoyed taking raw material and a crew of men and producing good results. I worked hard at it ten to twelve hours a day and Saturday mornings. I got up at five. so as to get to my office at the mill before six, where I had coffee with the supervisors, went over the plan for the day, and took a reading on how they felt about things in general, a routine I followed for twenty odd years. After operations started at seven, I would drive downtown and have breakfast at a café next to the Ritz Theater. I usually went back to Chapman late in the morning to check with various people, tend to my security responsibilities, and get a good lunch at the Rocky Creek Inn with the gang of regulars there.

I learned a lot from the people I dealt with on a regular basis. I got along with most of them and was interested in observing their styles. Walter Poole operated a small truck line on a shoe string and was our trucker of choice. A neat, nice-looking, trim man in his thirties with closely cropped, curly brown hair, he had served in the Merchant Marine during the war. He hadn't been to the Harvard Business School, or even to any college, but he was extremely intelligent and dedicated to succeeding in the trucking business. He knew everything worth knowing about it and built his company into one of the top hundred truck lines in the country, then sold it for big bucks shortly before the Interstate Commerce Commission deregulated the business. He had the knowledge and intuition to see this coming and got millions for the rights to operate all over the country just a short time before they became worthless.

Mack Casey, one of the independent loggers who cut on company land a lot, was a clever schemer. A little smaller than medium size with an aggressive personality, Mack looked something like a hamster, with small, close-set eyes on either side of a lumpy nose above a weak chin. Back then he always wore a little short-brimmed cap made from brightly striped awning material and bib Duck Heads. In his early thirties at the time, he had been exempt from service in World War II as he had married very young and already had several children when the draft started. He took good care of his brother Joe who resembled him and was his constant companion on the job in the woods. He was pleasant and indulgent with me, and I think had me figured for a dumb rich kid to be used to best advantage. One of his scams was to see me in my office when he came to pick up his weekly check every Friday afternoon to explain some imaginary financial difficulty that had him in a bind and could only be solved with an immediate loan, which always amounted to $500. I always gave it to him since I knew his production would secure it, and it was always repaid before the week was out, when the process would start all over again. The purpose of these loans as far as I could see was to convince me that he wasn't making any money from his small operation but was credit worthy. Mack was seriously smart in his way and very ambitious, and he was quoted back then as saying that he would be the first millionaire to walk down Commerce Street in Greenville in a pair of overalls, a boast he made good just a few years later. Somewhat like Julian, he had an intuitive ability to anticipate trends in land and timber values. I guess he figured that since he had nothing to start with he wouldn't be any worse off if he went bust, and so he took a lot of chances buying into a rising market on borrowed money. I saw his statement twenty years later, and he was worth millions by then. Like Walter Poole, he had never seen the inside of a college, but he perfected a way of buying and selling rural properties that paid off handsomely for him for a number of years.

Mr. Dempsey Moore from Dozier, a laid-back, country-looking, wise, and decent man, sold us lumber from his peckerwood mill. He seemed old at the time but was always friendly and talkative and glad to give me relevant, useful information. T. M. "Red" Phillips ran a neat little sawmill and did his own logging. Successful, friendly, and gregarious, he talked a lot but carefully said absolutely nothing. Our distant relatives in Andalusia, Charley and Solon Dixon, were bigger operators of the same stripe. They ran a large, ramshackle lumber company that I liked to visit to see what they were doing and gain some insight and intelligence from their experience with the markets. They always made time for me, and we had a good many friendly conversations in their little office. They were fairly old with grey hair and wrinkled, leathery faces, and they dressed like countrymen in khaki trousers with their shirts buttoned up to their chins, giving no clue to their wealth or education (Solon had taught engineering at Auburn), and I always left knowing even less than when I arrived. They were multimillionaires when they died, having made a fortune in land and timber. Noted for being cheap during their lives, they created a foundation that has made important gifts to their alma maters and operates the handsome Dixon Forestry Center on a large parcel of land they donated south of Andalusia.

Knowing people like these showed me that substance mattered more than style in the real world and that people's looks, behavior, and generosity—or lack of it—had little to do with their brain power or finances. Times were changing, and many who were making it big were not the polished, educated business, financial, and legal people whom I had been around in the world my father and his family inhabited and knew best.

THE STRIKE CONTINUED, BUT it was winding down, except for one more notable case of violence with bizarre overtones. Early on the morning of June 1, 1956, John B. Moseley, a young white man in his twenties, was driving his pickup through the woods to work on the little dirt road that parallels the L&N for a couple of miles south of Bolling to Williams Crossing just north of Chapman. He stopped when he came to a tree limb lying in the road and got out to pull it out of the way. While engaged in this activity, Moseley looked up to see a strange and frightening figure running out of the deep woods toward him—a black man with a woman's stocking pulled over his head, who was approaching quickly despite wearing high-heeled shoes. He carried a .22 automatic rifle, which he started shooting at point-blank range. Hit repeatedly with the small-caliber bullets, which shattered both bones in one leg and the knee cap in the other, Moseley went down in the middle of the road. Before he could react, the masked man reversed the rifle and swung it at him, breaking the stock over his head and knocking him out. The assailant quickly removed $72 from Moseley's wallet and left the scene. Moseley was found a short time later and taken to the hospital, where he spent the next forty-four days. He eventually recovered and came back to work where he was assigned a light-duty job as a night watchman.

I came down to Chapman as soon as I heard about this attack and met with Paul Hartley, the gum-sucking Butler County district attorney. I took him to the crime scene, which was relatively undisturbed. Moseley's blood was drying in reeking puddles on the light sand of the road, where the hulls of nine .22 short bullets and a piece of rifle stock lay. Imprints of a woman's shoes were clearly evident in the sandy soil, entering from the woods on the west side and exiting through the thin strip of trees that joined the railroad right-of-way to the east. After we spent a few minutes taking all of this in, Paul, deep in thought and sucking his gums, followed the trail toward the tracks, and I tagged along with him. We walked out of the woods and crossed a weed-covered ditch, then climbed up the embankment where we stood in the middle of the single-line tracks in the bright, cool morning sunlight. The shoe imprints had become invisible against the slag and wooden cross ties of the road bed, and as Rube the bloodhound was long gone, I wondered how we could take the investigation any further. Paul stood still for a minute, then looked up at me and said with perfect confidence, "Come on. He went south." We walked down the rails about fifty yards to a small trestle that went over a little pond, maybe twenty-five feet across, a deep place in a wet weather branch. When we got to the middle of the span, Paul stopped and announced that the rifle was at the bottom of the pond, made invisible by the muddy, stagnant water. He asked me if I could get the pond drained, and mostly to humor him out of respect for his past cooperation, I told him I would see what I could do. When we returned to Chapman, I went to the mill and found the company plumber, Wes O'Ferrell, and asked if he could help us. Wes, a genuine character given to spinning great tales, brightened and told me not to worry as he had just the solution, pointing to a big gasoline-powered industrial pump sitting on the bed of his crew truck. He got right on the project, and by noontime the pond had been pumped almost dry. Paul and I were on hand when the waters receded to reveal the rifle lying on the bottom. By the middle of the afternoon, the serial number on the weapon had been traced back to the Western Auto Store in Georgiana where Irv Gruenewald had a record of its sale to Henry Simmons. Simmons, free on $10,000 bond for dynamiting the house of Roland Spann, foreman of the Carpenter Crew, the previous August, was picked up and put in the county jail before night fell. That fall, after making a full confession, he was convicted of assault with intent to murder and sentenced to ninety-nine years in the penitentiary.

THE MILLS HAD BEEN back in operation for more than six months when the concluding event of the strike came on June 20, 1956. On that day the National Labor Relations Board dismissed the last of four unfair-labor-practice charges against the company (the previous three had also been dismissed), effectively dashing any lingering hope the striking employees may have held of getting their jobs back. While the union maintained a picket station manned around the clock at the north entrance to Chapman for another twenty-one months, it was all over at this point. A dark circle in the grass left by their warming fire left a grim reminder, visible for many years. They had lost, and we had won. They played loose and dirty in gangster fashion. We had operated on principle and achieved a victory through a strict adherence to the law and a willingness to use the guts and treasure necessary to win. I was very proud of my father and his brothers for having the will and mettle to see us through this trying time. It was the end of an era for Chapman as many of the old employees were out for good, and the strike had pointed

Floyd, Rosa, and the children, from left, Norman, Tucker, and Lucy.

up the problems associated with employees living in a company town hard by the plant. Those of us who went through the experience bonded in a way that could have helped the company for many years to come.

Greeley and I moved into our new homes that summer. My finances were very limited, and I could only afford a basic 1,400-square-foot house: three bedrooms, two baths, a kitchen, and a living and dining area with a fireplace. It was well laid out, handsome, and comfortable in its way. I put very pretty, random-width, clear beech V-edge paneling in the living room, and our friend Arthur Stewart, a prominent artist in Birmingham, painted a couple of decorative sprays of pine boughs on doors in the entry and bar. The floors were finished with oak planks made in Chapman. Rosa and I were proud of our little place, which she did a fine job of decorating. We raised three children, did a lot of entertaining, and had many happy times there. We didn't have a lot of money, but we lived a good life.

We spent a few days at the beach at the beginning of the summer. The coast east of Ft. Walton was still unspoiled, and we enjoyed the beautiful beaches and water. One night after dinner we went skinny-dipping at a deserted beach near Destin and retired to a blanket on top of a dune with a bottle of wine. Our daughter Tucker was conceived under the stars against the backdrop of the surf's murmur.

Mama had been diagnosed with cancer a few years before and undergone a mastectomy. Stoic and brave, she always exuded her usual charm and wit, but I am sure worry about it was always present in her mind. She was intelligent with a natural affinity for medical matters and probably understood the likely consequences of her condition as well as her doctors did. Symptoms of a recurrence had arisen in the spring of 1956, and I am sure she understood that she had a very limited expectancy from that point. She and my father loved to travel abroad, especially in England, and they planned one last trip together in August. She seemed upbeat and cheerful when I told her goodbye for the last time. She became ill a few days later when they were staying at the Lygon Arms in the beautiful little village of Broadway in the Cotswolds, near Oxford, and died a day or so later at a hospital in London. Earl had flown over to be with my father upon hearing of my mother's hospitalization and ended up bringing back the cremated remains a few days later. Greeley had left a day after Earl and got as far as New York, when he learned of Mama's death and turned around. I felt very lonely and excluded and numb to the point of not showing signs of grief, but her passing affected me very deeply. My childhood had not been particularly happy, but my mother had always supplied what nurturing I got. I always loved and respected her, and her loss meant more than I realized at the time.

BACK IN THE FALL of 1955, shortly after I came back to the company, Julian hired Roy Morgan, another person who indirectly, but profoundly, influenced my life. About forty years old at the time, intelligent and well grounded in the technical and practical forestry knowledge of that time, Roy had been educated at Louisiana State University, then worked for the U.S. Forest Service and the T. L. James Company in Ruston, Louisiana, before joining W. T. Smith. Julian hired him as our chief forester tasked specifically with developing a 10-year cutting plan for the company lands based on the forest inventory his Pomeroy & McGowin company was scheduled to conduct in 1956. I had a good working relationship with Roy, who taught me a lot about forestry as it related to our lands, although we were not very close personally. He learned of my interest in flying and strong desire to incorporate it profitably into the company's activities. One morning, while we were drinking coffee at the hotel, he told me about his idea to use a small airplane to map southern pine beetle outbreaks in our timber stands. He believed that the dying trees would be easy to spot as their needles faded and turned red among the rich green backdrop of the healthy pines and could then be marked accurately on photomosaic property maps for subsequent salvage.

Roy and I presented the idea to Julian and got his blessing to spend several hundred dollars testing the idea using a small aircraft rented from Montgomery Aviation. I had been flying a little with them working toward a commercial license and knew owner Bob Hudgens and his staff. Roy made up map boards using Soil Conservation Service aerial photographs on 20 × 20 inch plywood squares covering a township (6 × 6 miles) back to back on each side, a total of seventy-two square miles with each board. I rented an 85 hp Aeronca Champion on February 19, 1956, and with J. D. Brown in the back seat made the first of thousands of such flights over the next thirty-eight years. We made two more flights using this plane over the next few days, because it was the cheapest to rent, but while the results were promising, navigating precisely was cumbersome because the photo map was behind me, and we had to communicate by shouting at each other. Montgomery Aviation had just gotten a brand-new four-place Piper PA-22 Tri-Pacer, which J. D. and I used on March 3. The cockpit was a

Harvesting equipment.

little tight, but J. D. sat to my right where I could see the map board, and we realized immediately that we were onto something. We flew the section lines east-west at a thousand feet above the ground on 12-mile legs with J. D. observing out of the right side of the airplane and recording the red-topped trees he saw directly on the photo with a red grease pencil. He had a lot of experience with maps, aerial photos, surveying, and the company lands, so staying oriented down to a relatively few feet was not a problem for him. He had trouble with airsickness on the first few flights but got over that and became very effective at accurately recording what he saw. It was quickly obvious that in addition to providing regular, comprehensive surveillance of the property, this patrol flying was also highly profitable in salvage proceeds. The photos were transposed to large-scale maps prepared by Pomeroy & McGowin and given to the four salvage contractors. They were paid a premium logging rate, but many of the salvaged trees were large and valuable, and at times cutting them stopped outbreaks of bugs from destroying more timber. This practical, cost-effective method made a good deal of money for the company over the years and was later widely copied by other companies and by the Alabama Forestry Commission. In October, we switched to a Cessna 170, which was larger and more comfortable and a better plane for the job. We got our own 170 in 1958, followed in later years by a new 180 and 185. The bug patrols were flown regularly from 1956 to 1994, and the aircraft were also used very effectively to direct forest fire countermeasures on the ground many times in the years before the state gained that capability. The thousands of hours devoted to these activities were profitable and appreciated by those who understood what we were doing.

If Roy had not come up with his idea for forest flying, my dream of becoming a real pilot would have been much harder and taken much longer to realize. This work gave me my start in professional flying and enabled me to get good time and experience rapidly, as the flights typically ran over three hours. Flying became my second career running in parallel with my primary work, and I ended up with whatever benefits the equivalent of holding down two complicated, full-time jobs at the same time bestows. I operated under the theory that "hours spent flying should not be subtracted from one's lifespan" and am very glad that I was given the opportunity to realize a dream I wanted so badly. Charles Lindbergh said, "Ten years spent as a pilot on an airplane is in value worth more that an ordinary lifetime," a sentiment I agree with.

THINGS CONTINUED TO GO well in my job running the plant in Greenville, but I played the role more of caretaker than innovator. I bought a few items, such as a lift truck or two, but the facilities were old and labor intensive, and there were no plans for updating them. My brother had investigated log debarking machinery in Sweden after his time at Oxford, and W. T. Smith became the first U.S. lumber operation east of the Mississippi to employ this revolutionary technology. The bark was stripped from the logs by the machine as they entered the sawmill, and the clean waste wood was conveyed to a big chipper, which turned it into chips that met paper mill specifications for pulping. The brothers struck a deal with St. Regis that pegged the chip price to the weight equivalent of a cord of pulpwood delivered to a rail yard. This concept became the industry standard used by all the other paper companies as sawmill chips became a universal, and at times the only profitable, part of sawmill production in the South.

All the Greenville plant's wood supply came from peckerwood mills too small to employ debarkers and chippers, and four of them depended on company timber for their raw material. The area road systems were gradually being hard-surfaced, making it economical to truck logs longer distances. The brothers correctly figured that closing Greenville and concentrating all of the production at Chapman would accomplish several objectives: 100 percent of the mill waste would be converted into a profitable product; pressure to cut company timber would be reduced, making it easier to realize the objective of growing more than was cut each year and garnering economies of scale at Chapman; finally, some of the competition for saw timber off local, privately-owned land would be eliminated as the nearby peckerwood mills would lose an important outlet for their lumber, making them less competitive in the timber market and ultimately putting them out of business.

I was told of this decision late in the fall and instructed to get ready to take the plant down in the early part of 1957. I couldn't argue with the logic of my orders but regretted having to put so many of our loyal, hardworking people out of work. I was able to arrange jobs at Chapman for several of the supervisors and some of the better hourly paid men, but the majority wound up out on the street. I made a point to address the entire crew, telling them what was going to happen, letting them know how much we appreciated their attitude and help in difficult times, and going over what little I could do to make their lot easier. I felt terrible and awkward and sorry at the same time. It was the first of a good many situations over the years in which I had to lay people off or fire them. It was never pleasant, but I learned that if people believed that you were fair and in the right, they almost always took it well.

I had learned a lot in a short time between being a player in one of the worst strikes in modern American history, cubbing for Mr. Jackson, and managing the operation at Greenville, which taught me the basics of the lumber business. I discovered that while often scared, I could do what I needed to in tight situations and that I wanted nothing out of work so much as to be responsible and accountable for results, to always work hard, to do my best, and to lead by example. We closed down the operation on about March 1, 1957, and I reported to Julian in Chapman to work directly for him. It was another defining crossroads, the end of one chapter and the beginning of another, which had a profound effect on the balance of my life.

8

Lumbering Along

In the spring of 1957, I was given responsibility for supervising all of the pulpwood production on company land. Rosa and I had settled into our snug little house, very happy to have our own place. Tucker was a new baby, and Norman was three. I didn't make much money, but we always seemed to have enough to do what we wanted. Chapman was a tiny place, but as the seat of an important independent company, it attracted a steady stream of interesting business and social visitors, a cosmopolitan mix from all over the country and Western Europe. During that time, the family was as tight-knit as ever. We were frequent guests at my father's house and usually had Sunday lunch there. Greeley lived next door to us with his wife, True, and Rosa and I maintained close ties with Earl and Ellen and Julian and Betty, often visiting them in their homes. Nick had a well-established law practice in Mobile, and he and Elizabeth liked to take us out when we were down there. Miss Essie was still physically strong though starting to show early signs of Alzheimer's disease, the terrible malady she passed on to three of her five surviving children, who were affected by it in their old ages.

I enjoyed my job overseeing the pulpwood production and found it helpful in broadening my knowledge of the business, but I also found it very frustrating in that it was impossible to do a consistently good job. Julian had the entire forest subdivided into 40-acre units, or "40s," and I was kept supplied with data on those that had been logged by Roy Morgan, which gave an idea of the pulpwood volume and logging conditions. The company contracted with Branco Wood Products, run by Troy Brannon and his brother-in-law Pat Hayes, to hire producers, or independent crews brought in to cut and move the wood. These crews usually worked with nothing more than manpower, saws, and single-axle trucks. During the strike, I had come to know Troy and Pat, along with Ben Dubberley, the man in charge of Branco's operations on the Smith lands, and I saw Ben daily. He was a tall, nice-looking man of about thirty-five, steady and deliberate, with a stern look that belied a good sense of humor and appreciation for people. He understood and was fond of the poor men who accounted for most of the producers and their labor and knew how to get the best results possible out of them. About once a week I gave him a handful of 40 cards so that he could assign producers to cut them. Often considerable rain would have fallen in the interim between the logging and pulpwooding, which meant that a lot of the acres were inaccessible, given the limitations of the producers' equipment, and sometimes the wood spoiled before we could clean it up. When Ben determined that a 40 had been completed, he would return its card to me, and I would physically walk over as many 40s as possible in an ongoing quality check. I often found considerable wood left behind, usually from a lack of access, and overall I doubt that we recovered more than two-thirds of the total wood available for harvest.

I worried constantly about the quality of the harvesting. I knew that Ben was doing all he could and quickly figured out that he wasn't getting much support from his principals. Troy and Pat came for lunch about once a week, and Ben and I used these meetings to try to beef up their support for the operation. In their mid-thirties, both were attractive and smart, but the similarities stopped there. Troy, who had considerable Indian blood, was handsome with very black hair and a swarthy complexion. He always looked like an Orvis model, passing for a country gentleman suited up for the next high-roller quail shoot on the big plantation. He had built his late father's business into one of the largest wood dealerships in the state and had yards in Georgia as well. He was also a polished bullshitter. Troy's often repeated statement at these lunch meetings was, "Floyd, I'll have a bulldozer [sometimes two] up here Monday, and we'll get those 40s all cleaned up." I didn't need to hear this more than a few times to realize that, like Santa Claus, there was no bulldozer. By then Troy was resting on his successes and delegated most of the grunt work to Pat, who saw to the business end of Branco. Pleasant-looking with an alert, quizzical expression, Pat was intelligent, capable, hardworking, and well meaning, a thoroughly decent man whom I liked a lot. Had Troy been a big enough man to delegate the important decisions to him, their business might have continued to prosper, but this was not to be. Troy loved drinking, gambling, and fancy hunting and sought the company of the society sporting set. He ended up moving to Montgomery and buying a big house near the country club where he lived with his wife, Ann, who came from a prominent Birmingham family.

After watching all this play out over a few months, I went to Julian to recommend that we let Branco go and operate the pulpwood business as a company dealership. He adamantly refused to consider this then and on later occasions, fearing contingent liabilities from being one step closer to the producers from a legal standpoint, particularly with regard to compliance with federal and state laws and lawsuits from the producers' employees for work-related injuries or death. He told me not to worry too much about wood being left behind to rot, saying, "You can't make an omelet without breaking a few eggs," a favorite rule of his, which he often invoked to excuse mistakes and errors in judgment. He must have thought that I was doing a good job with the pulpwood since he gave me, as an additional duty, responsibility for running the eighteen small loggers contracted to W. T. Smith.

I had a good idea of the situation with the contract loggers going into the job, and the first thing I did was to sit down with a legal pad and make a brief analysis of each of the eighteen cutting company timber regularly. I made notations about their staffing and equipment, average production, dependability, competence, desire and motivation, character, and potential. Several things became obvious, the most important being that the pie was cut up into so many small pieces that none of these loggers could produce enough to make more than a bare living, much less generate enough cash flow to support additional mechanization and better capability beyond their very small and basic production units. Additionally, some had a character that made me uncomfortable, and others seemed to lack the motivation or talent to do better. My feeling right from the start in business was that I wanted people who worked with me as employees, contractors, landowners, or even vendors to value the relationship, to be glad of it and profit from it. I figured that if I took care of them, they would take care of me. People who didn't have the character to play by my rules and got greedy or showed their ass in other ways always made this obvious, which was usually sufficient reason to terminate the relationship.

After studying the contractor situation for a short while, I decided to terminate twelve of the eighteen and take good care of the remaining six. Telling these people that the working relationship had ended was difficult, but after worrying a lot, I got this unpleasant job done. My idea was to let the remaining six bulk up in size and capability, make good money, and become capable, dependable specialists in doing the cutting jobs that the big company crews were unsuited for. It worked fine, and very soon the six were working full-time and wide-open, having doubled their previous production.

As another collateral duty, Julian charged me with cleaning up the land-line cases that were still in play. These involved land along the edges of our properties that adjoining landowners occupied and used as their own but that by survey, based on the original nineteenth-century field notes, belonged to the company. Julian had been hard at getting all the hundreds of miles of exterior boundaries resurveyed with proper monuments installed to mark the corners and remarked with yellow paint, a process that had taken more than ten years. This was no easy undertaking for a variety of reasons: the original surveyors' field notes marked corners by referencing trees long since dead or cut that could only be located by digging down into the soil to find the charcoal remains of the stumps; the surveyors had used old and very basic, primitive gear, at times when they had been drinking heavily; and they worked in small parties in wild, empty country populated by bears, panthers, various snakes, and at times hostile Indians, who occasionally massacred white soldiers and settlers, which was reason enough to hurry. Considering this background, these surveyors were remarkably good, but far from perfect, and many townships had small and/or irregular, or skewed, sections along one edge to compensate for mistakes, so the result was not a perfect grid.

In addition to those relating to deficiencies in the original survey, many problems were caused by past actions of the company itself and its agents. In the first fifty years, company land had been accumulated as a by-product of acquiring standing sawtimber (i.e., the erstwhile owners had not wanted to pay taxes on the denuded land after the timber was sold off, so they made

"Old 14"—W. T. Smith Lumber Company locomotive.

the buyer take the land too for a nominal value). On many occasions, an owner would "borrow" a few acres of our adjoining land for a garden or an extension of his pasture, sometimes, but not always, receiving advance permission from the company. Others built their fences so as to infringe on our property, either in error or on purpose. Under Alabama law, a person who had used land uncontested for his own purposes and paid taxes on it for ten years or more could claim title through adverse possession. Because of the sheer scale of our land holdings and the many murky, grey areas in land use versus the legal description and the fog of time, this situation represented a big mess when Julian took over. I'm sure that all this offended his sense of values, and so he set out to clean it up totally over time.

Julian's plan started with identifying the problems based on resurveys of the properties where appropriate. He used company surveyors and personnel for these, and I had participated in more than a few as an unskilled summer worker. He evaluated each case and usually sought to get the landowner in question to agree to relocating the property line to where our survey said it should be, usually with the proviso that the company would bear the expenses incurred in the transaction to include moving fences and remarking and painting the new lines and corners. Some balked at returning acres that in many cases they had grown up using or at changing lines that their fathers or other antecedents had shown them, which almost always seemed to imbue a sort of holy correctness. Often negotiations proved fruitless, at which point we would hand the case over to our attorney in that county. The lawyers would try to gain a settlement, and if this was unsuccessful, they would enter a lawsuit and go to court as the ultimate remedy. The program to get the property lines in good order had been aggressively pursued and whittled down to a few of the most difficult cases by the time I got involved. Maybe Julian felt that sending in a fresh face might help settle some of the remaining disputes without our having to go to the court of last resort. In any event, my work in resolving these remaining hard-line problems was not marked by any great degree of success, and I remember it as probably the most disagreeable and frustrating project I took on during my years at W. T. Smith. A couple of cases best illustrate the nature of the task I confronted.

The home of a widow named Mrs. Will (Abbie) English was located on a 240-acre tract about ten miles from Chapman. The company owned all of the land around her property, which amounted to a two-and-a-half-mile shared boundary. The lines were irregular, marked by meandering old fences and some straight sections, which were skewed in and out to fit improperly located corners. This was just the sort of situation that begged to be cleaned up as doing so would make maintaining the land and cutting timber easier for both sides in the future without an ongoing dispute. Mrs. English, a stout, squat, tough-looking woman who wore a man's hat, resembled Tugboat Annie. Her eight grown sons and daughters all took an interest in the place, and all were tough, vocal, challenging people to deal with. I made it a personal goal to negotiate a neat settlement, bending over backwards to be fair, which entailed torturous and protracted negotiations and a lot of work and expense on our part. The family was universally suspicious and skeptical about the company's motives, and each step had to be explained to and agreed on by various combinations of family members. The old lady was their respected matriarch, but they did not trust each other. I hired Erastus Talbert, the licensed surveyor in Greenville who did all the court-ordered surveys, to run the lines and establish the corners using the same protocol as the court assignments. Afterward, I eventually gained the approval of the various Englishes to erect new fences and paint the lines per the survey, which was recorded at the court house. They wound up with five or six acres more than they had started with, a sturdy, straight fence around the property constructed with new wire and treated posts, a fine copy of the survey map and notes inscribed on parchment, and a recorded agreement that settled the matter permanently, all at no expense to themselves.

Another case involved old man Robert E. "Bob" Crew, a hermit who lived in a little, unpainted, square frame house on Highway 31 a few miles north of Greenville. The company owned the three-quarters of a mile around his place that were not bounded by the road, and the line as marked by Crew's fence was very erratic. One hot summer morning I drove up there with J. D. Brown, one of our main forestry men. We parked on the side of the highway and climbed steps cut into the red clay bank leading up to the house. When we gained the front porch, I knocked on the front door, and after a while we heard someone stirring around inside. Finally, the door jerked open a few inches to reveal a ragged figure with wild eyes, unkempt white hair, and a scraggly beard. The apparition asked what we wanted, and when I mentioned the land lines, he said, "Wait just a damn minute," and slammed the door. I noticed that J. D. had eased away from me to poise himself on the front edge of the porch but didn't think anything about it. In a minute, Crew reappeared armed with a fresh chew of tobacco and proceeded to tell us that he would see us in hell before he changed his lines. We beat a retreat and turned the matter over to the lawyers. I remember asking J. D. why he had backed away from me on the porch, and he answered, "Hell, Bo, I thought the old son of a bitch was going for his gun, and I wanted to be able to jump off!"

The land-line problems were resolved for all practical purposes during this period. I would guess that a little more than half of the cases were settled in our favor. Was it worth it? I guess so, but I'm sure that this whole program of getting the property lines in order would have benefited from another approach. In any event, we wound up with a much less contentious operating environment for the future.

THE YEAR 1958 WAS a busy one for me. The patrol flying had proven itself, and so it was time to figure out how best to do it on a permanent basis. A small landing field had been built on the Edgefield property in 1930 to accommodate army planes from Maxwell Field flown by friends of the brothers who taught there and visited Chapman frequently. I got Elbert Taylor, the county engineer, to survey the site and develop an improvement plan for making the field, last used in 1940, useable and safe. Elbert was an ideal man for the job as he had spent World War II building airfields, winding up a colonel of engineers. Engaged to do the work as a private commission from the company, he did a perfect job, laying a smooth, 2,200 × 150 foot strip out in the solid red clay, which was as hard as concrete. We did the earth moving and grading with company personnel and road-building equipment over a period of several weeks for an out-of-pocket cost of about $3,500. When this was finished, I got John Sherling, a friend and local farmer, to seed the field with common Bermuda and then had several truck loads of noxious-smelling chicken shit from local broiler houses spread on it for fertilizer. This powerful stuff would grow grass on the moon, and after a few days of terrible smells, clouds of flies, and a rain or two, a beautiful stand of green grass covered the field.

I had developed a friendship with Henry Barclay, who did most of the company's accounting, having taken the job over from his partners Jake Lehmann and Joe Ullman. Henry supported my interest in flying and told me that I should buy his client Andy Allison's almost-new 1956 Cessna 170B airplane, as Andy's health had gone down, and he could no longer fly. Henry and I drove over to Andy's country place near Livingston to look at the plane. It was in perfect condition with only 200 hours on it, and I traded with him for $8,000 on the spot. Andy's speed boat was in the hangar alongside the plane, and Henry took the opportunity to buy the beautiful Gar Wood handcrafted mahogany inboard runabout for his lake place at Guntersville for a lesser sum. I pledged the company stock I owned to the First National Bank to finance the purchase and arranged to use the plane for the patrol flying at a rate that let me come out on it. The J. G. McGowin heirs, who owned the Edgefield property, built a small wooden hangar, which I rented. This whole project was handled harmoniously and constructively, further testimony to how the family got along in those days. The field, now lengthened and much improved, is one the oldest surviving airports in Alabama and has been in daily use for more than fifty years since its rebirth. It proved an asset to both the company and the family, and it certainly had an important bearing on my life.

Very interested in what I saw going on around me in the forestry and harvesting areas, I worked hard and tried to learn as much as possible. Toward the middle of the year, Julian gave me additional responsibilities for the company logging crews and their associated trucking operations, the log yard, the log maker (a live deck cutup system that processed tree-length logs into optimum lengths to fill current mill orders), and the large central shop that maintained all the mobile equipment for the above operations, as well as the rolling stock operated by the mill departments, such as straddle carriers and forklifts.

The logging job consisted of two large crews that had not changed much since they were set up to replace railroad logging in the mid-1930s. I conducted an initial survey that told me several things: The equipment, all of it, was too old and rundown and, in the case of the trucks and trailers, too light as well. The two foremen, old men past due for retirement, were neither eager nor well motivated. There was little in the way of a planned maintenance program. Equipment was just operated until it broke down or tore up; then it was repaired and went back into service until the next time it failed or until it wouldn't run any more. There was no policy for orderly replacement of the equipment based on its economic service life. Julian liked the program because almost all the machinery had long-ago been paid for and was off the books. People and their associated cost didn't seem to count for much—perhaps this was a holdover from Depression-era thinking—and nobody thought much about the expense associated with lost production from downtime and expensive repairs. On the plus side, most of the employees were solid and hardworking. I retired the old crew bosses and installed in their places Travis "Trav" Lee and his brother-in-law Sam Smith, two tough, fair, early-middle-age countrymen of the old school, who knew how to motivate and work the kind of labor we had in those days.

I surveyed my other responsibilities and began to firm up ideas for improving them. The log yards were in the location of the mill ponds, where I had gigged frogs at night under the watchful red eyes of Julian's pet alligator, which used to follow us boys around, looking into the beam of our flashlight. The initial fill and stabilization of the area to convert it from wet storage to a compacted, well-drained, smooth area hard enough to sustain heavy machinery, trucks, trailers, and piles of logs had been poorly planned and executed; thus, except in the driest parts of the year, the yards were a boggy mess reeking of rancid water. While we tried to keep a week or more of reserve inventory piled up, most of the trailers were unloaded directly onto the live deck feeding the log maker to avoid the need to handle the logs twice. Three or four Pettibone Cary Lifts were used in this work, and one or more was always in the shop for repair as the soft, uneven yard surface and their heavy loads of long, tree-length logs constantly overstressed and twisted the rather small machines. All this made for a very inefficient, high-cost operation with many other drawbacks, among them considerable delays in getting the trucks unloaded and turned around to go back to the woods, which hurt productivity.

About this time, Earl was ramrodding a program to get the manufacturing facilities modernized and functioning more efficiently. This work included rebuilding old Number Two Sawmill, adding a new long side carriage and fully electrified machinery, as well as rebuilding the log maker and replacing the debarker with a more modern, maintenance-free machine. I was able to plug my needs into this program, which took considerable lobbying on my part with the brothers, but I kept at it and successfully sold them the three main things I wanted: first, a rebuilt yard, well drained and hard enough to support the heavy traffic; second, log-handling machinery big and tough enough to unload the trucks safely and quickly, move large turns of logs in and out of storage easily, and pile logs high to take full advantage of the limited storage space; and third, a system for scaling the company timber accurately and economically so that we had real, not estimated, numbers to keep score with. None of these issues had obvious solutions, and my involvement in coming up with the best answers was both challenging and fun.

Earl made a lot of use of John Patton, who had worked for him as chief engineer when Earl had served as director of the Alabama Department of

Conservation. John had a lot of accumulated leave, so he could take time off to do private consulting. I made good use of his professional services in planning and executing the rehabilitation of the log yard. This involved a lot of excavation and hauling away of rotten fill, which was replaced with large quantities of slag mixed with red clay. In addition, we constructed a series of reinforced concrete runs with heavy backstops installed at their rear for log storage. This work took several months and ran into a good deal of money, but it was absolutely necessary and paid off over an extended number of years.

We investigated log-handling machinery in concert with the yard work and came up with an exciting and novel solution. Old man R. G. LeTourneau had sold his earth-moving-machinery manufacturing company to Westinghouse and was precluded from getting back into that business by a five-year noncompete agreement. This frustrated him so much that he got around it by adapting his basic formula of diesel-electric power to large machinery outside of road building. His machines were massively built, strong, and heavy, with large capacities. The big diesel engine powered ac and dc generators in the frame of the machine, which supplied electricity to motors that powered each wheel, as well as every other moving function, individually. There were no clutches or hydraulics to wear and tear up, and the articulations of the various functioning parts were all mechanically operated by rack and pinion or cable-operated winch and drum. His first family of products built in his factory at Longview, Texas, comprised huge rubber-tired mobile cranes for moving crashed or damaged airplanes on aircraft carrier decks, in some cases throwing them overboard to clear the fouled deck quickly so that other planes low on gas could be recovered. This product was very successful but addressed a limited market, so Mr. LeTourneau turned his inventive energy to log-handling machinery and designed a "log stacker," in essence a modified crash crane. This product was new at the time and few had been sold, but it sounded very good to me, especially since it could pick up an entire load of tree-length logs at one bite and pile logs higher than any other product. We investigated the concept very thoroughly over a period of some months. Julian and I flew up to Sumter, South Carolina, and watched a stacker work at a lumber plant. Soon after, we bought the machine, and it was a good choice, the first of many big-buck LeTourneau products to become part of the Chapman scene.

The third issue I wanted to address was the log-scaling problem, and once again Roy Morgan, the chief forester, came up with an innovative concept that we saw through to a successful conclusion. Pulpwood, a commodity product, had been weighed to establish a cord equivalent for years, but sawtimber was measured by the Doyle Log Rule in our part of the South, a size-related measure, so variables other than weight had to be introduced. Roy and I had some rough ideas about how this might be done, but neither of us had the knowledge or means to perfect it. Roy had known Dr. Sam Guttenberg when he worked for the U.S. Forest Service and contacted him at their Southern Forest Experiment Station in New Orleans to ask for his help. The two of us flew down in my plane and met with Sam, who had thought through the problem and come up with a proposed solution. The criteria was for us to take a random sample of one hundred loads of tree-length logs, have the test loads spread out on good ground with each tree precisely measured and scaled in log lengths using calipers and measuring rods for extreme accuracy, and record the results carefully. Sam created the formula for converting the data, and arrangements were made with the University of Georgia Forestry School, which had an early computer, to crunch the numbers. Implementing this solution took time, as we had to sell the brothers—not hard in this case—on the idea of building a scale house and facility, then have it certified, and finally try out the new system and prediction tables, which matched piece count per load with product weight to come up with a Doyle board-foot equivalent. We weighed and scaled many more loads and found that the system worked flawlessly. This was another first I was part of, and it gave us not only good information but also added protection against fraud. It worked well for years until the industry largely shifted to pure weight ton equivalents, which work well as long as quality standards and size specifications are adhered to.

I worked on another interesting project with Roy Morgan in the spring of 1959. At that time, hardwood pulpwood was a very low-value commodity, and the demand for it was considerably less than for pine in our area. The majority of the mills made Kraft paper used in bags, wrapping paper, and liner board for boxes. Our pine went to one of these, the St. Regis Mill at Cantonment, Florida. Our dealer, Branco, had no outlet for the hardwood on our land. We had an area comprising several thousand acres a few miles southwest of Greenville that was timbered with a sparse overstory of loblolly pine and nothing but scrub oak underneath, which crowded out the natural pine reproduction. Roy thought that if the blackjack oaks could be killed economically, then the pine seedlings would be released to grow with plentiful sunshine, water, and nourishment. W. T. Smith had been running girdling crews for some years. The cull hardwood trees were ringed, or "girdled," with a gas-powered tool that cut through the bark down to the wood, blocking the tree's circulation and eventually killing it. Another technique we used was to inject the trees near the roots with a herbicide that was supposed to kill them. Both of these slow, labor-intensive, and very expensive methods produced spotty results. Roy's idea was to spray 2-4-5-T over the timber stand from a fixed-wing crop duster that could cover several hundred acres during a relatively short flight. 2-4-5-T was a selective herbicide that killed broad-leaf (deciduous) trees without harming the pines. It was the infamous Agent Orange used to defoliate large areas of jungle in Vietnam and subsequently outlawed in the United States as a possible carcinogen. (I was sprayed with it on several occasions during the course of the work, and none of us who came into contact with it suffered any ill effects.)

I got a good bid from Paul LaRue, an established aerial applicator in Foley, Alabama, to do the flying part of the job. His pilot for the work was Russell Ost, then in his late thirties. Rusty flew one of the early production G-164 Ag-Cats from our field. The spraying worked out well enough, but it entailed a lot of work on the ground to be sure it was done right and represented a significant exposure to liability—it was dangerous to use near property belonging to others as it killed cotton and other crops. Plus, we correctly concluded that markets would develop for our hardwood pulpwood in the not-to-distant future. Thus, we discontinued the job, but its most important effect was that it led me to hire Rusty Ost, who spent the next six years in Chapman as our maintenance manager and pilot.

Russell Ost seemed a clean-cut, squared-away, capable man with a good personality. He was a Connecticut Yankee who had been a cadet in the final phase of pilot training at Napier Field in Dothan, flying AT-6s and P-40s, when World War II ended. He married a young woman from Gordo, Alabama, and they wanted to remain in the South. He had worked at Waterman Airlines in Mobile as an apprentice mechanic (unlicensed) and also owned and operated an 18-wheeler hauling produce from Baldwin County up the East Coast to New England. He later spent several years training air force pilots as a civilian instructor at contract schools at Greenville, Mississippi, and Marianna, Florida, flying the T-6 during the big buildup occasioned by the Korean War and its Cold War follow-up. When I met him he had been an Ag-pilot for LaRue for several years, living in a neat little house in Foley with his wife, Elaine, and two young children. I was interested in Rusty, as he seemed to be a good solution to two pressing problems. The maintenance facility I had taken over was a critical part of the operation at Chapman, supporting a large and very diverse fleet of rolling and crawling machinery. There was a lot of money involved, and I hoped to turn the big good-old-boy shade tree operation I had inherited into an effective, reasoned program with good records and cost controls. There wasn't much rhyme or reason to the running of the shop and equipment, and I had reason to suspect that one of the principal supervisors had a racket going with a tire and recap supplier that amounted to stealing from the company. In addition, the brothers were making increasing use of my little Cessna airplane that further taxed my already overextended schedule. Rusty was an excellent stick-and-rudder pilot with strong skills for the kind of flying we did at that time. I made up my mind to hire Rusty and set about selling the brothers on him. Papa and Julian backed my judgment, though Earl asked me why I thought Rusty's background qualified him to be a high-level supervisor responsible for a good-sized department. I argued him down on this point, and he went along with good grace, although he was at least partially right as it turned out.

My instincts were telling me that Rusty was just what we needed. Besides his background working on and operating trucks and airplanes, enough to establish his mechanical bona fides with me, I sensed that he had a strong desire to settle down in a good job that promised him a future and security for his family. As it turned out, he was an improvement over what we had, and he performed well, making some valuable contributions on the technical side. His problems centered on his dealings with his peers and underlings. He was adept at cultivating people with power and authority but exhibited something of a mean streak toward some of the people he worked with as well as his children and dog, whom he was prone to discipline by severe applications of a wide leather belt and a piece of chain, respectively. I didn't see this part of him in the beginning and welcomed him with open arms into our company family, expecting great things.

I SPENT THE FINAL year of the 1950s pulling my operational responsibilities together and making plans for improving them. All this amounted to a total reorganization, which was complicated by the fact that Julian was my immediate boss. I liked and generally related well with Julian and made a practice of communicating with him informally several times a month about operations and problems in my area. I was around him a lot both in my W. T. Smith work and also on regular flying trips for business to Arkansas and other places. He was usually pleasant and interesting to be with, and he seemed to trust me, but he could be petty and mean-spirited on occasion. He always took care of my expenses on trips for first-class food, drink, and lodging, but I never had a personal expense account during the time I worked for him. He and I were in almost constant negotiations over buying new equipment, which was complicated by the fact that what we had was mostly obsolete junk without any plan for orderly replacement. This could get actively unpleasant at times, and once he told me heatedly that if I worked for a big company, I would have to do things differently, that they operated with sophisticated budgets and I wouldn't be able just to walk in and ask for what I needed in such a well-controlled environment. He got pretty worked up on that occasion and volunteered that if I wasn't who I was, he would fire me on the spot. I had talked to the other brothers on various occasions about what we needed, and they were generally more open to my suggestions. Though the brothers usually agreed on most issues, my program clashed with Julian's desire to save money, while the other brothers were more interested in running a competitive business.

Julian perceived my discussing my ideas with them as an attempt to go over his head to solicit approval for my program of improvements, and on the afternoon in question, he warned me not to do it again.

I left his office, got in my pickup, and drove up to Williams Crossing and west across Rocky Creek on the main dirt road through the big company timber. I turned off to the north after a couple of miles on a side road I had come to know as a child and drove a little way around a curve, parked the truck, and got out. I started walking and trying to think in the solitude of the forest. I was twenty-eight, married with two small children and another on the way, treading water in a low-paying job that seemed to be leading nowhere, and working for a powerful man whose ideas and plans seemed at complete cross-purposes with mine. I walked for about forty-five minutes, alone with my black thoughts. I didn't know what to do and felt pretty hopeless. I knew one thing: Julian could run my ass off, but he could not make me quit. I turned around and started back to my truck deep in thought and close to tears. I looked up when I was getting near to see Julian approaching in his car. He stopped, got out, and while shaking my hand, said he was sorry. He asked me to come on back, told me not to worry about it, and promised to try to be more supportive. Nothing like that ever happened between the two of us again, and this was the only time I ever saw him make anything like an apology or tacit admission of being wrong about anything. After that, I was able to carry out my program to completion, and if I didn't always have his unqualified support, at least he didn't block me. Julian must have known that I was working as hard and as smart as I knew how to further the company's interests, and I think he paid me at least grudging respect for these qualities. His one weak spot was a healthy admiration for the quality and value represented by Caterpillar products, and he always gave in easily when I sought approval to buy new Cats on the theory that whatever happened, they would still be worth a lot of money.

Around this time, I also became one of the founding members of the Alabama Loggers Council, a group sponsored by the Alabama Forest Products Association, of which I was a board member. Some of us, including Roger Bruce at Allison, M. C. Hamilton at Scotch, and Hank Wilson at Alger, were very interested in trying to bring more respect to the harvesting business by cleaning up its image and promoting better equipment to improve things in the woods and on the highways. I believe I was the second president of this organization when we staged our annual meeting and a fairly elaborate equipment show in the big company timber west of Rocky Creek. I had to address a crowd of several hundred people at this event and managed to get through my speech, although I am sure that my delivery was stilted and a long way from inspiring. Shortly afterward, I gave another talk to a large group on operating log yards and inventories at the Southern Pine Association meeting in New Orleans, and I had several stiff drinks at lunch beforehand to summon up some Dutch courage for the oratory, which went fairly well, although I was again acutely uncomfortable.

I mention these events because they had an important effect on my subsequent career. I was so ill-at-ease speaking before large crowds that I made a point of avoiding participation in groups and associations that might ask me to do more of it, and this probably prevented me from making friends and contacts in the industry who might have been useful to me and my career. Many years later, I attended a concentration camp–style, total-immersion cram school run by a psychologist who had trained drill instructors for the Marine Corps. He had schools in Chicago and New York, and I attended one in the Chrysler Building with fifteen other senior executives. The course lasted several long days, seemingly from dawn to dusk, and I stayed up late, totally sober, each night working on projects for the next day, which involved making presentations to the group with no written material allowed (flip-chart pictorial graphics to convey core ideas were okay). The instructor personally supervised everything, recording our performances on closed-circuit video, and any gaffe drew heated heckling. It was a trial by fire, and the results were impressive. I went from feeling terrible and being terrible in my presentations to mastering the tricks for communicating to groups effectively and confidently. I was surprised to find that I had come to actively enjoy this kind of activity and have often wished that I had received this training as a younger man as it is very necessary if you want to succeed in a lot of situations in the business world.

I didn't have trouble in smaller situations as a rule, although I still had some shyness, probably left over from being just a face in the crowd in my early school years without much in the way of positive accomplishments to build up personal confidence. I served as a director of the Southern Guaranty Insurance Company headquartered in Montgomery and vice president and director of the Greenville Broadcasting Company, WGYV-AM, and I had no trouble in that kind of business situation.

Rusty took over management of the maintenance facility and began to reform the operation, bringing some organization and planning to it. He and I were both familiar with aircraft maintenance, which we thought offered a pattern for optimizing the care for our fleet of rolling stock. We put in the basic changes necessary to start tracking the life history and operating costs of each piece of equipment and sought to improve the quality of the mechanics' and welders' work, as well as that of the support people who did the cleaning, washing, oil changing, and tire maintenance. This was a big job that represented a totally new direction for the operation, and we achieved some limited successes. The first 75 percent or so of these changes were basic improvements in methods and discipline, something like learning to block and tackle consistently well in football, and were not too difficult to master. The remaining 25 percent of the potential improvement we gained in small increments, and it took twenty years and several managers before I felt it was good enough to be proud of, probably up to 92 percent or more of optimum performance. Rusty was enthusiastic and wanted to do a good job, but spotty people skills held him back.

I didn't know much about trucking initially, but I learned pretty quickly. The big Ford and GMC gas burners we used were poorly made and did not hold up well on the job. I began substituting more expensive B-42 Macks, which were also gas-powered, single-axle tractors but with much stronger frames and good cabs and sheet metal. We bought them from a nice young man named Bill Morehead, who was from a wealthy New York family and had taken the Mack franchise in Montgomery. We had good relations and enjoyed doing business with him, and we were impressed with the design and quality of the Mack product. I bought our first tandem diesel, a B-61, about this time, which was a quantum leap forward and a fine truck. Montgomery was not a good location for selling big trucks in those early days, and Bill went out of business a year or so after we met him. We were notified that the Mack factory store in Birmingham would handle our account. A short time later, we began having chronic difficulties getting the Mack-built parts we needed for our B-42 trucks' rear ends and transmissions, sometimes experiencing as much as six weeks' downtime waiting for spares, a clearly unacceptable situation. My people seemed unable to get anything done about this and told me that they were continually frustrated in getting any satisfaction from the functionaries at the house dealership. I wrote the manager Bill Wooten, whom I had never met, a strong letter to the effect that we had standardized on Macks, always paid our bills promptly, been in business for a long time and planned to stay in it, and needed better cooperation, help, and results from him in servicing our account. I heard nothing by phone or letter, so about a week later, while I was in Birmingham on a trip flying Earl to a board meeting, I used my waiting time to go to the Mack place to meet Wooten. He turned out to be a tall, sparsely built man a little older than I was with black hair, glasses, and an unremarkable pasty face with a weak chin. I introduced myself to him in his office, reminded him of my letter, and asked him what he planned to do. He condescendingly informed me that the knowledgeable people operating trucks had gone almost exclusively to diesels and since they didn't sell many B-42s any more, we would just have to be patient and take what we could get when we could get it. I didn't bother to tell him that I had just recently bought the first diesel-powered truck, the B-61, that anybody in Butler County or the surrounding counties was using to haul logs and that many knowledgeable locals supposed me to be a fool for so doing. I thanked him for his time, returned to the airport, and never again considered buying another Mack. I subsequently bought close to two hundred Class 8 18-wheelers worth close to $14 million at today's prices.

Later in 1960, I was invited to attend a week-long seminar on logging at the Yale School of Forestry, and Julian agreed to let me attend at company expense. It was a good trip that brought back a lot of memories, and it was the only time I ever went back. The flight from Atlanta to New York was aboard a brand-new four-engine Convair 880, which, recently put into service by Delta, was then and probably remains the fastest of the subsonic airliners. I was impressed by the quiet, smooth ride high above the bumps and weather that marked travel in the piston-engine airliners in use before jets took over. Nobody ever seemed to get airsick on the jets, a common occurrence on the earlier planes. I had done several flights in the radar operator's position in Marine F3D Skyknight (a.k.a. the "Drut") two-man night fighters, which were rough rides with uncomfortable moments and almost useless as a frame of reference when compared to the quality comforts the classy commercial jet offered.

The seminar was interesting but dealt with such lofty ideas and theories that I found little in the material of practical relevance, although the school at that time still focused mostly on forestry as opposed to the environmental whacko curriculum that gradually took over in later years. The other attendees were mostly smart people in their prime years who held key jobs in harvesting with some of the best companies. As with most high-powered short courses, a lot of the real value emerged from the interplay of words, ideas, and experiences that came out while socializing with the other students over drinks and meals rather than from the formal course content itself.

I used my free time to visit my old mentor, former Lawrenceville assistant head master Alton Hyatt, who was retired and living in a comfortable house in the suburbs. I also saw my cousin Stallworth Larson, Estelle and Keve's son, who gave me an insight into what the undergraduates were thinking. When we finished on Friday, I made my way to his parent's home on Long Island where I had spent so many pleasant visits before.

Rusty Ost called while I was in New Haven to tell me that Karl Roesch had invited him to visit the Autocar truck plant in Exton, Pennsylvania, west of Philadelphia, to see the trucks being built and give their engineers firsthand information about conditions in the Southern logging industry. They hoped I'd be able to meet with them there the following Monday. Mr. Roesch was the White Motor Company vice president in charge of the Autocar division, and Rusty and I had been talking about looking at their equipment as an alternate and improvement to the Macks in the company's truck operation. Autocar made premium-quality heavy-duty rigs for the construction and logging industries, and they weren't often seen in our part of the country. Since they would provide Rusty's tickets and cover his other trip-related expenses, I told him to accept as it would be a valuable learning experience. I called Julian to ask if I could add a couple of days on to the end of my trip to cover this meeting, but he told me to come on home. I told him that I felt strongly that I should go and would do so on my own time by using two days of vacation.

On Sunday, I took the train down to Philadelphia, where I spent the night in Thruston Thayer's family home in Newtown Square on the main line. Thruston had been a good friend in Pierson College at Yale, and I hadn't seen him since he had visited us a time or two in Chapman on weekends while he was in flight training at Pensacola before going to sea to fly carrier-based F2H Banshee night fighters in the Med. He lived with his attractive widowed mother in a big white mansion. A pleasant, laid-back guy who poured with a heavy hand and liked to party, Thruston got me pretty drunk that night without much trouble, one of the last times I ever did that.

The next day, I took the train to Exton where I met Rusty and toured the small, neat, and modern Autocar plant. They completed five big trucks a day, so we could take in the whole operation easily. They built trucks to the customer's specification with any engine, transmission, power train, and rear end requested. This meant that the operator could get most of the parts he needed during the life of the equipment from multiple sources, which made for improved availability and better prices. Companies like Mack, Caterpillar, and LeTourneau used mostly proprietary items of their own design and manufacture to lock the customer into their tightly-controlled and high-priced parts-distribution systems. LeTourneau went so far as to thread their bolts to their own pattern to keep customers from buying in the open market, and Mack and Cat built their own engines. A friend at Cat confided in me that they would do fine if they just broke even on new equipment sales (actually they made a ton on them in those days) because the replacement parts they sold during the life of each machine were so lucrative.

We had a very productive session with the design engineers later in the day and put together on paper a unit optimized to W. T. Smith's needs. We operated in mud a lot, and our dirt had no natural rock or gravel to promote traction, so the trucks and trailers often had to be towed to a more stable road by Pettibones or Cats. This put a lot of stress and strain on the frames

Floyd and Rosa.

and front ends, and I told them that they needed to engineer a feature into the product that would protect the truck while it was being towed in bad conditions. This requirement piqued their interest, and they designed a pull-hook device that equalized the stresses coming out through the front bumper, and this later become a standard feature on most of their line.

Mr. Roesch had us for dinner that night at his attractive house in the country, and we had a fine evening. We all got along well and established the kind of lasting relationship that makes for an effective operational partnership. For some years after that, before our taking delivery, Autocar always had a new unit with our corporate logo centered on each door and in our colors—bright red cabs with a white top to reduce cab temperature and flat black on the top of the hood to reduce glare—in their exhibits at the machinery shows in New Orleans.

We flew back from Philadelphia to Atlanta on an Eastern Airlines prop-jet Lockheed L-188 Electra, my first of many trips in this fine airplane. Commercial flying was still literally a first-class experience as most all the planes operated by the large trunk airlines were configured only for full-fare, top-of-the-line comfort. Rusty and I sat together in two of the comfortable, wide seats in the main cabin that held sixty-six passengers. This was long before computerized seat assignments and the hysteria over smoking—you sat where you wanted and, except for landing and takeoff, were free to light up and puff as you pleased as long as it wasn't a cigar or pipe. The Eastern Electra even had a six-seat horseshoe-shaped lounge in the rear, and we moved back there soon after takeoff to chat with the attractive hostesses, then uniformly young, trim, and unmarried.

Rosa and I had become good friends with Aubrey Sweezey, an Eastern captain, a couple of years before when he was about thirty-three. Aubrey moonlighted for the Insurance Company of North America as a safety inspector evaluating their aviation risks (insureds), and he used to fly into Chapman once or twice a year in his Cessna 195 to see us. He and I imme-diately recognized each other as kindred spirits, what I call "True Believers," or hardcore aviation people. He had been saved from a hard, poor, dull life on the family potato farm in northern Maine by World War II and ended up flying a B-25 twin-engine bomber at the tail end of it, winding up in Japan. He had to struggle for some years following the war—he drove a bus in Boston, flew for Panagra as a DC-3 copilot in South America, and instructed air force students in T-6s at a contract school in Kinston, North Carolina, before finally starting a long career at Eastern. When we met, he was based in Charlotte and flying Martin 404s and Convair 440s. Strong-willed and independent, he was very capable and confident about his flying, but in a nice way without arrogance or unattractive egotism. Once when he came to see us, he said that he had equipped the 195 with the necessary gear to fly IFR (instrument flight rules) safely in bad weather so as to make his travel schedule more dependable. Very interested, I asked him what he had installed, and he said in all seriousness, "A football helmet and a parachute." I had never flown a 195, and one day when he asked me if I would like to fly his, I jumped at the chance. We took off with me in the left seat of the big radial-engine plane, and I went around the pattern to make a perfect landing back on the grass runway. He looked at me and said, "I don't believe that. Let's see you do it again." So I did, which I think impressed him. The 195 had a bad reputation for its landing and ground-handling manners, and the plane later put the skillful Aybrey "in the ditch" from a botched crosswind landing that ended with a ground loop and some damage. He got into numerous scraps with the FAA over the years, both while he was with Eastern and on his own; at the same time, he was greatly respected by the Feds and gave flight training as a contract instructor to a lot of their inspectors over the years.

Aubrey was a heavy-set, tall man with long arms and big feet, which were normally clad in Florsheim chukkas (semi-high-tops) or wing tips, light tan with a pebble grain finish that resembled his weather-beaten complexion. His sparse hair was cut short, and his weathered, craggy face looked like it had spent time before the mast at sea. It had a sort of tough, mean look that belied his cheerful attitude and innate, full-ahead friendliness and good humor. I learned a lot from him over the years and was proud to be his friend. Rosa, a natural judge of people, liked him from the start and was always glad to see him at home or on the road. Besides being an aviator of the highest order, he was a genuinely nice person and a real character, sort of a legend in his own time in the aviation community. He was well known by many of the Eastern flight attendants, so I asked one of the women working our flight if she was familiar with him. "Know him!" she said. "You mean the man with the face that looks like it has worn-out a thousand bodies?" I wasted no time in passing this backhanded compliment back to Aubrey who, face not withstanding, was a ladies' man of the highest repute among the distaff side of the company, his charm easily overcoming any shortcomings in the looks department.

Over the next five years, we pushed the program of retiring all the old equipment and replacing it with state-of-the-art, well-maintained machinery sized and optimized for our conditions. We wound up with a cost-effective, safe, and dependable logging and trucking operation, which probably reached 85 percent, if not slightly more, of the excellence possible at the time. In the end, we standardized on the tough Autocars. As we trucked only logs in those days on a very short average haul of less than twenty miles, tough-ness was more important than fuel efficiency. We got rid of the homemade trailers and wound up with a fleet of pole and double-deck frame units engineered for our job and supplied by Nabors in Mansfield, Louisiana. They had the same big 10:00 × 20 tires as the trucks, plus air brakes and turn signal, stop, and marker lights, as well as all of the safety and most of the efficiency of units made today. John Sly, a tall, white-haired Southern gentlemen of the old school, was sales manager at Nabors, and we formed a close working relationship with him and his staff. We enjoyed doing busi-ness and visiting with each other, sharing mutual respect, confidence, and trust. Old Mr. Burford and his son Lamar in Montgomery owned the Cat dealership for South Alabama, and they had a fine group of old-line sales and service employees who played an important role in our success, as their D-6 crawlers and bulldozers were the backbone of our logging operation for many years.

I enjoyed making these changes as well as the personal relationships that grew out of them. Some of the contractors and other local experts widely assumed that these changes were stupid and ill advised and, as such, would prove expensive mistakes. I never paid any attention to this kind of criti-cism, and over the years, I watched the whole local timber industry adopt comparable equipment to what we had introduced to the point that it became 100 percent the norm.

It took me several years to get my areas of responsibility to function at something close to their full potential, and it was a great learning experi-ence. My drive and consuming ambition to get the jobs done in the best, most efficient, cleanest, and safest way possible counterbalanced my lack of knowledge in engineering and the nuances of timber production systems. While they never talked about this kind of thing with us, I believe the brothers realized that the company was lacking in forward thinking in the methods and technology that were becoming available in its operational and marketing areas. The brothers weren't interested in going outside to recruit talented and expensive professional management, which often as not fails to work out, especially in privately-owned companies, so they gave Greeley and me the opportunity to fill this void. Neither of us was perfect by any means, but we rose to the challenge with all the brains and effort we had and were effective in the main. I used to tell myself that I was doing twice as much work for half as much pay as an outside professional, but I never regretted my situation and relished the responsibility and the opportunity to make things happen on a daily basis. The knowledge and maturity I gained as a result helped me to continue steadily on my chosen path over the next several years, weather a particularly nasty storm, and move forward successfully into the future.

9

Barbarians at the Gate

The year 1960 was a big one in my life. Our third child, Lucy, was born in February, almost exactly three years after her sister, Tucker. Norman was almost six, and he took his little sisters in stride with good cheer, although he was not above playing tricks on them as they got a little older. Probably on account of Rosa's deep-rooted family values and wholesome nurturing, none of our children ever showed any signs of jealously or meanness to each other and continue to show mutual love and support to this day. I was working so hard that I didn't get to spend a lot of time with them, but I was available to exert discipline when needed.

Besides seeing to my various company responsibilities, I played hard and was lucky to be blessed with a strong constitution. Rosa and I were on the tennis court often and swam together. A good athlete and competitor, she was better than I at both, but I was strong and tried hard in anything I did. Our social life was active with our circle of close friends as well as a steady stream of mostly interesting visitors who came either to see the family or to do business with the company. I smoked a pack a day of unfiltered Chesterfields and had two or three stiff drinks of Scotch or bourbon every night, plus some wine on occasion, practices I maintained for some twenty-five years, seemingly without ill effect. I was constantly under a lot of stress between family and financial worries, plus the considerable strain of my work at the company and flying schedule. I had to watch my weight as I have always liked to eat, but I was able to get down to 185 pounds in those days and maintain it. I read constantly and always had a book going, usually a novel or something to do with flying or the sea. In my mind, I was friends with Ernest Hemingway and William Faulkner, Herman Wouk, Thomas Heggen, Kenneth Grahame, James Jones, Robert Lewis Taylor, William March, Ring Lardner, Mark Twain, and Sir Arthur Conan Doyle, as well as Charles Lindbergh, Ernest Gann, Richard Hillary, and Marine

Colonel John W. Thomason. I read most all of their books several times or more and like to think that much of my worldview synthesizes their outlooks and values. Reading, like flying, remains a passion to this day.

By 1960, my little airplane had started to play an important role in the company. I was becoming more sophisticated in the niceties of the flying business, which made me understand how little I really knew. Weather plays a crucial part in flying, and back then meteorology was a complicated, black art understood by few nonprofessionals. The first weather satellite was about to be launched, and the weather forecasts on the murky TV sets of the day were poor from a graphics standpoint and difficult to follow. The weather-men (WSFA's was a trained meteorologist, but he was abruptly terminated, supposedly because he was a Communist or a sympathizer) drew fronts and air-mass symbols with highs and lows on a chalkboard while you watched, but the whole thing was probably less then a third as informative as current weather presentations and the superb Weather Channel. The government still maintained Weather Bureau branches staffed with real meteorologists at all the main airline airports, like Montgomery, and they were available for weather briefings, but the pilot had to know enough to ask the right questions diplomatically to get good results from talking to them.

My plane was equipped for basic instrument flying, but I lacked the specialized knowledge and skills to take advantage of this capability, which coupled with almost constant worry about the weather and its effect on flying safely, detracted from the plane's dependability, as well as my plea-sure and peace of mind, on anything other than short trips. I determined that I had to do something about this and started taking instrument flying lessons from Jim Perkins out of Montgomery Aviation. He and Jack Hale were working there temporarily and were both high-class professional pilots only a little older than I was. They had been instructors for Central Ameri-can Airways Flying Service at that company's Augusta, Georgia, contract school that trained army pilots for instrument ratings. Like all the school's instructors, they were required to have Airline Transport Pilot (ATP) ratings, the top license and rare in those days for anyone except captains flying for scheduled air carriers. Jack and Jim recognized me for a True Believer, and both recommended that I get the company to send me to their old school for an intensive course instead taking widely spaced, short lessons. This was some of the best advice I have received in my entire life, and following it transformed me from an amateur into a professional. It has kept me safe and been the critical foundation on which I built the rest of my flying skills.

I had just under ten hours of instrument instruction with Jim in the early spring in my Cessna 170. The brothers bought into my recommendation that the company send Rusty and me to the army contract school in Augusta to obtain instrument ratings. I went first, driving Rosa's big new Ford station wagon over many miles of narrow, crooked rural roads through the east part of Alabama and across central Georgia, which took all day. I checked into a nice new Admiral Benbow Motel on the south side of town seven or eight miles north of Bush Field on Highway 56 and settled in for a two-week stay, determined to give the school my best shot.

I presented myself to the school's manager, W. K. "Robbie" Robinson, promptly at eight the next morning on August 8. Bush Field, a big airport built for World War II, had an unusually pretty terminal and a good restaurant, with lush green lawns and towering pine trees all around. Central American Airways Flying Service had its headquarters in a lean-to built into the side of the southernmost big ex-military hangar, and their academic and Link Trainer departments were in a separate building between the headquarters and two large army hangars to the north along the flight line. Mr. Robinson, a spectacled graying man of about sixty, walked with a cane and a bad limp, the result of a serious crash in the distant past. He was courteous but direct, with little to say except for what was necessary to cover the business at hand. Jack Hale had told me that Mr. Robinson had every rating issued by the FAA, all of the pilot and mechanic tickets plus exotic ones like "Master Parachute Rigger." He ran a no-nonsense tight ship. Besides the academic and Link departments headed by Bill Puttuck and H. L. Kohlemeyer, respectively, he was assisted by Carl Morgan, the chief instructor, who was a handsome man in his late thirties, an ex-captain who had been a paratrooper before becoming an army aviator. Mr. Robinson told me that since his instructors were tied up with the army students, he would personally work with me and that we would start immediately as I needed to get through in minimum time.

Mr. Robinson gave me the schedule for my flying, classroom, and Link work for the next two weeks and took me out to the flight line between the hangar and the FAA control tower, where we stopped in front of one of the twelve Beech Bonanzas, all practically new H and J models. They were fine airplanes, perfectly maintained, and equipped with first-class instruments and radios for "blind" flying in bad weather, communications, and navigation. The army students took six weeks and sixty flying hours to complete the course, so I had my work cut out for me. Mr. Robinson walked me through the thorough preflight inspection required before every hop and then climbed into the copilot's seat on my right to talk me through the start, his walking stick wedged between us. I fell in love with the Bonanza and had no difficulty at all flying it. I was a good stick-and-rudder pilot, and with my considerable tail wheel experience, the modern tricycle-gear Beech was very easy to land and maneuver on the ground.

The earlier lessons I had with Jim Perkins, previously an instructor for Mr. Robinson, had covered the basics. I was ready to get to the heart of the matter, that is, to navigate and make approaches for landing solely by reference to the instruments, my vision restricted to the instrument panel by orange goggles and clear blue plastic on the windows, making everything outside the cockpit look pitch black to me. The Bonanza was an excellent plane for this purpose, being tough and efficient with good handling. It was fast and clean, which meant that it would pick up speed and a high rate of descent rapidly, leading to a graveyard spiral if an inattentive or poorly trained pilot let his instrument scan wander. More than a few were destroyed like that over the years, which earned the plane the nickname "The Fork-Tailed Doctor Killer" as it seemed to specialize in doing away with arrogant, rich medicos.

My flying with Mr. Robinson went well. I was highly motivated and enjoyed the professional-level training very much. My lack of experience meant that I had no frame of reference to gauge how well I was progressing, so I just hoped and prayed that I was doing okay in carrying out the old man's sparse instructions. One day, about halfway through, I was eating lunch with him in the terminal, and I got up my nerve to ask how I was doing. He looked directly at me and said, "I'll let you know if you are doing anything wrong," which was all he ever said about it.

The flights averaged a little over two hours each, and the school's policy was to launch any time the weather permitted the airline DC-3s to fly. I never flew in any terrible weather while I was there, just through a lot of bumpy summer cumulus that sometimes got pretty rough around building thunderstorms. The idea was to hand-fly the airplane (no autopilot was fitted) smoothly and precisely to small tolerances in maintaining heading and altitude while navigating and communicating using a handheld mike. The navigation radios—one very-high-frequency omnidirectional radio (VOR) receiver ("Omni") and one low-frequency automatic direction finder (ADF)—were high-quality professional models. In those days, they were hand-tuned "coffee grinders," which meant that you had to crank in the frequencies manually and then listen to the coded identification each time you changed stations to be sure you had the right one. We did cross-country flying along the airways and a great many approaches, including precision Instrument Landing System (ILS) approaches, which brought the plane down a glide slope to the end of the runway with a two-hundred-foot minimum ceiling, and nonprecision VOR and nondirectional beacon approaches using the Omni and ADF, which had higher minimums, generally three to four hundred feet above the ground. We also practiced "flying the beam" on low-frequency radio range legs and making approaches off them. These first radio navigation aids used by the airlines had come into being in the early 1930s. As they depended on one's listening to an aural tone and Morse Code signals, they were somewhat difficult to use and thankfully went away a few years later. These were exactly the procedures used by the airlines, and we were taught to their standard in proficiency and minimums. It was something like a budding professional musician learning to read music: you had to apply and execute exactly the data and procedures on the en route charts and approach plates so that you could follow these directions with consistent precision anywhere. There was no room for error. It was hard, exacting work that took intense concentration in the beginning, and I felt as busy as a one-armed paper hanger.

The training slowly came together as the lessons progressed and my experience level built up so that I knew when I was flying correctly. All the takeoffs and climb outs were done "under the hood" or "blind" (meaning that our vision was restricted to the instrument panel inside the airplane), and toward the end of the course, I was doing ILS approaches to touch down solely by reference to the instruments, procedures taught only in the really professional schools. The days were usually routine but did have their moments. One morning we were flying some pattern over the big lake about thirty miles northwest of Augusta at 6,500 feet in bright sunshine. I was concentrating on the instruments and flying straight and level when Mr. Robinson said with as much urgency as he ever showed, "Floyd, pop your hood!" which I instantly knocked to the top of my head with my right hand. There, framed in the windshield just in front of us, were four beautiful air force North American F-100 jet fighters locked in tight finger-four formation heading directly at us with a tremendous rate of closure. I held my course, and we slid between, and about ten feet above, the flight lead and his number-three man on his right wing. They never saw us as the lead ship never flinched, which would have been an automatic reaction if its pilot had spotted us, and the other three had their eyes only on the plane they were keeping station on. We were so close that for a brief instant, I saw the pilots' colorful hard hats and oxygen masks, and then they were gone as suddenly as they had appeared. Neither Mr. Robinson nor I said much about the incident as these kinds of things just went with the business.

Besides flying every day, usually once but sometimes twice, I went to class and "flew" the Link Trainer. Bill Puttuck had been a sergeant pilot in the Royal Canadian Air Force during the big war and, more recently, had trained air force pilots in the States before coming to Central American. A small, intense man with blond hair brushed straight back, very neat and precise in dress and deportment with piercing blue eyes, a serious demeanor, and erect posture, he had a husky voice influenced by Camel cigarettes and spoke with a clipped, faintly British delivery. He had refined his lectures on FAA rules and regulations and the theoretical side of instrument flying to a finely polished product that brought the sometimes complex material to life, making it interesting as well as understandable, thus easy to retain. A big part of his course, probably close to 50 percent, was about meteorology, the whole theory and practice of what made the world's weather and how we pilots should predict and analyze it. When he stepped to the blackboard to illustrate his points, the piece of chalk in his hand effortlessly rendered perfect illustrations that looked like they had leaped right out of a textbook. He wove in stories about his own experiences with icing and other flying weather problems to illustrate in practical terms the theory he was teaching. My time with him was all one-to-one personalized instruction, a very interesting and effective ground school.

I had eleven Link periods with Mr. Kohlemeyer, a young, German-looking man with short blond hair and pink cheeks. The Link was a little play airplane perched on a pedestal where it could turn 360° as well as rock nose up and down to give a primitive imitation of flying. It was the first-generation synthetic trainer and the grandfather of the present-day full-motion simulators that are much more realistic, capable, and expensive. Airline and military pilots now effectively learn to "fly" their specific model aircraft in them. The Link student climbed up into the pilot's seat facing a complete panel of functioning instruments as well as a control yoke and rudder pedals with a power quadrant at hand on the left. When seated and strapped in, you donned earphones and lowered the lid of the "box" over your head to face the "clocks" on the panel that were lit up by strategically located lights. The instructor sat at a desk alongside and communicated by headset and mike. The desktop had the same instruments as the trainer and was overlaid with a large-scale map of the area covered by a sheet of glass. An ink-tipped stylus, the "crab," projected from a moving metal arm over the desk so that the track of the Link's "flight" was faithfully drawn on the glass over the pertinent navigation fixes as well as everywhere else the student chose to go. The trainer wasn't much like a real airplane, and I never had much difficulty flying it, but it was a valuable tool in practicing air work making precise, timed patterns involving changes in heading and altitude and for practicing radio navigation. After each flight, you dismounted from the stuffy, claustrophobic "box" and got a critique from the instructor who had been filling out a log detailing your performance all the while. Besides his comments and the log, the results were plain enough to see on the glass top of the desk. If you had flown well, the lines were straight and direct and the holding patterns neat and symmetrical. I liked instrument flying from the beginning and found the Link helpful in reinforcing what I was doing in the real airplane.

The motel had a good dining room, and I went straight back there late every afternoon to take a shower and eat an early dinner by myself. I had nothing to drink the whole time I was at the school, not even a beer, and went back to my room to study weather and rules and regulations every night until about 9:30, then turned in for eight hours of sleep and started all over again the next morning. Saturday was a workday for me like any other, with flying, academic, and Link periods. On Sunday I flew one period with Mr. Robinson and spent the rest of the day holed up in my room studying.

The following Thursday, August 18, I caught a ride in one of the Bonanzas with an instructor and his army student, who delivered me to the FAA Flight Service Station near the airline terminal at Columbia, South Carolina, about seventy-five miles to the northeast. I was there promptly at eight to take the instrument written test. I took the entire eight hours allowed and needed most of the time to work through the complicated questions on the very comprehensive test and used the rest to recheck some of my answers. I handed in my papers at 4 P.M. and walked outside, where another school airplane on an army flight promptly picked me up courtesy of Mr. Robinson's responsible arrangements. I went back to work the same as before with flying and Link periods on Friday and Saturday, then flew on Sunday morning before starting the long drive home to wait for the test results, which Mr. Robinson had gotten put on the fast track with a friend at the FAA in Oklahoma City, where they were graded. I got a telegram on Wednesday saying that I had scored a 96 on the exam. I flew to Augusta the next afternoon and had my last flight with Mr. Robinson and in the Link on Friday. On Saturday and Sunday, I flew with Carl Morgan doing a comprehensive review and prep, and he recommended me for the FAA check ride.

One Monday morning, Mr. Robinson took me over to Daniel Field, the old close-in city airport, in a Bonanza N619Q. We met Forest E. Boshears, a designated FAA examiner, who operated Augusta Aviation with his brother Buster. Mr. Boshears had extensive experience with Mr. Robinson and the products of his school, so the test was sort of an anticlimax. I just did the same stuff I had been doing so intensively and passed with no difficulty. We went back to Bush Field where I said goodbye to Robbie (I never called him that to his face) and the others, then cranked up the plane for the two-hour flight home.

In two weeks, I had gotten twenty hours of academics and twenty hours in the Link, as well as 33.4 hours of specialized, very professional training in the airplane, some of it in bad weather, and I had passed two arduous tests without difficulty. I was proud of myself for handling it well. It was a total-immersion, tough learning experience that I enjoyed in its entirety. I had a total of 863 hours flying time, forty-three of which were with instruments. Rusty Ost attended the school a short time later and got his rating. He had a lot of complaints and did not seem to enjoy the experience, which should have told me something as I thought it was absolutely first class in every respect.

AT THE END OF April. we had gotten delivery of a brand-new Cessna 180C, a big brother to the 170 and a really good airplane, which the brothers owned in partnership with me. It had an efficient, constant speed prop like the Bonanza, plus a much stronger motor, better radios, good instruments, much better weight-carrying ability and rate of climb, and more speed. It cruised at about 140 knots (160 mph), nearly as fast as the DC-3s, which still did a lot of the short-haul and local-service airline flying. It was a pretty airplane with good lines and a pleasure to fly with its light, precise handling and good stability for instrument work. The brothers liked it because it was economical and versatile; it was ideal for the forestry flying and a great time-saver in getting the brothers, especially Julian, to some of the places they needed to go.

As soon as I got back from Augusta, I started work toward a commercial pilot license to take advantage of my recent intensive training while it was still fresh. I worked through a study manual on my own and took the written examination at the Flight Service Station in Montgomery a few weeks later, scoring an 85. During September and October, I took 10.7 hours of dual instruction in the 180, doing the maneuvers plus various takeoffs and landings that had to be demonstrated on the flight test. This was low-key, low-stress flying, tweaking skills I already had. I had my first lesson with John Granger, an ordinary-looking guy whose mundane appearance masked a keen intellect and who could fly as well as anybody, but I got most of the training with Jack Hale. Ed Long finished me off with a couple of flights reviewing everything and gave me the written recommendation necessary to take the flight test. I had known Ed for about ten years and always liked him, as did Rosa. He had given her ten hours dual in a two-seat Cessna 140 at Montgomery Aviation. It was a demanding little tail wheel plane, and she gained a lot of confidence flying with him, although she had no interest in soloing. Ed was a good-natured, simple man with a marvelous sense of humor that ran to heavy-duty, ridiculous, off-color stories and jokes. He wound up working with Bob Hudgens for fifty-five years and had both Norman and my son-in-law Paul Moore as his doctors when he died in 1999 at age eighty-four, actively flying until a few weeks before the end. He did a great deal of low-level patrol flying under contract with Alabama Power in small planes and logged in excess of 64,000 hours, the world record for the most flying time and one not likely to be broken.

I flew the 180 down to Panama City, Florida, on October 29, where W. R. "Bill" Sowell gave me a 1.1 hour check ride that I passed with no trouble. He was a designated examiner who ran a large, fixed-base operation and flight school still in existence. For many years his advertisements featured an early picture of his girlfriend, a beautiful blond with sunglasses, wearing a scanty, checked bikini and come-hither look, but I never got to meet her. When we finished the test, Sowell issued me a temporary Commercial license with "airplane single-engine land" and instrument endorsements. I had logged 913 hours and felt that I was really flying skillfully, as well as knowledgeably and professionally.

I was committed to flying by this time, so much so that I was happily working what amounted to two full-time jobs simultaneously. If I had slicked my act up by spending more time politicking and getting elected to positions in trade and civic organizations instead of flying, I might have been better known in the forest-products business at the time, but that would not have been the real me. I have always felt a strong calling to move in certain directions and just as strong an aversion to other pursuits that did not fit my temperament or seem worthy of my time, and on balance I have never regretted dedicating a big part of my adult life to aviation. It was just something I had to do.

I planned to add a multiengine rating to my license as soon as I could afford the training, something all the "real" corporate pilots had and a necessary step if I was to realize my goal of adding a twin-engine plane to our flight department at the company. Bob Hudgens, the principal in Montgomery Aviation, was helpful in getting me started on this. They had a Beech dealership, and Bob had high hopes of selling us one of the new Barons that had just been introduced. Bob and I set up a series of demonstration flights for the brothers over several days at the end of March 1961. We picked up Julian in Atlanta on March 26 and flew him to Memphis on some of his Pomeroy & McGowin business, then deadheaded back to Montgomery. The next day we flew into our little field at Chapman, then 2,200 feet long with trees on each end, where we picked up Earl, who had an important meeting in Mobile. There is often a lot of weather in the Gulf South during March, and this was such a day—an unstable, juicy atmosphere with building cumulus everywhere east of a strong cold front. Bob flew the leg to Mobile, and when we got close, we found a violent thunderstorm anchored over Bates Field, the municipal airport and our destination. Earl was worried about getting to his appointment on time, and the commander at the air force base, General Cassidy, was a friend of his. Bob declared a weather emergency and the Brookley Tower cleared us to land, where a phone call got Earl instant VIP transportation downtown. Bob and I spent several hours at Base Operations filling out forms and waiting for the weather to abate enough for us to depart for Dallas, where we were to pick up my father at Love Field the next morning and fly him back to Chapman. Unable to get any gas from the air force, we finally departed late in the afternoon for the short 1.2 hour flight to Baton Rouge, where we could refuel and grab a sandwich.

We climbed out of Baton Rouge Metropolitan Airport toward a sun setting among massive clouds and headed for Dallas. The Baron was very nice to fly, even for someone like me who had no meaningful experience. It handled much like the Bonanza but was faster and climbed better. It got dark soon after we got to altitude, and we saw a lot of lightning ahead and to our right front. I asked Bob to get the weather for Shreveport, which was off our right wing, and also for Dallas Love, which we would get to in about fifty minutes. The controller, in a flat, unemotional tone, reported that Shreveport was experiencing a violent thunderstorm with three-inch hailstones. As for Dallas, they had a thunderstorm with tops to 63,000 feet as measured by radar and wind gusts to fifty knots. Nobody was getting in, and he asked our intentions. Both ready to call it a day, Bob and I decided to duck into Lufkin, which was still open and not far ahead. I touched down and parked near a Trans Texas DC-3, also bound for Dallas, which had just landed to put its passengers in a motel for the night. We rented a car and headed off for the drinks and dinner we craved only to face another frustration. Texas had strange liquor laws in those days, and it was beyond our power at that time of night to come up with any booze, legal or bootleg, so we were cold sober when we finally got to sleep as neither of us had had the foresight to pack a survival kit, a mistake I never made again. We got up early the next morning for the short flight over to Big D, where we landed and pulled up to the beautiful new General Aviation Terminal, just built by Southwest Airmotive, one of the nicest in the country. We met Papa, who had been visiting his first cousin Mary Smith, an important stockholder in the company. We had a nice, two-hour and forty-five minute flight over to Chapman in bright, clear weather.

All the brothers liked the plane, but being very conservative, they found the price, almost $70,000, too rich. In addition, the Baron was too much airplane to be operated safely off our short runway on a regular basis, so it was just as well that we didn't buy it, although I was disappointed at the time. On the plus side, I found that I could fly the bigger, more complicated twin in normal operations with no difficulty, and Bob signed off on ten and a half hours of multiengine dual instruction in my log book. It was a valuable, real-world look at what a lot of my future flying would be like—at no cost to me.

I had enough money saved up by July 1961 to get the training I needed to add a multiengine endorsement to my license. Montgomery Aviation had a three-year-old Beech Travel Air used for charter flying and flight instruction, and I got 2.4 hours of dual in it early in July with Jack Hale. A consummate professional, Jack introduced me to the problems inherent to flying a twin on one engine: A twin flies basically just like a single, except there are more levers, mechanisms, and fuel tanks to manage, none of which is difficult as long as everything is working properly. When twins lose half their power due to a bad engine, they demand to be flown properly and by the numbers, especially the low-powered ones like the Travel Air. General aviation twins below a certain weight were not even required by regulation to be able to climb at all on one engine, although all the better ones did have some reserve performance if flown correctly. The heavier Transport Category prop planes like the Martin 404s and Convairs then in use by the airlines had to meet greatly enhanced performance criteria so that, in theory, a well-trained crew could cope successfully with the loss of the critical engine at any stage of the flight and still land safely. Lacking such a large reserve of power, the small twins demanded faultless execution of the proper procedures in the event of an emergency, and their accident record has always been poor as a result. Many pilots flying the little twins had only marginal initial training to be rated and little or no recurrent training after that (all airline and military pilots get this follow-up training frequently), so the fatal accident rate was, and remains, grim.

Mindful of the above, Jack gave me a solid foundation in coping with the little Travel Air's bad moments, and we constantly "lost" an engine during every phase of the flight. We made balked landings followed by single-engine go-arounds (very difficult), practiced minimum control speeds ground and air (VMC) again and again, and repeatedly performed feathering drills, where we actually shut down one of the engines for real, as opposed to simulating engine failure with a retarded throttle. After two good periods of this training on July 8 and 10, Jack said I was ready for the rating ride.

On July 12, I flew the 180 back to Panama City, where I had an appointment at Sowell Aviation to be checked out in a Piper PA-23/150 Apache and take the test. The Apache was a tired, old original model of the small twin, with little 150 hp engines and less redundancy in its systems and performance than the Travel Air. It would just barely maintain altitude on one engine without having much, if any, reserve power. It had low stall and critical speeds but was still very demanding, so, though it was a bad airplane for practical purposes, it was a good one for training since everything had to be done correctly to avoid an ugly accident. After four short flights totaling three hours, the instructor signed off a recommendation in my log book and took me to his boss. Bill Sowell gave me a 45-minute check, which went well, and issued me a temporary Commercial license, which added "airplane multiengine land" to my other ratings. I had 1,108 hours total time, which included just under seventeen hours flying twins with an instructor. After the flight test, I did five takeoffs and landings in the little Apache by myself to validate my accomplishment, and this was, thankfully, the last time I ever flew one.

John Granger flew for Burford Equipment Company, our Caterpillar dealer in Montgomery. They had been operating a Beech Twin Bonanza, a big husky twin with excellent short-field performance. Mr. Burford and his son, Lamar Jr., who was about my age, were making a lot of money in their thriving business and wanted to step up to a larger, cabin-class twin. Beech had roughly the same reputation for quality in the airplane field that Cat occupied in its markets, so it followed that they chose a Super 18, one that the manufacturer's chairperson, Olive Ann Beech, had used as her personal transport. I happened to be at Montgomery Aviation the day the new ship arrived, and the Burfords eagerly grabbed me and took me into the main hangar for a guided tour. The plane represented top-of-the-line quality and comfort at that time. It was a little private airliner, and almost every major U.S. company that had an airplane operated one or more of them. It was a classic tail wheel design like the DC-3, an elegant, medium-sized plane with graceful twin vertical stabilizers with a low wing and two 450 hp Pratt & Whitney radial engines. The cabin was large and comfortable with five big individual chairs, a little toilet in the rear, and a small galley forward, the whole area finished in light blue, one of Mrs. Beech's personal trademarks. The cockpit was a separate area that could be closed off forward of the main cabin with comfortable, fully adjustable crew seats, duplicate instrument panels for pilot and copilot, all the latest and best airline-quality radios, a good autopilot, and a weather radar. The Burfords were impressed with the plane because of the statement it made about them and their company (i.e., solid quality representing big bucks), which they could use to advantage in making a good impression on their best customers. I was probably more impressed than they were, as I understood all of the above and also appreciated all of the good equipment the plane carried. I thought it was the finest and most wonderful airplane I had ever seen, little knowing that I was to become very familiar with it in the future as one of its pilots.

I did quite a lot of flying for Burford over the next fifteen years in the Super 18 and later their Beech King Air 100 as both copilot and captain, and I enjoyed their full trust and confidence during that time. My interests in doing this were manifold: I wanted to get experience in heavier airplanes, add to my night and bad weather time, and take advantage of the free and recurrent training that came with the territory. In the back of my mind, I was also interested in the possibility of having a heavy-equipment truck or aircraft dealership at some future time, and flying for Burford gave me the opportunity to see more of how their business operated as a quasiemployee getting a sort of worm's eye view behind the scenes. I never accepted any pay, just expenses and training, and flew with them mostly at night and on weekends. I covered trips occasionally during the workweek when John was sick or off on personal business or when people from the company were passengers. I had many memorable flights crewing their airplanes, which often resembled steering a sort of airborne "ship of fools" around the country, at times producing good-quality TV comedy worthy of the BBC's best efforts. The first trip I flew with John on the Twin Beech was representative of many of these.

My first trip on this plane involved a multileg flight for customer entertainment and a factory visit in Peoria. We left Montgomery on a Sunday morning and flew to Chicago with intermediate stops in Birmingham and St. Louis to pick up one passenger and drop another one off. Lamar Jr. and James "Hutch" Hutchens, who coordinated new machine orders at Burford, were aboard with two customers. We flew the trip up in good weather with no problems, and I enjoyed working in the nice cockpit and getting familiar with the airplane. By then, I was strong and current in instrument flying and radio navigation and was beginning to have a highly developed talent for sensing weather, so most of my copilot duties were routine. The airplane was not totally unfamiliar, as I had acted as copilot in the SNB (the military version of the Twin Beech) on a few flights with pilot friends at Cherry Point and in Korea. The Super 18 was a highly developed, heavier version of that Marine utility transport. We landed at Meigs Field just east of the Loop alongside Lake Michigan after 5.2 hours in the air, put the plane to bed, and took a short taxi ride to the big Drake Hotel where we checked in and cleaned up. Lamar took us to the Stockyard Restaurant, a fine steak place for drinks and dinner. The plan was to spend a free morning on Monday shopping at Marshall Field's, one of the best department stores in the country, and seeing a little of Chicago, then to depart for the short flight to Peoria after lunch. It got very cold and overcast during the night with some snow and sleet, and Monday dawned drab and raw. John went to the airport ahead of the rest of us and greeted us with some bad news when we arrived at about 2 P.M. Moisture had frozen in the primer line going to one of the engines as the plane sat outside overnight, and weren't going anywhere until it had been thawed out by a small gas-fired heater. This took almost two hours, and it was almost dusk when we finally took off at about 4 P.M. John had done the flight planning and hadn't mentioned any problems to me, so I was looking forward to the flight in blissful ignorance and antici- pating a nice evening in Peoria with an interesting morning the next day at the Cat headquarters and main plant before flying back to Alabama. We climbed up through a cold overcast and got on top at 8,000 for the short hundred-mile leg. We had to use the deicing boots and windshield and prop alcohol in the clouds, but everything was serene and beautiful in the dark clear air above the cloud deck as the trusty airplane droned southwestward. In a short while, we were in range of Peoria, and Chicago Center handed us off to Approach for the decent. I got us an approach clearance, and we had no sooner started down when the controller told me that the airport was now closed due to ice on the runways and asked our intentions. After conferring with John and Lamar, I told him that we would proceed to our alternate, Springfield, about sixty miles to the south, where we could leave the plane and drive back to Peoria. We went though the same drill approach- ing Capitol Airport, only to have the field go below minimums in blowing snow, with poor braking action reported by an airliner, before we could land. After another brief conference, we decided to give up on Peoria and fly directly back to Birmingham, which seemed practical as we had started with full tanks, at least that part of the planning having been good. When I got back to the center to request this clearance, they said that the weather was going down rapidly due to a major weather event along our projected route down the east side of the Mississippi Valley and that we should check it out and advise them of our intentions.

It turned out that everything was down to below minimums, or zero-zero conditions, along our route and in Alabama, which closed out that plan. I told the center that we didn't care where we went and requested clearance to the closest airport still open, which turned out to be Chicago Midway six or seven miles southwest of Meigs, where we had started out.

I turned around in my seat and motioned for Lamar to stick his head in the cockpit, where I briefed him about our intentions with the idea that he could reassure the passengers that we were en route to a safe haven and not to worry. Lamar was a nice enough person but not the strong and capable man his father was. He had attended Auburn for several months when he was eighteen before dropping out and returning to the safety of the family tractor company, where his daddy created a position for him. He was well on his way to developing a serious dependence on liquor, and it wasn't surprising that his response to the problem at hand on this flight was to pour another round of strong drinks for every one in the back. By the time we started our approach down through the snowy, icy overcast, none of them was feeling any pain.

We were cleared for an ILS approach to Runway 31 Left (now 31C) at Midway via the Kedzi radio beacon, number one with no delay, which was fortunate as the ceiling was not much above the 250-foot minimums and dropping fast. John and I discussed this on the way to the beacon and both agreed that we would fly the ILS to touchdown, regardless of the actual weather, as we really didn't have anywhere else to go. We got established on the localizer leading to the runway and dropped down to 1,800 feet in solid clag with ice from the props bouncing off the sides of the airplane, while the boots pumped away shedding ice from the wings and tail. We passed the beacon located about three and a half miles from touchdown and started down the glide slope, thankfully breaking out at minimums with the welcome high-intensity approach lights popping into view just in front. Then, we saw the edge lights of the 6,500-foot runway stretching out like beautiful twin strings of pearls beckoning to us. Our flight from Meigs to Midway had consumed two and half hours. When we parked at the ramp, the group in the back rapidly deplaned, and when I was coming down the air stairs in the cabin door, I saw Hutch get down on his knees and kiss the frozen concrete. Lamar and the others went to drop all the bags off at the Drake and told us to meet them at the Playboy Club after we had taken care of the airplane.

John and I were soon in a cab headed for the club, which had opened earlier that year at 163 East Walton Street, not far from the Drake. It was the crown jewel in Hugh Hefner's developing empire, a lavish, glitzy place that catered mostly to single men—men who were not the marrying kind being married already. It was finished in an expensive, glaringly decadent style in the mode of a make-believe upscale whorehouse. We sent word in by the doorman that we were joining Mr. Burford's party, then stood waiting outside under a heated marquee. The red door was locked as it was a key-holder's club; if you didn't have a key, you couldn't go inside, except to join a member. Neither John nor I had ever been there, and we had visions of strong drinks and steaks served by legions of big-busted, Nordic blonds from the farms of Minnesota. The door opened, and we were beckoned inside by a beautiful, tall, buxom, Swedish-looking woman wearing a black satin swimsuit, stockings, black high heels, bunny ears, and atop her well-developed, attractive derriere, a fluffy round tail. She led us across the thick black carpet adorned with trademark gold bunny heads and up a wide staircase to the dining room by the bar, where she seated us at a table for two at the side of the room by the wall. Lamar and his group waved at us from their own table for four and raised their drinks in salute. They were well into their cups, celebrating their deliverance, and I was just as glad that we didn't have to fool with them. After a brief interval, a bunny who introduced herself as Cynthia came over and said that she would take care of us. She was the only black woman in the place, and I thought it a fitting, ironic finale for two sons of the South with no desire to change their luck at the end of a hard day when nothing seemed to go right.

The next morning we met the bleary-eyed passengers at the plane and made the 4.6-hour flight back to Birmingham and Montgomery in much improved weather. The lack of planning on this trip by John, and more especially Lamar, set the stage for many more just as memorable. In the future I was always careful to do my own flight planning and weather checking so as not to get caught again in an ascent during a maelstrom. For all the foolishness involved in this escapade, John was a good friend who taught me a lot and played an important part in the aviation side of my ongoing development.

In the spring of 1962, Bob Hudgens sold Red Blount a new Baron and took a 1960 B-95 Travel Air in on trade. Red was Earl's buddy who built Blount International into a large construction and manufacturing corporation. He had flown B-29s, was an accomplished pilot, and later served in Nixon's cabinet as postmaster general. The Travel Air was an attractive little twin painted in Blount's trademark green color scheme that all his company planes carried. It had only 700 or so hours on it and had received excellent maintenance. Its radio equipment and instrumentation were first-rate, although it did not have weather radar or an autopilot. Bob called me when he took possession of Blount's Travel Air and suggested that the company consider buying it as an economical entry into twin-engine operations to cover our executive flying. He had a firm price of $35,000, which seemed fair to me. The plane had the excellence that characterized Beech products in its design, manufacture, and handling. The four-cylinder, 180 hp Lycoming O-360 engines were a little weak but made up for this defect in reliability. They were almost bulletproof and seldom quit due to mechanical problems, although I did lose one on final approach from carburetor ice one time in an earlier model. Our little field was also fine for this plane as long as both engines were working, but it would have been dangerous to lose one on takeoff. I presented the deal to the brothers, and as conservative as they were, they took several weeks to consider it before finally telling me to go ahead.

Without telling Rusty, I made arrangements for both of us to attend Flight Proficiency Service at Dallas Love Field for a thorough initial checkout. I knew about Flight Proficiency from Jack Hale and Jim Perkins, who had earlier steered me to the Army Instrument School in Georgia, and I had great trust and respect for their judgment in matters relating to business airplanes. Created, owned, and operated by Tex Barry, Flight Proficiency was headquartered in the Southwest Airmotive complex at Love and had a branch office at Houston's Hobby Airport. Arguably as good as there was for high-class, professional flight training, the young Flight Safety operation at New York's LaGuardia Airport was the company's closest competition. Flight Proficiency counted Fortune 500 companies, as well as many smaller businesses and some individuals, as customers, and in those days, they had contracts with Beech and Aero Commander to do all the training for their in-house pilots. In addition, they trained pilots for some government agencies and CIA operations like Intermountain Aviation out of Marana, Arizona (I worked alongside some of their people on several occasions). There were also some colorful Mexican corporate pilots who flew strange and exotic airplanes, like a four-engine British de Havilland Heron and a converted Martin B-26 Marauder.

One Monday morning on June 18, 1962, I took delivery of the Travel Air at Montgomery Aviation, where I was met by my first cousin Keville Larson and his bride, Eloise "Weezie" Echols (Greeley's sister-in-law). I had been one of the groomsmen in their wedding at the Episcopal Church in Greenville on the previous afternoon. We had a nice flight to Dallas, the first leg of their honeymoon, stopping for lunch in Shreveport. Rusty had driven out in my company car with Elaine and his children, who visited her relatives in another part of Texas while we went to school. He was surprised and pleased when I showed him the plane.

Tex Barry was a big, tall man in his fifties with a little mustache and a large gut that stuck out like the cowcatcher on a steam locomotive. Always dressed in a suit and tie, he cut an imposing figure. Tex had been a captain in Pan American's Latin American Division and later ran the training for Panagra. He had picked up some sort of parasite while living down there, and his health was never very good as a result. He combated the invaders in his system with large amounts of booze and red-hot Mexican food. As far as I could see, Tex never did anything except tell stories to his customers and employees, but he must have had plenty of talent to conceive the business, set its high standards, and assemble its superb staff. His wife, Nina, an attractive, nice woman, usually came to work chauffeuring their big Cadillac from their home in Fort Worth to keep a watchful eye on him. Meredith Alexander was the extremely capable office manager who really ran the place and helped Nina with Tex. Then about thirty, she knew and related well with the customers and had an answer for anything they needed. I used to go to lunch with her and Tex occasionally at one of his favorite Mexican joints, and I liked them both and enjoyed his endless stories about the "Red Caps" (secret police) and other strong characters out of his past in Brazil and assorted Latin American countries.

I did all my flying with Philip J. "Jeff" Graves, the chief flight instructor. About forty, Jeff was a tall, taciturn man with an expressionless face set under a closely cropped, military haircut. He was very focused and intense and economical in his speech—when he spoke, his words meant something. He had flown four-engine C-54 (DC-4) Transports in the war and later in the Berlin Airlift, and he had copious experience in flying the line in all sorts of bad weather and difficult conditions. Nice enough in his quiet way, he was nonetheless a hard taskmaster with very high standards covering everything we did together. When his students were flying an assigned altitude, he used to lay his extended index finger against the designated number on the face of the altimeter, and he wouldn't put up with the big hand moving more than the width of his digit (about fifty feet) on each side of the target value. We were expected to fly smoothly and precisely during all phases of flight and to operate the power and brakes very gently on the ground so as to give passengers nothing to notice or worry about. Emergencies were to be handled in the same manner—very low-key with the airplane flying a precise heading and altitude regardless of what was going on. Slick Slaughter, another great instructor who had flown "the Hump" over the Himalayas between India and China in the war, once told me as he was cutting an engine, "Handle it so the folks in the back reading their papers won't even know that there is a problem." In other words, during a flight's cruise phase, when there is plenty of altitude and airspeed, it's unnecessary to make abrupt changes in power or attitude before feathering the bad engine and securing it in good time so that no strange noises or swerves can be heard or felt.

Jeff was a very hard worker, and during training I would often fly with him for two periods during the day, plus one at night after we'd had a supper break, and he was carrying other students besides me. He and his wife had a cattle ranch a good distance from Dallas, and he only got home on weekends.

Learning to fly precise instruments and approaches and handle emergencies of all kinds in multiengine planes is largely a matter of repetitious training plus the pilot's own building experience level. When Rusty and I started the program, our ratings were the equivalent of learner's permits, and we had the opportunity to gain a sophisticated competence if we took advantage of the program and worked hard. We knew what we were doing, but the ability to execute all the procedures with effortless smoothness and economy of movement to keep the aircraft exactly where it should be at all times was still a ways off in the future, at least for me.

I loved every minute of the training and saw it as an opportunity to advance to the ATP rating as soon as I accumulated the flight-time requirements, and Rusty and I passed first-class flight physicals to be sure we met that prerequisite. The program was an intense, cruciblelike experience, throughout which I fueled myself with a lot of coffee and cigarettes during the long days. Rusty complained the whole time: the water was making him sick to his stomach; he and I could already fly safely without all the attention to petty detail and precise tolerances that the program entailed; anyway, he preferred flying the Cessna, so I was welcome to take as much of the Travel Air flying as I liked. In reality, his ego was in rebellion. He felt put on the spot when people with much deeper backgrounds than his own scrutinized his flying and aeronautical knowledge. He muddled through the training on this initial occasion and during the six week-long sessions that we attended together over the next three years, and he always got acceptable grades on the reports Flight Proficiency sent to Earl (our nominal boss for flying) and the insurance company. Still, he never seemed to appreciate the chance he had to improve himself and never was truly happy about anything. He told me that getting an ATP rating was a waste of time since all we needed for our work was the Commercial with instrument and multiengine endorsements that we already had. I should have paid more attention to his attitude and personality, but I liked him and respected the fact that he had more flying experience than I had. Years later I found discovered that the instructors at the school had had little use for him.

I flew eleven periods with Jeff during the seven days we worked at the school (16.6 hours) plus 5.1 hours in one of their Link Trainers. We had very thorough critiques after each flight from Jeff and the other instructors, plus ground school on weather, regulations, and aircraft systems. I quickly realized that getting the ATP rating would be piece of cake after several of these training events. The flying started out with testing the aircraft to determine the actual stall speeds and other performance values. The Travel Air was an excellent multiengine trainer as it would perform well and climb acceptably with one engine, but only if the proper speeds (±5 knots) were used and the correct procedures followed. It stalled cleanly and sharply and had a lot more bite than the fat winged Piper that I got my rating in. We did a great many instrument takeoffs "under the hood" (which stayed on throughout the flights), plus stalls, slow flights, steep turns, single-engine slow flights, regular and aborted takeoffs and landings, holding patterns, ILSs, manual (emergency) gear extensions, canyon approaches (a difficult maneuver then used on the ATP test, which involved descending, maneuvering, and climbing out of a confined space—the "canyon"—on one engine), time/distance solutions (this being before distance-measuring equipment and all the other fancy equipment that makes precise navigation so easy now), spot landings, VOR and ADF approaches, single-engine approaches, circling approaches, unusual attitudes, loss of flight instruments, radio failures, loss of lights at night, and many other situations and problems normal and abnormal. In those days, the training was very aggressive, and we "lost" a lot of engines near the stall speed and at critical stages of flight, situations that are simply not simulated in real airplanes anymore as they are viewed as too dangerous. Now, flight simulators are used to teach a lot of the bad stuff, but the way we did it on many, many occasions in training in Dallas over the years made real pilots out of those of us who applied ourselves. The school never had an accident, although I later knew two highly qualified instructor pilots, one an ex–Pan Am captain, in other states who were killed in Barons giving engine-out training.

We stayed at a nice new Holiday Inn on the other side of Lemmon Avenue, which was a couple of blocks up the street across from the big Braniff headquarters and maintenance complex next to Flight Proficiency. We didn't have time for any socializing or entertainment. We had a good lunch every day at the restaurant on the second floor of the Southwest Airmotive Terminal, where we were treated to a constant panorama of arriving and departing airline and business aircraft and a few military ships on Runway 13 (now 13 Left), which could be seen through the floor-to-ceiling plate-glass window running along the entire south side of the room. Those were good days, and I was as happy as a pig in clover, reveling in getting a king-sized dose of real professional flying.

Before I left, I told Tex about Bill Puttuck, my ground school instructor in Augusta, and suggested that he try to hire him as the army had centralized all its training at Fort Rucker and closed the contract schools. We set up a schedule for Rusty and me to come back twice a year for recurrent week-long training sessions, and I was glad to see Bill in the classroom the next time we were there, doing his classic presentations on weather and instrument procedures and regulations. He made them a good employee and was very happy to be back in aviation doing what he loved.

We went back twice in 1963, and I tried to learn all I could in the ground school periods relative to things I needed to know for the ATP written exam, which one had to pass before taking the flight test. The curriculum was not specifically tuned to getting that rating, but a lot of the training material was related, and the standards used in the flight portion were to the highest degree of excellence and 100 percent germane to the ATP practical test. At the end of that year, I bought a Pan American Zweng manual, a thick study guide for the ATP written test, and worked through it on my own time at home. The test (which changed frequently to prevent pirating) always used one of the large transports for a "flight" that the questions were worked around. I had to learn a lot of theory and procedural stuff about these kinds of airplanes and their operations in a highly regulated environment totally outside my working experience. One had to compute weight and balance problems involving various loads of passengers, cargo, and fuel on the big airplanes to know if the proposed flight was legal and safe. Handheld calculators had not been invented then, so the problems were done the old-fashioned way—multiplication and long division to eight or ten decimal places using a pencil, eraser, and sheet of paper. In the spring of 1964, I finally completed all the experience requirements for the ATP when I logged my hundredth hour of nighttime flying and became eligible to take the test. It was another day-long ordeal at the Flight Service Station, the hardest test for me because a lot of it involved things that I had only studied theoretically, as opposed to actual experience. For instance, a lot of questions dealt with arcane topics like the required number of flight attendants, life vests and rafts, and emergency oxygen bottles relative to the number of passengers, as well as crash axes and first aid kit requirements. The plane on my test was a Douglas DC-6, a four-engine, pressurized piston transport, a lot bigger, faster, and more sophisticated than anything I had ever flown. I passed the test on my first go with a 76 (70 was passing) and am satisfied that virtually everything I missed involved the minutia associated with airline equipment and not flying, navigation, or weather.

During our second recurrent period in 1964, Jeff got me ready for the rating ride, which he scheduled with the FAA out of their headquarters on the south side of Love Field. At 8 A.M. on July 23, 1964, I taxied up to the FAA building, a two-story, red-brick structure, and went in to meet Fred Shine, who was in charge of the General Aviation District Office. A pleasant-looking, trim man in his forties, he asked me lots of questions while perusing my logbooks and paperwork in what amounted to a loosely structured oral exam. I was well prepared and pumped up and enjoyed answering the questions to his satisfaction. After a while, he gave up and with a smile said, "Come on, let's go fly before it gets really hot out there." He watched me do a walk-around and preflight on the airplane, after which we got in, fired up, and took off. The flight consumed an hour and fifty minutes, of which I spent a little over an hour hooded. We did all the things Jeff had drilled into me, including the canyon approach, and I flew well, without any nervousness, as I could see that Mr. Shine appreciated that I knew what I was doing. It was getting hot and a little bumpy, but the little airplane was several hundred pounds below its maximum gross weight, and by flying all the speeds correctly, I made it perform well in the engine-out cases. John Granger, himself a designated examiner for the FAA for a time, told me once, "I can ride with somebody for ten minutes and tell if they know how to fly, usually even before they takeoff," which I think is usually the case, and I was pretty sure that I had passed the test before we got very far into it. As soon as we did the minimum to satisfy the test requirements, Fred Shine told me to take off the hood, and as one colleague to another, he proceeded to show me some of his personal pet tricks and ideas for getting optimum performance, little things not in any canned program that he had picked up on his own over the years. We made three landings under various types of engine failure and emergency scenarios, then taxied back to his office and debriefed over coffee and cigarettes while he wrote me out a temporary license that added the rating "Airline Transport Pilot, aircraft multiengine land." I had accumulated a grand total of 2,140 hours flying time. I had just turned thirty-three and was holding up well under hard work and stress. I was in good shape physically and had my weight down to 175 pounds. Back then, fewer than 25,000 pilots had the ATP rating in the United States, and most of them were airline captains. A lot of the dedicated top corporate pilots had the rating, as did some of the younger True Believers like me, and it was a prestigious thing, a sort of aeronautical equivalent of a PhD. Nowadays, between five and six times as many pilots hold ATPs (about 138,000), including most applicants for airline jobs, so it doesn't seem like such a big deal anymore. Back then, the airline companies provided their copilots with the training to get the ATP rating when they were ready to upgrade to captain. I got it because I wanted to be all that I could be as a pilot, and I wanted to take advantage of the opportunity I had. In addition, I felt that it would, to some extent, compensate for my lack of military flight training and give me an edge on possible future employment in a flying capacity. I was thrilled to have finally achieved the top rating, which I felt established my bona fides as a pilot without question.

IN THE MEANTIME, A lot had been going on back home in the early 1960s. My end of the company was becoming more efficient due to improved equipment, planning, and management, and the sawmill and some other areas of the plant were being modernized as well. In general, the whole company was enjoying a sort of renaissance period. And yet, differences were emerging among the key family stakeholders in the company, and as a result, the family, hence the business, was starting to come apart at the seams.

Over the years, Greeley hadn't been idle and had become the de facto manager of our manufacturing, sales, and retail yard operations. In this capacity, he had made some significant changes both in the scope of these activities and in personnel. He had a good mind for envisioning the strategic direction the business should head in and was innovative in planning these changes.

My old boss Gene Jackson was retired to make room for Max Spann, who took over as sales manager with responsibilities for selling our mill's production as well as a lot of wholesale lumber and plywood, a business he and Greeley had gotten the company into. Max had been around us from earliest childhood, as he and Greeley had been best friends as boys. Handsome, intelligent, and seemingly very self-assured, Max knew the lumber business and could have used the opportunity his new and very responsible job at the company gave him to make a real success of himself. For all his attributes, however, he had a fatal flaw, which manifested itself in various jealousies that bubbled to the surface and asserted themselves in far-out, sometimes crazy ways. He had a deep-seated complex about his place in the world's social structure, which led him to say and do bizarre things. I always thought I liked Max growing up, and he was a groomsman in Rosa's and my wedding, but after my return to Chapman following my stint in Korea, my former fondness began to give way.

I remember one night before Christmas in 1955, Rosa and I went to Greeley and True's house for drinks. Max, then a lumber salesman living in north Alabama with his wife, Carolyn, was with them. After we had some routine talk and ingested several shots of bourbon, Max started in on my case, egged on by Greeley, a continuation of the bullying they had delighted in subjecting me to since I was a very small boy. Something snapped in me, and I reacted in an instant without regard for the consequences. I hit Max in the jaw with a right cross as hard as I possibly could, deriving extra energy, I'm sure, from years of frustration. This could have resulted in a dangerous, unpleasant fight with permanent serious consequences as Max was tough, strong as a bull, and a natural athlete, but a strange thing happened. I was prepared to hit him again and then defend myself, but he disarmed me by standing still, shaking his head as if a horse fly had bitten him. Then his face broke into a toothsome grin. He stuck his paw out to shake hands with me and said, "By God, Red, you're all right, and I'm proud of you. Anybody who's got the guts to hit the Blond Bomber is okay." This broke the tension, everybody got another drink, and the atmosphere improved immeasurably. Still, I was beginning to tumble to the fact that this guy wasn't the trustworthy, admirable pal who had my back that I'd long supposed him to be when I was growing up.

I also figured out that he was an inveterate liar, even about inconsequential, meaningless things, and his tales sometimes produced highly unusual consequences. Often when Carolyn was out of town, Rosa and I had Max for dinner at our little house. One time while we were enjoying drinks on the patio, he was entertaining us with some way-out story of his exploits— he was always the artful hero—and he happened to mention something about his graduation from Alabama. Now, I knew he had passed out of the university without a diploma after four years in residence. He had forgotten that he had told us about getting an incomplete in a course the spring of his senior year, which prevented him from graduating. Needing to start the job he had been promised at the company, he'd left, assuming, probably correctly, that most people would think him a graduate. The incomplete grade was occasioned when one fine spring afternoon while the professor was writing on the blackboard with his back turned, Max had hopped out the window of the ground-floor classroom so as to get back to his fraternity house in time for a poker game and the attendant cold beer. He had been proud of this when he first regaled us with the story some years before, and like most liars of consequence, he sometimes had trouble remembering exactly what he had said to whom. I called his bluff and told him I would bet him a $100 (a lot of money then) that he was not a graduate. He thought about this for a short period before coming up with a cock-and-bull answer to the effect that he had misplaced his paperwork and would have to get a duplicate transcript and diploma from the school to prove his point. As these kinds of things took time in academic bureaucracies, if I would give him six months to be on the safe side, he would take the bet. I correctly figured that he would contrive an inspired scam to get out of the hole he had dug himself into, but I figured that it was worth a hundred bucks to see how he would do it, and in addition, I would have the satisfaction of being responsible for getting him a college degree.

I didn't hear anything else out of Max for a long time until one day, just before the six months ran out, he gleefully came to me with a certificate and diploma evidencing his bachelor's degree from Alabama. Only after he had the money in hand did he reveal his modus operandi, which, while troublesome and expensive, had worked perfectly. He had signed up for a correspondence course that would yield the credit he needed, made Carolyn read the study material and send the completed lessons in, and then recruited a graduate teaching assistant to take the final exam and sign his name to it. I don't remember how much this last cost, probably about the same as the bet, but I'm sure the travel and time were billed to the company. Stuff like this was all in a day's work for Max, and as time wore on, I came to realize that this seemingly charming eccentric was actually neither charming nor eccentric but self-absorbed and just plain nuts.

At the company, Max had young assistants like Bart Rainey and Billy Wood, plus some more seasoned people, including Melvin Brown, Al Wallace, Fred Faircloth, and Jack "Farouk" Warren. Max was big on personality and flamboyant style characterized by heavy drinking and gambling—he placed bets on all manner of sports, games, cards, and dice—overlaid with a lot of outrageous and profane language. This was sometimes funny, established him as a character, and probably helped him with some of the customers, at least until they got to know him better and had been disappointed by some of his failed promises and neglected orders. He did a lot of entertaining for his customers from northern Alabama and their friends at the hotel and sometimes at our hunting place south of Chapman. Camp Cohassett was nothing fancy, but it was in a remote, beautiful setting in a longleaf pine flat at the convergence of the Sepulga River and Pigeon Creek. Some of this was probably effective in promoting sales and customer loyalty, but a lot of it was just an exercise in heavy drinking and tacky, over-the-line conduct. Some of the younger salesmen, like Bart Rainey and to some extent Billy Wood, were impressed enough by Max and his shenanigans to try to emulate him, which never came off very well and did little to help their personalities or careers. Farouk was by nature something like Max in his own right and played the role of the roué and rogue effortlessly, which lent credit to his nickname coined by Max. Jack, portly, jowly, and porcine, bore a close resemblance to the one-time playboy king of Egypt and had a penchant for living on the edge in a series of financial as well as comic and tawdry romantic escapades. He also had a keen wit.

Soon after Farouk came to work for W. T. Smith, he flew to the West Coast with Max, and I believe Bart and Billy, to spend a week calling on mills in Oregon and Washington to meet key people and get better acquainted with their products. Max was in his glory as the knowledgeable boss, well versed in the culture and geography of that lush, fertile area that was new territory to Jack and his other companions. Max lost no opportunity to unload his wisdom on them, always prefaced by, "Now, you boys don't know nothing about this, but . . . " This went on all day, every day, as they drove through farm- and forestlands in their rental car, going from one mill to the next. Max was particularly repetitious about explaining the local farming methods and equipment, which in those days were much advanced over those used in the rural South. Each farm had silver-painted cylindrical tanks holding pressurized liquid nitrogen used as fertilizer on the fields and pastures, which particularly impressed Max as symbols of the advanced culture he was earnestly explaining. One morning toward the end of the trip, Farouk was dozing in the passenger seat next to Max, nursing a hangover, the result of a lavish dinner followed by a late night of carousing. Just as a sharp gas pain hit his expansive gut, he spied another large dairy operation unfolding around a curve in the road, complete with distant tanks shining in the bright sunlight, and a plan formed instantly in his active mind. He bided his time until they got to what he considered an appropriate distance, based on his recent experience with the Blond Bomber, where upon he raised up slightly on one hammy cheek and eased out a silent but generous, cloying, oily emission of flatulence, maintaining a straight face while watching Max. He reported that Max's nose began to twitch eagerly as they pulled even with the tanks where he smiled and inhaled deeply and happily, saying,

"Now, you boys don't know nothing about the liquid nitrogen over there that I been telling you about, but you can even smell it sometimes." They never let him live that one down.

By 1964, Max had built a nice Colonial-style house in a subdivision the company had opened under Greeley's direction off Fort Dale Road in Greenville, a good address. He referred to his columned manse as "Mount Vernon" and was proud of it, but he didn't get to enjoy it long. He had gotten seriously involved with one of his customers' wives in Mississippi, and both their marriages came unglued. Carolyn took their young son, James, back to her home in Asheville, where her father was postmaster and also chairman of the Republican Party in Alabama. She was an attractive, sweet person, nothing like the Bomber. She realized her mistake and filed for divorce. Max had his new friend stashed in a motel in Andalusia. He may have had an early midlife crisis (he was about thirty-eight), or maybe his large quota of craziness took over, but he was going through a rough period with a lot of heavy drinking and very bad conduct. He even managed to get kicked out of the Greenville Country Club for his obnoxious and rude behavior—no small feat as the club's membership included a number of con men and rogues, several devious attorneys, and at least one certified murderer.

Max's time at the company eventually came to an end when Greeley fired him and replaced him with Bart Rainey. Greeley later told me that no one specific event or situation pushed him to get rid of Max; rather, it was an accumulation of problems. I have no reason to doubt him although he did have a selective memory and lack of recall at times about past problems he was involved in. I surmise that Max, for whatever reason, had lost his liking and respect for Greeley and had become insubordinate and lax in following direct orders. It was obviously a gut-wrenching situation for both of them as they had been best friends since early childhood. Max was out of control at that point, and I am sure that Greeley had to do what he did. Neither one of them said much of anything to me at the time, and I was not sorry to see Max leave. Greeley's hiring him in the first place, as well as Max's long tenure, in a way reflected developing conflicts of interest and character within the company command structure that would ultimately generate fissures in the family's tight bond.

By this time in 1964, other company issues simmering beneath the surface finally started coming to a head. In the late 1950s, I started hearing discussion between the brothers and their advisors regarding strategies to better position the company and its stockholders for the future. Bill Harrigan, my father's close friend, operated Scotch Lumber Company at Fulton in southwestern Alabama. Scotch owned about 150,000 acres of pine timberland around its mill, a slightly smaller version of W. T. Smith. Bill and his sister each owned 47 percent, and an elderly uncle owned the remaining 6 percent. Henry Barclay did their tax work and was a leading expert in timber taxation and dealing with the IRS in related matters, usually very successfully. They had carried out a liquidation under Section 331 of the U.S. tax code, which removed the timberland from the corporation and resulted in direct stockholder ownership of the land. Bill and his sister reformed the lumber company as a partnership, subsequently enjoying a totally improved situation in their personal tax and financial affairs. The operating company ran in the black while providing them with a controlled market and the means to economically and efficiently maintain their properties, forestry programs, and a logging operation tailored to its characteristics.

As far as I know, Bill Harrigan and his sister had little or nothing to lose and everything to gain in electing the 331 liquidation, and in effect they lived happily ever after, both extremely wealthy. All this was closely observed by the brothers, who besides being close to Bill, had Henry at their side in Chapman on an ongoing basis while he did his routine audit and tax work. All four of the brothers were smart, honorable men who felt a fiduciary responsibility to the stockholders and initially saw a Section 333 liquidation as their pot of gold lying in a green pasture. A 333 liquidation would have entailed transferring ownership of the timberland directly to the stockholders with a minimum of adverse tax consequences. My father and Earl devoted a great deal of the time and effort over the next several years in a sincere and exhaustive attempt to see their way into adopting this plan. They had the support of Nick, who did considerable legal work on the project, and their brother-in-law Keve Larson, who was a vice president of Weyerhaeuser at the time. Julian was deeply committed to the idea from the word go, and I believe it fit right in with ideas he had been secretly entertaining for years to divorce the land from the operating company. From the time he was a young man, he had espoused the idea of operating the company's land holdings as a separate business, either as a legal entity or at least for accounting purposes. At least ten years before the company's eventual sale, he was strongly committed to a crash program to get the property records and boundary lines in perfect shape, which was good business, but also suggests that he was getting his house in order to accommodate a future plan. Like many solutions to complex problems, confusion and disagreement emerged out of consideration of the 333 liquidation plan. The devil was in the details, and the plan was studied from every side to try to make it fit the situation without success.

The Chapman McGowins were a close-knit family when I was growing up, so I had a longstanding familiarity with the players. On a professional level, I interacted with my father, Earl, Julian, and Greeley in countless ways and observed them in all sorts of situations, some very stressful and critical. The continued discussions between the brothers and the company's outside directors and stockholders about a Section 333 liquidation or some other means of getting the timberlands and the wealth they represented into play sowed the seeds of discord. Very sure of himself about being the guiding light to bring the 333 plan to fruition, Julian became very active and outspoken in courting the ownership outside his immediate family (siblings) in this regard. The situation was beginning to sour behind the scenes, and for the first time bad feelings started to develop. Julian was particularly negative toward Earl, who had the temerity to question him in meetings and memoranda about the wisdom of continuing his very conservative forestry practices. The focus on a light cut that removed the poorer trees and saved most of the best growing stock had severe bottom-line implications, making it hard for management to deliver large dividend payouts to the stockholders. Julian had always had the ultimate say-so on anything pertaining to our land and timber, and he deeply resented having to defend his policies and mostly stonewalled Earl. He also started keeping a diary of Earl's time away from Chapman, which usually had to do with serving on various boards and other civic undertakings, although he did make a good many high-visibility junkets on his private railroad car, *The Finest Hour*,

which may have piqued Julian. All this was troubling and seemed a bit
hypocritical as Julian himself also spent copious amounts of time pursuing
his personal and lucrative Pomeroy & McGowin work, as well as serving
on boards at the state Chamber of Commerce, banks, and hospitals and
taking long vacations in Cuba every year.

By 1964, the issue of control had become the dominant theme at the
company and prevented much serious consideration of alternatives other
than the Section 333 liquidation or sale to the highest bidder. Julian had
every confidence that the liquidation idea made the most sense and saw
himself in the ongoing role of manager of the property, initially split into
between fifty and seventy-five legally separate ownerships. This would have
provided him with a lucrative power base in the forest-management and
consulting business independent of Pomeroy & McGowin. By necessity, this
management would have been on a retail basis and enormously complicated
and expensive to administer. I was privy to Julian's property division plan,
which Roy Morgan and Harry Hitchcock in the Forestry Office worked
out using stand data from the 1956 P&M cruise and subsequent cutting
records. Harry, christened "No Brain" by Max, had been hired a couple of
years after Roy. He was a nice-enough guy with a bachelor's and master's in
forestry from Syracuse and Penn State, respectively, as well as a surveyor's
license; he was very intelligent IQ-wise but light on common sense and
judgment. Roy and Harry's plan purported to allocate the land equitably
between family groups and individuals but ignored important factors such
as location, access, road systems, local politics, site index, timber quality,
and so forth, all of which influence an individual tract's value significantly.
When I asked some questions about these points at the time, Julian in effect
told me to shut up as he believed that the overall objective overshadowed
the detailed particulars. I believe that had the plan been adopted, the question of fairness would have arisen fairly quickly, possibly with legal rami-
fications—or at least with a lot of hard feelings. The question of expense
allocation from such necessary activities as road building and maintenance
would have made for ongoing arguments. Julian thought that the suspen-
sion of manufacturing at Chapman or the substitution of markets by new
operators presented no real problem. In truth, it probably would have

become a buyer's market with depressed prices as the new owners sought to cash in their timber on a stepped-up basis. I have seen a good many cases of long-term timber leases floated in the industry from time to time in an effort to address the above problems, and in every case, they have failed to yield fair value to the landowners over time, often resulting in legal actions to break the agreement.

Julian was absolutely committed to the liquidation, but he lacked the political skills required for high-pressure negotiations with his lifelong family partners, who refused to rollover for him. In effect, he lost his cool and his patience, refusing to see the liquidation through in an orderly way if it was meant to be. Somewhat like a latter day Joe McCarthy, he had a good idea and a lot of the facts on his side, but he wound up short of his goal due to his hardball tactics, which used criticism of the opposing players as ammunition in his campaign. His frequent dealings in the South's timber industry through P&M work gave him an insider's perspective on future trends in the business, which served to fine-tune his clairvoyant certainty in the supreme value of outright ownership of timberland compared to other types of investments.

The developing scenario was not lost on the staff and employees, and more than a few were worried about, and embittered by, what they saw. Many had invested their whole lives in the company and Chapman and felt great loyalty to, and affection for, the family, town, and business, which were all interrelated. Max's solution, which he put forth on many occasions during the daily rap sessions among the staff over coffee at the hotel, was to volunteer me to make the supreme sacrifice for the cause, namely to accidentally-on-purpose have a fatal accident kamikaze style on one of the trips I frequently flew Julian on. Max had names for everybody, and in his lexicon, Earl was "the Eagle," a tribute to his noble style and handsome appearance. Julian was "the Hawk" in deference to his cold-blooded, predatory operating practices and keen vision in observing and exploiting others' weaknesses. Some also referred to Julian as "Roach" because of his resemblance to a villain of that name from the *Dick Tracy* comic strip.

Like everyone else, I was worried and uncertain about where I might be headed. I was working in the family business in Chapman because it was

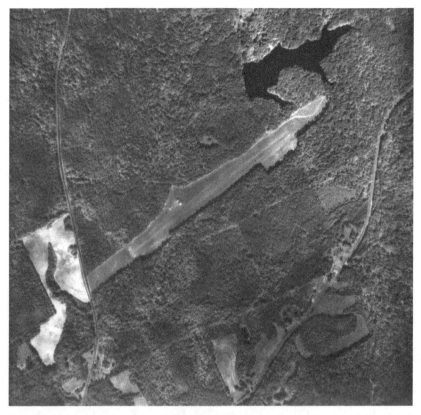

Satellite view of McGowin International Airport.

a calling, a sort of tar baby I could not get loose from. Flying was the only other thing in my life that meant as much to me, and I was doing a lot of it right along with my other work, so I thought I had the best of both worlds at the company. I decided that it might give me a new career, and so I began to consider my options. I was going into the big Atlanta Airport frequently, often twice a week, and one day, I went to Delta's little employment office to put in an application for a pilot's job. I got no further than the woman behind the counter, who asked how old I was (thirty-three), then told me that twenty-eight was the maximum age to be considered for the job. Earl wrote his Business Council friend Juan Trippe, chairman of Pan Am, and enclosed my resume. Mr. Trippe wrote me a nice letter, saying that he would consider me for a pilot's job but that he could not recommend in good conscience that I take it as advancement was very slow in their company for flight crew. He did say that they were excited by their developing air cargo business and would be glad to consider me for a job in that part of the company. American and United in particular were hiring pilots with less experience than I had, but something about their cultures put me off, and I never applied with them. I had reconnected with an old friend from my squadron in Korea, Don Kelly, who was flying for Braniff in Dallas, and I often saw him when I was there training. He told me that the CIA was hiring pilots for their operations in Southeast Asia and introduced me to a couple of his Marine Reserve pilot friends, who knew all about it. Following their lead, I applied to Air Asia at a Washington, D.C., address and furnished a lot of detailed information and references.

Civil Air Transport had been started by Claire L. Chennault in China after World War II and moved to Taiwan in 1949 with Chiang Kai-shek and the Nationalists when the Reds took over the mainland. They had regular airline and charter services and also ran a lot of "black" operations for the CIA in Korea and in support of the French in Vietnam against Ho Chi Minh and the Vietminh. One of its legendary pilots, James McGovern, a.k.a. "Earthquake McGoon," was killed during the siege of Dien Bien Phu when Communist antiaircraft artillery shot down his C-119.

By 1964 American involvement in Vietnam was becoming serious, and Air Asia and Air America were bulking up to provide increasing service flying funny people and cargo to funny places, mostly from bases in Laos. Possibly as a result of reading too many Hemingway novels, I continued to carry some desire to prove myself in a trial by fire, and I was still smarting over being denied the opportunity to be a Marine pilot. My thinking, as far as it went, was that I might go to the Far East for a year or two, get some priceless experience and make good money, then take time out to consider and reshape my options. At the time, it seemed worth doing, and if push came to shove, I needed something to go to.

I got a telegram from Air Asia a couple of days before the annual stockholders' meeting—at which the stockholders would vote on whether to adopt Julian's plan—offering me provisional employment as a reserve captain at an initial salary of $38,000, twice what I was making. I found out later that the work would likely have entailed flying planes such as the Helio Courier and Pilatus Porter and maybe Twin Beech 18s and that some of the pilots were making as much as $5,000 a month. I had flown the Helio and Twin Beech and liked them both, and the Pilatus had a good reputation, so I wasn't worried about the planes. Of all my references, only Bob Hudgens at Montgomery Aviation talked to me about my application, and he said that the FBI had interviewed him exhaustively. If memory serves, I also gave as references my Memphis friend Rich Wilson, Tex Barry at Flight Proficiency, and my close friend, college counselor, and groomsmen Dr. Alan Henry. Al held a very high security clearance at Westinghouse's Atomic Energy Division while working on power for Admiral Rickover's nuclear submarines. In later years, I met several pilots who had been turned down by Air Asia, people with military time in big iron with more experience than I on their resume. I guess Air Asia liked what they saw in my background, and I did have a lot of tail wheel experience in small planes. The telegram gave me some added confidence and a needed ego boost. One almost never sees the name Air Asia, and I guess they did the stateside administration for Air America, the company I would have been flying for.

Julian counted his hand and was confident that he had a majority locked up by the time of the annual stockholders' meeting at the company early in the fall. The day before the meeting, Albert Patrick, Marian McGowin's husband from Mobile who had some previous experience running his own small lumber company in Covington County, had walked in Earl's office and told him, "You better take a good look at your desk [an antique from the New Orleans Customs House] while you can, because its going to be mine after tomorrow." Julian had asked Grady Aplin, the plant superintendent, if he would work for him, and Grady reportedly told him, "I guess I will. I have to work somewhere." Julian made no secret of the fact that he intended to remove my father, Earl, Greeley, and myself from management as his first act upon assuming control of the company when the votes were counted at the meeting, which was to be a defining moment in my life as well as the lives of many others. I was sick and disgusted by then, and if Julian took over, I wanted to get as far from Chapman as possible and absorb myself in another world and value system. I had given everything I had to give for the company, as had Greeley, only to be run down by Julian and his followers, and I had had enough. Julian later even blocked a move by some of the directors to give Greeley and myself vice president titles to help us with future employment.

Julian was defeated by a narrow margin at the stockholders' meeting by a last-minute defection of one of his adherents, Edith Fisher in Dayton, Ohio, who had wired my father her proxy the night before. It was a bitter blow for him, and he immediately left the company and moved to Mobile. I assumed his operational responsibilities and was sitting at his old desk the next day. I notified Air Asia that I would not be coming with them due to a change in my personal circumstances and thanked them for their confidence in me and kind offer.

We in management knew that the company would be operated under our control only for as long as it took to shop the market responsibly and effect a sale. We continued business as usual. The plant and equipment were maintained in good condition right up until the end, and the cut of company timber likewise followed our normal practices. Given the situation at the time, a well-executed sale of the company was the most feasible alternative, a remedy that would provide the most tangible benefits to the most stockholders in the shortest time. Papa, Earl, Julian, and most of the other key owners were of the age that something needed to happen, and soon, if they were to enjoy the golden eggs. The estate tax was also an important influence pushing toward an outright sale as few of the families involved were wealthy enough to handle the tax consequences that the death of one of the major owners would trigger. Besides Julian's liquidation plan and a speedy sale to the highest bidder, every other possible alternative was studied carefully by some very sophisticated people without any positive results.

I was now able to implement some changes that I had been wanting to for a long time. Number one on my list was to replace Branco Wood Products with our own company-operated dealership, which I figured would give us more profit, better control, and a more complete cleanup of the remaining useable wood after removal of the saw logs. I flew down to Pensacola one morning and met with Joe Brewster, the St. Regis procurement manager.

Joe was a forester and married to a daughter of Mr. Estes, the prime wood dealer in the truck wood zone in about a fifty-mile radius of the mill. He was also very close to Troy Brannon, and they socialized, fished, and drank together. I met with Joe in the airport coffee shop, and his stiff attitude and lack of interest or friendliness made me ill at ease from the start. He stonewalled me, saying flatly that he had no intention of dealing directly with the company and that our arrangement with Troy and Branco was inviolate as far as he was concerned. This was the first, and thankfully the last, face-to-face dealing I ever had with Joe, as he seemed to be as sorry in person as he was by reputation. When I got back to my office, I called Mark Rawls, the man in charge of all of the St. Regis woodlands. I told him that I had been disappointed in a negotiation with his man Joe and that I thought the best thing was for the two of us to get together. I flew down to Jacksonville a couple of days later and had a pleasant meeting with Mark and his chief of staff, Noah Jackson. Noah was also one of Troy's frequent drinking buddies, but I always liked him and found him to be smarter than most of the paper company foresters, at least when he was sober. I went over what I wanted and why with the two of them. I never had to talk tough, but I got the point across that Joe's demeanor was totally unacceptable and that if they wanted to continue receiving our pulpwood and chips, we expected forthwith to take the business over from Branco on the same or better terms. Mark and Noah readily agreed and were subsequently always good to deal with. I went back and hired Ben Dubberley to run the operation on better terms than he had with Branco. He liked Troy and Pat Hayes, as I did, but he knew their business was going downhill and that his future prospects with them were dim. We hired Duane Coburn to run the wood yard and do the scaling. Duane was my age, and I had known him slightly while growing up. He had good experience with International Paper Company. He was intelligent and an excellent, extremely accurate scaler. He liked to drink, but that was not a problem at the time.

The wood dealership with St. Regis was immediately profitable, and the net from it was enough to cover my annual salary five or six times. Ben immediately got the company a dealership with International for our hardwood, which gave us a badly needed market outlet and turned a previously largely wasted asset into clear profit. The pulpwood business was still very primitive, but it was fun and a great learning experience that would prove valuable to Ben and me in the future. Troy and Pat were miffed and very cool, but I felt that it was something I had to do in the company's best interest, and they were smart enough to realize that. Pat and I became very good friends and did a lot of work together running an insurance fund for the Forestry Association in later years. I knew something about this, as my first action when we took over was to get workers' compensation insurance coverage on favorable terms with the company's carrier for all of the producers and their employees. They were the first pulpwood producers in the state to enjoy the badly needed benefits it provided. We learned a lot about safety and its management from this and enjoyed a competitive advantage in years to come because our insurance premium was a lot lower per cord than the rate other dealers could get at the time.

Troy used to stop by and visit with us from time to time, but he was drinking so much that he had a black man driving him. The booze eventually cost him his marriage and his business, and he died at a relatively young age. Pat came into a wonderful income when gas and oil were brought in on some of his family property, which seemed to further embitter Troy. At some point during those years, Eddie Brooks, a friend of Ben's who ran the Branco office in Brewton, told him, "Every night Pat goes to bed, and when he wakes up the next morning, he's $27,000 richer."

The second change I made was hiring John Wood to help with the contract loggers and pole sales and to back up Bill Parmer with the company crews. John was a local boy about thirty years old from Pigeon Creek whose brother Billy was already working for us as a salesman. He had attended the Florida Ranger School at Lake City on a scholarship that Julian or P&M provided, earning a junior-college degree in forestry. John had worked all over the South as a crew chief for P&M cruising timber on big acreages for paper company acquisitions. He was married and starting a family and wanted to get back home and work for W. T. Smith, but Julian would never agree to this. John got a good job managing a 50,000-acre tract that some of the T. R. Miller Mill Company principals owned near Brewton. I got to know him when P&M was cruising the company lands in 1956 and thought he would fit in well, given his experience and strong motivation to join us. I never knew why Julian refused to let me hire him. It could have been that he didn't want John to leave P&M, or maybe he was shrewd enough to see possible problems with John's personality and work ethic, or maybe it was a combination of both of these factors. I brought him on board with the assurance that if he did a good job, he would get a shot at succeeding Mr. Parmer as logging superintendent, which was his lifelong ambition. John did excellent work during those first years and was an effective contributor to the profitability of our operations, though, as it turned out, his pleasant personality and intelligence masked a lot of phobias and prejudices. His brother Billy was handsome, slick, and very smooth, while John was of medium height and build, with a tough-looking face under a flat top. Most people liked him, and he seemed a sort of diamond in the rough, illustrating the old saw about how you can take the boy out of the country, but you can't take the country out of the boy. He wasn't afraid of hard work in those early days, and his experience and skills complemented our little organization.

Shortly after Julian left, I faced a truly fortuitous situation that greatly improved the potential of our aviation operations. Earl had been director of the state docks, a cabinet position in Governor John Patterson's administration, and while acting in that capacity, he used his political muscle to get the state to build a first-class road, which it turned over to the county (Country Road 37) to serve as a connector between U.S. 31 at Chapman and Alabama 106 west of Georgiana. It ran through our property for several miles and crossed the railroad just south of the mill site by a handsome, high bridge with long approach ramps on either end. It was popularly called the "Earl McGowin Superhighway" and much appreciated and anticipated by all of us supplying Chapman as well as the general public. W. S. Newell Construction Company from Montgomery, the low bidder by a wide margin, was awarded the job. I had flown Billy Newell—a shrewd, tough man about ten years older than I was with an eye for making money—on the Burford plane. He had split off from the family business and was doing very well on his own.

I was sitting at my desk the day after the bid letting when Voncile

Leyseth stuck her head in and said that Mr. J. E. "Big John" Shows, Billy's superintendent, was outside and needed to see me badly. I knew him slightly and liked him, so I asked how I could help him. He didn't make any bones about his distress and laid his cards on the table, saying "Mr. Floyd, Billy is off dove hunting in Mexico, and I assumed that the fill dirt for the railroad bridge was going to come off company land at each end, but the specs call for it to be hauled from a pit over four miles from here, and that is why I left so much money on the table. If you don't let me get the dirt right next to the railroad, I might as well kiss my job goodbye because Billy will sure as hell fire me when he gets back and finds out what happened. I'll do anything I can to square this up with you all if you will help me out." My nature in business then and in the future was to treat people the way I would like to be treated. We had a hell of a lot of land—221,000 acres—the largest private holding in the state, and the road and bridge would be a great cost saver and safety benefit to us. I told Big John that I would help him out and give him the dirt if he would do one thing for us while he had his big earth-moving and -compacting equipment in Chapman. The company would pay his direct cost (fuel and labor) if it wasn't a high figure. The job I had in mind was to extend our airport runway from 2,200 to 3,000 feet by placing several hundred feet of fill on each end, which amounted to a lot of dirt moving and stabilization. Combined with cutting some timber to improve the approaches, this would give us a much safer field that could accommodate a wide range of business planes. Big John rode out, took a quick look, came back to say that he would be glad to do it at a cost to us of $5,000, and left very happy when I told him to go ahead. This got him out of a jam, and he worked on happily with Billy. It made our airport, one of the oldest in Alabama, one of the nicest and prettiest anywhere, and it would cost a huge amount of money if created from scratch today.

As soon as the runway extension was completed, we traded the Travel Air in to Combs Aircraft in Denver for a fine two-year-old A-55 Baron, which had been traded in on a new one by John Love, the wealthy ex-governor of Colorado. Our cousin Wayne McGowin Brown was president of Combs and a good man to do business with. Combs was then the largest Beech distributor in the country and took care of its customers. The Baron gave

I. UNITED STATES OF AMERICA   XI.

Department of Transportation – FEDERAL AVIATION ADMINISTRATION

THIS CERTIFIES   IV.

THAT   V.   NORMAN FLOYD MCGOWIN JR
PO BOX 35
418326486   CHAPMAN   AL   36015   VI.

DATE OF BIRTH	HEIGHT IN	WEIGHT	HAIR	EYES	SEX	NATIONALITY
05-20-31	72	221	RED	HAZEL	M	USA

IX. HAS BEEN FOUND TO BE PROPERLY QUALIFIED TO EXERCISE THE PRIVILEGES OF

II.   AIRLINE TRANSPORT PILOT   III. CERT NO   1114278
   RATINGS AND LIMITATIONS

XII.   AIRPLANE MULTIENGINE LAND
CE-500 DC-3
   COMMERCIAL PRIVILEGES
XIII.   AIRPLANE SINGLE ENGINE LAND*

VII.   _Norman Floyd McGowin_   X. _Donald D. Engen_
   SIGNATURE OF HOLDER

X.   DATE OF ISSUE   03-15-85   VIII.
AC Form 8060 2 (1 85)   ADMINISTRATOR

DEPARTMENT OF TRANSPORTATION
FEDERAL AVIATION ADMINISTRATION

STATEMENT OF ACROBATIC COMPETENCY

PILOT
Norman Floyd 'McGowin

TYPE CERTIFICATE/NUMBER
ATP 1114278

ISSUANCE DATE	EXPIRATION DATE
2/20/85	2/28/86

GENERAL AVIATION OPERATIONS INSPECTOR (Signature)
Bobby Lott

FAA Form 8710-7 (5-78)

MANEUVER LIMITATIONS

NONE

ALTITUDE LIMITATIONS	AUTHORIZED AIRCRAFT
Surface	Any aircraft in which qualified and current

I understand that this statement of competency does not authorize deviation from FAR 91 except as defined by waiver thereto, or to the terms of Special Provisions contained in any waiver to FAR 91.

PILOT (Signature)   Norman Floyd McGowin

Floyd's Airline Transport Pilot rating.

us much greater speed, and because it had plenty of power, it was a lot safer in an engine-out situation. Precise speeds were not quite as critical with it compared to weaker airplanes, which gave one a little more time to get things sorted out and squared away in an emergency.

Interstate 65 was being constructed at this time, and I concluded a deal with the appraiser in charge of right-of-way acquisition, Paul Corwin, to sell our land between Garland and Greenville on the highway route. This amounted to about 250 acres of prime pine timberland, as we owned on both sides of the projected road for six or seven miles. Corwin had a good reputation and impressed me as a straight shooter. I took his price for the land, as I thought it was in the public interest, and we logged off all of the merchantable timber, which was reserved by the company after Papa and Earl went along with my recommendation. I believe that if Julian had still been in charge, he would have extracted every possible dollar for the land as that was his style of business, and company land was very special to him.

I engaged Pomeroy & McGowin to do another forest inventory to provide up-to-date information to assist management in negotiations with potential buyers of the company. I handled this through the P&M staff in Arkansas whom I knew well from frequent trips there with Julian in the past, and I had total confidence in their work. I had no contact with Julian relative to this extensive job.

I showed the land and its related statistics to some eight or nine interested parties, all major national corporations ranging from Standard Oil of New Jersey and Freeport Sulphur to more likely buyers like Container Corporation of America and Union Camp. This was a period in big-time corporate America when diversification was fashionable, but it was also before such business entities as large insurance companies and pension funds were very interested. The traditional buyers were pulp and paper firms with manufacturing facilities and occasionally extremely wealthy families such as the DuPonts, who owned substantial forest acreage near Chapman. I spent a lot of time with the representatives of these various companies in show-and-tell sessions, sufficient for them to make an informed opinion about me and my operating style. Container emerged as the high bidder, barely topping Union Camp at about $45 million. None of us liked this,

Above, Rosa and Floyd with his USMC SNJ-6 airplane. Left, three generations of McGowins—Floyd, Norman, and Floyd Sr.

and Papa reached Hugh Camp the next night at the Charlottesville Country Club and asked him if he wanted to reconsider their bid. Mr. Camp told him he would bump Container's offer by a $1 million, and they signed off on the deal over the phone.

Soon after this, Mr. Camp, who was in Chapman wrapping up the details of the transaction, visited me in my office. He told me that they had no desire to be in the logging business and had concluded that I might like to form a new company to do the logging job, maintain the rolling stock, and serve as a sort of master dealer for pulpwood harvesting and wood procurement. He said that they would let me buy back the equipment at a fair price and take anyone I wanted for the new organization. I had never really wanted to work for Union Camp, but I was bonded to Chapman and my profession, so I thanked him and told him that I would be glad to take it on. My father joined me initially as a nonmanagement partner, and we went into business on April 13, 1966, concurrent with the sale of W. T. Smith. I got the name Rocky Creek Logging Company from the original lumber company and ran it as a successful operation for the next twenty-five years, the last fourteen as a Union Camp subsidiary. The company was the largest of its kind in Alabama and well respected. I had thirty-six years of continuous service in Chapman.

Greeley and I learned a tremendous amount working for W. T. Smith. I became a seasoned player in several disciplines at an early age and presided over the nuts and bolts of the largest real estate transaction in Alabama history. W. T. Smith was a class act in many respects, and any subsequent success my brother and I had in business was certainly influenced by what we learned there. It was an ethical business, the customer always got good value, and it was well respected by the employees, who showed great loyalty. It compared very favorably in the quality of its management and the way it conducted its operations to most of the large national corporations in the forest products business that I have observed over the years since then.

Greeley and I worked well together and supported each other at W. T. Smith, though we had separate operational responsibilities. I trusted him and often sought his advice and opinions. Greeley lived next door with his wife, True, and we were together a lot at family functions. We had a pleasant enough, but never close or intimate, relationship as our tastes were very different. Both of us believed, however, that W. T. Smith had a great future, and we worked as hard as possible to make our contribution. When Union Camp bought the company, Greeley made a good impression on their top people and was asked to stay on in Chapman as resident manager. In 1971, he was promoted and moved to Savannah, where he took responsibility for woodlands and building products as a vice president of Union Camp until he retired.

Papa had endured a tremendous amount of stress but managed to keep his head up and function well, with dignity and good judgment all the while. After my mother's death in 1956, he had several lady friends who were all heavy-duty people in their own rights, but he never remarried. He generally enjoyed good health but had various surgeries during this period, which put him through much worry and discomfort. The split with Julian must have been very painful to him as they had always been close. Through it all, my father kept his cool and did everything reasonable, and then some, to accommodate Julian and his allied stockholders. He sought the best advice he could get from some very sophisticated and seriously smart men.

Earl stayed his usual upbeat self during most of this debacle, which never seemed to get him down. His wife, Ellen, went through a long and painful bout with cancer and eventually died. He married Claudia Pipes Milling, a widow from New Orleans, in the early 1960s. Julian and he had become estranged, and Julian was very critical of him, which I don't believe Earl was ever able to understand. Like my father, he never lost his cool and always turned the other cheek. He stayed very close to my father through the whole dissolution of the company and of the bond between the brothers, as did Nick, Estelle, and Keve, and he did all he could to effect a fair and happy solution for the stockholders and the Greeley McGowin family. Union Camp put him on their board, where he served for the next ten years.

Julian was a complex man, and my remarks are based on my own observations and subsequent deductions. I was particularly close to him and worked directly under him for six years. He had taken an interest in me since I was a child and generally supported my career development. We had some mutual interests and enjoyed each other's company during most of the time we traveled together, which was often. I believe that he had also considered me a budding protégé.

He had an imperial manner in his approach to the company's future, perfectly confident that his recommendation, the 333 liquidation, was the best for all, whether they wanted it or not. He believed that the end justified the means in this case, and when his arguments did not prevail, he resorted to tough tactics that fractured the close family relationship. But that heavy-handedness had cropped up in his dealings with his siblings on other occasions as well. When the Edgefield furnishings were eventually divided, he demanded and got first choice as a condition of going along. The same was true of the property division of Mr. Greeley's real estate, and he exacted a double share from Earl when he bought the house from the heirs.

He was a very interesting man, different from anyone I have ever known and something of an enigma. He shared many tastes with his close family, but our value systems and operating styles differed from his. I believe his relations with his brothers and others who had always been close to him exposed a strong need on his part to rise above everyone else and assume the dominant role. I liked him most of the time, and he did a lot to help me and get me started, but he lost me during the final years at the company. I learned a great deal from him, but a lot of it was how not to do things. I have tried to figure him out ever since, and while closer to understanding, I don't presume to believe I have ever really fathomed his inner motivations. He came up in the same household as his siblings and was raised in a loving environment. He was separated from them for a period as a child when he lived with the old black man on Mr. Greeley's place, and he was sent to Atlanta for his last two years of high school. Earl was handsome and more outgoing, which may have provoked jealously, but I never saw any signs of this before the land-division scheme entered the family conversation. Julian remains an intriguing mystery to me to this day. When his health began to fail, he made a positive effort to reconnect with his people, including me, and adopted his old pleasant persona, as if nothing had happened. I don't know about the others, but I felt ambivalent. It was good to talk to him again, but it wasn't the same.

Then again, things in life do change, and aside from the manner of the company's and our family bond's dissolution, things in my life had changed for the better, and they would continue to do so. In the years leading up to the sale of W. T. Smith, I had grown from a small, insecure boy into the mature, confident, and competent head of my own family, then after the sale, of my own business. I'd overcome self-defeating patterns of behavior through discipline and dedication to become the man I'd wanted to be. Along the way, I'd developed and pursued great passions, and I learned to hold course, my internal compass steady, even when the ride got rough.

Epilogue: Rocky Creek

*Never underestimate the number of people who would love
to see you fail.*

— MARK TWAIN

The constraints of page count permit only a summary of what I have been about in the forty-two years that have passed since the events described in the preceding pages. The business I put together, Rocky Creek Logging Company, lasted a quarter of a century. It was an unheralded success measured in financial or objective terms. Being the CEO of a substantial and successful business you have started from scratch is a premier experience. It was often very stressful and sometimes acutely unpleasant, but it taught me a lot. The business played to a very limited audience, which was its fatal flaw, and politics and perceptions ultimately brought it down. It is interesting to note that Union Camp, Rocky Creek's customer and later (after 1977) its owner, itself failed to survive, being bought by International Paper in 1997 after years of declining results. Neither of the Union Camp executives who engineered my resignation and Rocky Creek's demise, John Albert and Jim Fendig, were kept on by IP when they took over a few years later.

The twenty-five years I operated Rocky Creek were marked by continuous improvement in all areas of the business. The company did well from the start but was always a work in progress. It ran close to an optimal level of efficiency by the time I left in 1991. The problems we had were largely of a cultural nature. As an independent contractor doing business exclusively with Union Camp, we were regarded as a sort of inferior race by the rank and file in the big company. Rocky Creek continued to maintain an entrepreneurial flavor after becoming a Union Camp subsidiary in 1977, something endorsed by corporate management, but not well understood or accepted by the careerists and apparatchiks who constituted most of the Woodlands and Building Products people we interacted with. For whatever reason, many of those people always looked at us askance, which made for a less-than-ideal relationship. We used to say that we spent 60 percent of our time defending our business from our stepbrothers in the parent company, time that could have been more profitably focused on beating the competition.

Rocky Creek was also a sort of incubator for talent and started more than a few on successful careers for themselves or in larger venues. It was also an entity that people enjoyed working for or with as employees, contractors, or customers. I think the people side of it is the thing I am most pleased about from those years.

By the time I left, Rocky Creek was about twice the size it had been on startup in 1966, with 145 employees and about that many more working for our subcontractors. We cut almost all the big timber from company land with our big company crew whose capability protected the mills operations even in extended wet times. They turned their log inventories some thirty-six times a year and never ran out of wood during my time. We made extensive use of contract loggers who mostly cut from private lands. We managed over 55,000 acres owned by clients who granted us a first right of refusal for the timber they sold in return for the management and aerial patrol services we provided. This was accomplished, on a handshake basis very, successfully for both the company and its landowner clients.

Rocky Creek did important work in pioneering first and second plantation thinning, using state-of-the art, high-tech Scandinavian cut-to-length equipment. These types of systems now account for about half of all logging worldwide but were almost unknown in the South at the time we deployed them. The Union Camp Woodlands people were strongly against what we were doing as their horizon was limited to clear-cutting the plantations at about age twenty-two for low-value pulpwood, a concept that had been beaten into them as a holy grail since forestry school. My brother Greeley and I, being traditional lumber people, knew that raising high-grade saw timber over a longer rotation made much more economic sense, and he had enough clout to protect our advances in this direction. Events in the ensuing years have proven that our thinking was correct and the techniques that Rocky Creek employed were superior in a silvicultural way to most of what now passes for thinning.

Another contribution Greeley made was to install a chipper canter mill in Chapman in place of the old sawmill. This was a small log mill that made small timbers and paper mill chips from what was essentially low-value pulpwood. My contribution was to develop the log specifications and pricing strategy, which resulted in our buying all the material we needed for just 10 or 15 percent more than the pulpwood commodity price. A great success that remains in operation, in many of the ensuing years it was more profitable than the big Chapman plywood plant. This type of mill is still very rare in the South, but our first cousin Mason McGowin built and operated a good one that he named Rocky Creek Lumber Company in Monroeville. His manager, Randall Robinson, had previously run the canter mill in Chapman, and his wood-procurement man, Jerry Middleton, had done that work very successfully for me at my Rocky Creek. Mason sold his company for a big profit in 2006 just before the lumber market crashed.

Rocky Creek operated a good-sized trucking business hauling logs, pulpwood, and wood chips with a fleet of twenty-four fuel-efficient Freight-liner trucks, which used the equipment eighteen or more hours a day. A PhD-type looked over our trucking operation shortly before I left in 1991 and commented that it was the finest she had seen anywhere. The trucking was backed up by our thirty-two-person maintenance division, also double-shifted, which also maintained all the logging and plant equipment.

We had an excellent cost-accounting system that gave us a continuous snapshot of how we were doing in all areas of the business. By contrast, the Union Camp Woodlands managers operated sizable spreads of big equipment clearing land and building roads without any realistic yardsticks to measure costs and production, and their accounting did not even have a depreciation cost entry. This led to a lot of naive thinking on their part about the economics of the business and led to expensive practices. We employed numerous benchmarks to measure productivity, safety, attendance, and costs

in all areas. Our employee turnover rate averaged less than two percent a
year, and the employees averaged fifteen years seniority. Many still comment
that Rocky Creek was the best place they ever worked.

FLYING AND AVIATION COMPRISED my other great passion, and I got to do a
lot of interesting airplane stuff in the fifty-four years I was an active pilot. I
regretted not getting to fly as a Marine or airline pilot, but I believe I made
up for this in other ways. I have always had an intense interest in the business of aviation and have read about it avidly since I was a boy. My personal
flying library now numbers in excess of five thousand titles. I was fortunate
to get professional-quality training from some of the best in their respective
fields all throughout my years as an active pilot.

I managed the aviation activities in Chapman for W. T. Smith, Rocky
Creek, and Union Camp and was responsible for over 16,000 hours of
accident-free flying doing forest surveys, fire control, and executive transportation in small airplanes, notably the Cessna 180 and 185 and Beech
Barons, all very good types. I have also been much involved with various
aviation history programs and museums for the last twenty-five years. This
has enriched my life immeasurably through the good friends I have made
among what I call the "True Believers" who share my interests.

I have always gotten great peace and a sense of well-being, even elation,
from doing good flying, often in difficult circumstances. There were plenty
of challenges over the years in flying hard instruments as a single pilot in
small airplanes; being the first one to "get in" when bad weather had caused
the airport to shut down from low ceilings, rain and fog, and the like; and
getting the trip done despite en route weather problems if there was any
practical way to do it. I was also active as a professional air show pilot for
ten years in the late 1970s and 80s. Like single-pilot instrument flying, air
show work is another challenging, demanding discipline. I read recently
in a column in an aviation paper, "Air shows glorify low flight, and 10s of
thousands flock to them. They're thrilling. Air shows also have the highest
fatality count of any organized sporting activity anywhere, except perhaps
bullfighting."

My only accident in all those years of good flying was a serious one in my little Great Lakes biplane on takeoff at Montgomery in 1996. It was caused by a mechanical problem with the airplane. I was unhurt but trapped in the inverted wreck for eight minutes until the crash crew and fire truck got there. The airplane had a full tank of gas, but, very fortunately for me, there was no fire.

WHEN W. T. SMITH WAS sold in 1966, my Uncle Earl restored my grand-father's mansion, Edgefield, and moved in. He rented us the "Lodge" next door, and we lived there happily for the next seventeen years. It was a pleasant, comfortable house built by Mr. Greeley in 1919 for use as a weekend place on his farm.

In 1982, we decided that Chapman would be our permanent home. My father had died the year before after a long illness, and we bought Eastwood, the house that he and my mother had built down the hill from Edgefield in 1949. We remodeled it extensively and have enjoyed being there. Our son, Norman, the surgeon, now lives in the Lodge. That same year I also built a new hangar and office at the airport, which I have enjoyed ever since. We kept the Beech Baron and Cessna 185 that were used in the business, as well as my Stearman, Great Lakes, and newly restored SNJ there. They were all high-class airplanes.

MY BROTHER GREELEY WAS named resident manager for the Building Products facilities in Chapman when Union Camp took over in 1966. Several years later, he was made a vice president and moved to Savannah to be in charge of the Building Products and Woodlands divisions. He held this position for some twenty years before being unhorsed by his erstwhile protégé, John Albert. He stayed on in a caretaker capacity for a year or two before retiring at age sixty-five in 1992. He continued to live in Savannah but maintained a residence in Chapman until he died in 2000 when he was seventy-three. His last major project was conceiving and doing the basic research for a very good company history, The W. T. Smith Lumber Company, written by John Appleyard in Pensacola. I helped with this, and since 2000, three editions totaling 3,500 copies have been printed.

OVER THE YEARS, I made some good money in the stock market, largely negated by what turned out to be foolish investments in small venture-capital situations, dreamed up by bright people with fatal flaws. My mistake was thinking that because I had talent and some success in one field, I was good to go in anything that presented, a very ignorant supposition in the light of hard-earned experience. Discouraged by two or three such failures, I let the perfect situation slip by in 1972.

Some years before, Greeley had gotten W. T. Smith into a glamorous new business fabricating high-quality laminated beams and arches out of good pine lumber. Architects favored these in buildings like churches and schools and some structural applications. Though this had turned into a decent small business, it was not of a scale to fit Union Camp's grander designs, so they decided to sell it. The plant was located on the company's old Greenville sawmill property, my old stomping ground. Henry Barclay and I took a cursory look at it and, still licking our wounds from recent bad experiences, decided to pass. An ex–IRS agent from Birmingham bought it for $250,000. He has always been an absentee owner and made his original investment back in less than a year. Carlton Whittle, then a young engineer at the "glue-lam" and now its longtime manager and my friend, recently told me that it soon started making really good money and now turns profits in excess of a million dollars a year.

I have always liked architecture and applications that show wood at its best. I believe this business offered me a perfect future, and I have always regretted this lost opportunity. It would have given me a wonderful venue to use my drive and talents for fun and profit for the rest of my active life, free from all the backbiting that was a constant around my situation with Union Camp. As my old friend and fellow director Greg Leatherbury on the Merchants Bank board remarked to me shortly before we sold out to First Alabama, "Floyd, life ain't fair!"

A Son's Postscript

"Plan your flight and fly your plan."

My father died on December 1, 2010, almost six months before his eightieth birthday. Interestingly, he had commented to me on more than one occasion that "I never was supposed to have lived this long."

He had a dominant personality, and until the end, he remained a force to be reckoned with. In many ways, he reminded me of a real-life version of Lt. Col. Wilbur "Bull" Meechum from the movie, *The Great Santini*, based on Pat Conroy's book. Papa knew how he wanted things to go, and in his opinion this was how things should go. Honestly, for most of his life he was able to pull this off through sheer force of personality and determination. He was definitely a unique individual.

Papa had a very keen ability to analyze other's strengths and weaknesses, while at the same time, introspection, flexibility, and empathy were not his strong points. Unfortunately, he died before this book could be published, but I think it gives the reader a sense of the fascinating character that he was and the times in which he lived.

— NORMAN F. McGOWIN III

Index